American Genealogical Research at the DAR
Washington, D.C.

by Eric G. Grundset and Steven B. Rhodes

DAR Library Studies in Genealogy and History, Number 1

National Society
Daughters of the American Revolution
1776 D Street, N.W.
Washington, D.C. 20006–5392

Published March 1997
Second Printing, December 1997

ISBN 0-9602528-9-4

(0397-2000-OP)
(1297-2000-OP)

★ ★ ★ ★ ★ ★ ★ ★ ★ ★ ★ ★ ★ ★ ★ ★ ★ ACKNOWLEDGMENTS

The President General, Mrs. Charles Keil Kemper, the Librarian General, Mrs. David W. Ulrich, and the entire Executive Committee, have been most supportive of the concept of this book from the beginning. The DAR Library Centennial Committee, Mrs. Richard Powell Taylor, National Chairman, has funded the publication costs through various projects, and its support of the Library's publishing efforts is greatly appreciated. DAR National Parliamentarian, Mrs. Frank B. Surber, kindly proofread the copy and made many helpful comments.

Many DAR staff members have provided insight and information on the workings of DAR offices and records. In particular, the following deserve special thanks for their assistance: Glenna Acord, Rachel Ashby, James E. Barker III, LaKeitha Clarke, Elva Crawford, Diane Dunkley, Janice Fitzgerald, Belva G. Geist, Kathleen Hale, Rose Hall, Betty Humphrey, Darlene T. Hunter, Hazel F. Kreinheder, Elisabeth W. Schmidt, Margaret Turner, and Gerald S. Walker. Edith Rianzares has taken the rough copy of the book and transformed it into a polished product.

Without the support for DAR collections from Daughters around the country for over a century, the research center which has evolved in Washington, D.C. would not be the storehouse of information it is today and this book would be unnecessary. Their dues and contributions have funded all the work to arrange this material since 1890, and their dedication to the purposes of the National Society have resulted in a long influx of materials to the Nation's Capital. With their books, periodicals, manuscripts, research notes, indices and files, DAR members have built a great repository of American history.

The public, which has had access to DAR collections since shortly after 1900, has also contributed greatly to the growth of DAR collections with donations of books and other materials. Many researchers have placed copies of their completed family histories and other works in the DAR Library to give these publications national exposure.

PHOTO CREDITS

Pages 6, 8, 12, 19, 21, 27, 36, 41: Eric G. Grundset
Pages 17, 29: Robert W. Fones, Jr.
Page 78: Helga Photo Studio; Mark Gulezian

Artwork on pages 11, 122, 123, 124, 126, 127, 133 135, 136, 138 and 145 is from Elroy McKendree Avery. *A History of the United States and Its People from Their Earliest Records to the Present Time.* Cleveland: The Burrows Brothers, 1908.

★ CONTENTS

his book actually had its beginnings in the late 1980s with proposals to write a guide to research in DAR collections. Unfortunately, many other projects had priority. With the celebration of the Centennial of the founding of the DAR Library in 1996, the composition of a guide to genealogical research at the DAR was a timely commemorative project. It is long overdue. DAR has "hidden its light under a bushel" for far too long. American genealogists need a clear understanding of the many family history treasures DAR owns and makes available for research.

Portions of the information contained herein have appeared in print in various DAR publications over the years. Finding it in all of these scattered places is not easy. Condensing over a century of collecting into a guidebook has been a fascinating challenge. With no precedent, we gathered everything from scratch over the past several years in preparation. Writing and research continued right up to the final minute.

The Washington Monument from the C Street Portico, Memorial Continental Hall.

Others have written guides to genealogical research in the major repositories in the Nation's Capital, including DAR of course. Such accounts of DAR's collections have been particularly lacking. These authors have generally not consulted the proper staff in each research center for the proper information. Consequently, emphasis has been uneven, accuracy has suffered, and omissions are glaring. This leads to misinformation for genealogists and difficulties for staff who assist them. To insure accuracy and to present the full picture of DAR's role in genealogical research, this guide is essential.

American Genealogical Research at the DAR is not a general guide to genealogical research in the United States. There are ample introductory and advanced guides on the market and in libraries nationwide. Instead, this new DAR publication serves as a manual discussing the collections at DAR Headquarters in Washington, D.C. within the broader scope of American genealogical sources and subjects. Explaining what is available at DAR and how a researcher will be able to use it in his or her search for their family's place in American history is the book's purpose.

Chapters on the major departments at DAR Headquarters which maintain genealogical collections, including the DAR Library, begin the guide and provide detailed information on holdings, procedures, and finding aids. Chapter 13 presents portions of these DAR collections arranged in subject categories to highlight the interconnections between the departments and to inform researchers of the many unique and less well known sources.

Many people assume that because of the appearance of the word "Revolution" in the society's name that only material on the American Revolution will be found here. While the War of Independence is, naturally, a major focus, DAR collections are much broader in their coverage and include materials from the past four centuries of American history. Recently, a colleague at another Washington research center was surprised to learn that the DAR Library owned a very large collection of American county histories. He had been telling researchers that these were only available in Washington, D.C. at the Library of Congress. Unfortunately, this is not atypical. DAR collections are not as well known as they should be — yet another reason for this publication. People simply do not know what is behind the marble walls and columns.

Similarly, many researchers are surprised to learn that DAR collections are not limited to famous individuals, supposedly "blue-blood" families, and those with colonial English ancestry. American history and records are the result of a great mixture of peoples and traditions, and the same applies to DAR collections. Interspersed throughout are major holdings relating to many European immigrant groups, to African Americans and to Native Americans.

The staff at DAR is always surprised that so many people are unaware of the fact that the DAR is open to researchers and has been since shortly after 1900. It is a common misconception, even among long-time Washington area residents, that only DAR members may use DAR collections. One does not need special permission to visit. The door is open to all.

Generally, DAR collections compliment and partially duplicate those of the Library of Congress and the National Archives. Although much smaller than these massive institutions, DAR is no less important to the average American genealogist. So much unique material resides at DAR that researchers frequently comment that they have found genealogical gold they could not find anywhere else.

The holdings themselves, which do not circulate, coupled with open bookstacks in the Library, quick processing of new materials for use, and major in-house finding aids, draw researchers from across the nation every day. *American Genealogical Research at the DAR* presents the DAR's research materials, gathered for over a century, to American genealogists with the hope that more will visit and find what ***they*** could not find elsewhere. After all, the point of building a historical collection is preservation for future generations. We are at once the future generation the DAR's founders had in mind when they began these collections and the preservers for still other future generations of Americans who will be likely be interested in their family history.

Eric G. Grundset
Library Director
February 1997

THE NATIONAL SOCIETY
DAUGHTERS OF THE AMERICAN REVOLUTION

The National Society Daughters of the American Revolution (NSDAR, and hereafter simply DAR) was established on October 11, 1890 by four women interested in preserving the memory of the men and women involved in the birth of the United States. It was incorporated under the laws of the District of Columbia on June 4, 1891 and incorporated by an Act of the United States Congress in 1896. Since 1890, over 776,000 women have been members. The DAR is a nonaffiliated service organization dedicated to the support of historic preservation, the promotion of education and the encouragement of patriotic endeavor.

Membership is by invitation to

> any woman ... who is not less than eighteen years of age, and who is lineally descended from a man or woman who, with unfailing loyalty to the cause of American Independence, served as a sailor, or a soldier or civil officer in one of the several Colonies or States, or in the United Colonies or States or as a recognized patriot, or rendered material aid thereto; provided an applicant is personally acceptable to the chapter. ["Bylaws of the National Society of the Daughters of the American Revolution, Article III, Section 1]

Memorial Continental Hall from the Ellipse.

The DAR is headquartered in a block-sized group of connected buildings in downtown Washington, D.C. a few blocks from the White House. Memorial Continental Hall (1905-1910), Constitution Hall (1929), and the Administration Building (1921-1923; 1947-1950) are the components of this complex.

DAR is comprised of nearly 170,000 members grouped into state organizations and local chapters; Units Overseas in the United Kingdom, France, Canada, Australia, and Mexico; and members at large. Many of the state organizations and some chapters maintain their own buildings and offices, but the National Society is the primary repository for the DAR collections examined in this guide.

The history of the DAR has been told several times. The most recent account, by Ann Arnold Hunter, *A Century of Service: The Story of the DAR*, was published for the National Society's Centennial and chronicles the development of the organization and its programs. *The DAR Magazine* serves as the official serial publication and provides both historic and current information on the National Society. It is available in libraries nationwide and by subscription.

During the past century the DAR has worked to collect, to preserve, to transcribe, to index, and to arrange much material documenting the historical development of the country and the genealogical history of its families during the past four centuries with a natural, but not limited, concentration on the Revolutionary era. The value of DAR materials has been known to researchers for the better part of the twentieth century, but the size of the collections and variety of materials has never before been presented in a collected fashion.

1.1
CONTACTING THE DAR

The DAR's address is 1776 D St., N.W., Washington, D.C. 20006-5392. The main telephone switchboard number is 202-628-1776. DAR's homepage on the Internet may be reached at www.dar.org.

1.2
GENERAL INFORMATION ON THE DAR

Readers interested in more information on the DAR may contact the Corresponding Secretary General's office and request some of the available literature and publications. See Chapter 11 for more information.

1.3
BECOMING A DAR MEMBER

Those interested in membership may contact the Membership Services Office for information on the process. Phone: 202-879-3205.

1.4
A DAR GENEALOGICAL TIMELINE

1890   The National Society Daughters of the American Revolution was founded in October.

1892   *The DAR Magazine* begins publication.

1895   DAR publishes volume one of its *Lineage Books*.

1896   The DAR Library was established in February.

1900   The "Genealogical Column" of *The DAR Magazine* begins.

1902   The public is permitted to use the DAR Library in its first home on F Street.

1905   DAR purchases the Chalkley Manuscripts of early records from Augusta County, Virginia.

1910   DAR moved into the Memorial Continental Hall in February. The Library was then located in the office now occupied by the Genealogy Department.

1911   After much debate, DAR publishes the Chalkley Manuscripts as *Chronicles of the Scotch-Irish Settlement*.

1912   DAR begins effort to urge the U.S. Congress to establish a national archives.

1913   Genealogical Research Committee established; name changed in 1932 to Genealogical Records Committee.

1919   The Bureau of the Census makes its first transfer to the DAR of original volumes of various special schedules from United States censuses.

1920   First book catalog of the DAR Library published.

1929   DAR Library moves into new quarters on the second floor of Constitution Hall.

1930   DAR transfers the special census schedules to the manuscript collection at Duke University's Perkins Library.

1933   Daughters nationwide urged the United States Congress to preserve, restore, and microfilm aging federal census records, especially those for 1800, 1810, and 1820.

1934   Congress appropriates money for census microfilming and preservation.

1936   The Works Progress Administration began donations to the DAR Library of its valuable guides to records.

1937   DAR receives another shipment of mortality schedules from the Bureau of the Census.

1939   The DAR Library's "wear and tear" fee begins for non-member researchers.

1939   DAR publishes the final volume, number 166, of the *Lineage Books*.

1940   Second book catalog of the DAR Library published.

1946	The DAR Library celebrates its fiftieth anniversary.
1947	The Library completed acquisitions of microfilm of the 1850-1880 federal censuses, a process which had been stalled by World War II microfilm shortages.
1949	The DAR Library moves into its present location in the converted auditorium of Memorial Continental Hall.
1950	The first genealogical index to *The DAR Magazine* appears: *Genealogical Guide*.
1956	The National Archives transfers original 1880 population census schedules for twelve states to DAR.
1956	Dr. Jean Stephenson begins writing articles of genealogical methodology in *The DAR Magazine*.
1958	First publication of *Is That Lineage Right?*
1962	DAR begins microfilming membership application papers.
1966	The first *DAR Patriot Index* is published.
1970	DAR's Seimes Microfilm Center is established.
1972	A two-year project by the Genealogical Society of Utah to microfilm many unique materials in the DAR Library comes to an end having produced nearly 2,800 rolls.
1977	Requirement begins for documentation for membership applications for the first three generations, including the applicant herself.
1980	DAR transfers its holdings of census mortality schedules to the National Archives and the 1880 population schedules to state archives or historical societies.
1982	The first volume of the third book catalog of the DAR Library is published: *DAR Library Catalog: Volume One: Family Histories and Genealogies*.
1986	The second volume of the third book catalog of the DAR Library is published: *DAR Library Catalog: Volume Two: State and Local Histories and Records*.
1986	The American Indian Committee and the Librarian General developed a new section for the Library, The American Indian Collection.
1989	The DAR Museum presents an exhibit, "Family Record: Genealogical Watercolors and Needlework."
1992	The third volume of the third book catalog of the DAR Library is published: *DAR Library Catalog: Volume Three: Centennial Supplement, 1986-1992*.
1994	The Centennial Edition of The DAR Patriot Index is published.
1996	The DAR Library celebrates its Centennial with publishing projects and development of a computerized catalog.
1997	*American Genealogical Research at the DAR* is published, the first detailed guide to the National Society's extensive resources.

COMING TO DAR HEADQUARTERS

*L*imited public transportation and minimal parking compli- cate a visit to DAR Headquar- ters, but the trip is worth the effort!

DAR Headquarters is located at 1776 D Street in the block bounded by 17th, 18th , C and D Streets, N.W. in downtown Washington. Use the D Street entrance to the building. The historic main entrance, now used only for special events, faces 17th Street and the Ellipse south of the White House. Besides the President's home, DAR's neighbors include the Red Cross, the Organization of American States, and the U.S. Department of the Interior.

The 1776 D Street Entrance to DAR Headquarters.

Access to the building for the disabled is at 1776 C Street. This entrance into the lower level of the administration building is in the center of the block behind the DAR Founders' Memorial. Presently, those with disabled license plates may park at meters without paying fees.

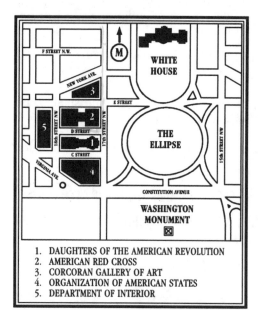

1. DAUGHTERS OF THE AMERICAN REVOLUTION
2. AMERICAN RED CROSS
3. CORCORAN GALLERY OF ART
4. ORGANIZATION OF AMERICAN STATES
5. DEPARTMENT OF INTERIOR

DAR's location is highlighted on this map of downtown Washington, D.C. and immediate neighborhood near the White House.

2.1
PARKING

Street parking in this part of Washington is very limited and fills up very early in the morning on weekdays. Parking meters only take quarters (no other coins!) and are only valid for two hours. DAR is not able to provide quarters for meters. There are no meter fees on Sundays, but events in Washington often result in full streets by the time DAR opens at 1:00 p.m. Parking restrictions may apply on some nearby streets. **READ POSTED SIGNS** to avoid tickets or towing. Meter readers appear very regularly. Parking around the Ellipse is by govern- ment permit only.

Frequently, the Metropolitan Police Department restricts parking on streets for specific hours or days. There is little advance notice of these closings. In addition, when major events such as marathons, parades, demonstrations, or rallies occur on the Mall or the Ellipse, parking is often banned, restricted, or at a premium. The police may also close streets to through traffic without notice.

One parking garage is located on west-bound New York Avenue, N.W. between 17th and 18th Streets, two blocks north of DAR. It often fills early in the day.

In short, parking can be a challenge. Public transportation or a drop-off are alternatives.

2.2
PUBLIC TRANSPORTATION

The DAR was not consulted when the Metro subway system was constructed or when bus routes were laid out! The park-like area which has been DAR's home since 1910, is several blocks from the closest Metro stations. These are:

Farragut West – 6 blocks due north at 17th and 18th Streets and I ("Eye") Street, N.W. on the BLUE and ORANGE lines
Farragut North – 7 blocks due north at 17th and K Streets and Connecticut Avenue, N.W. on the RED line

Metrobuses run during the morning and evening rush hours only on many of these routes. Midday service (9:30 a.m.–3:00 p.m.) was cancelled a few years ago. There is no Sunday service on these routes. For exact schedules, routes and fares call Metro at 202-637-7000.

Mornings
From the Pentagon Metro Station in Virginia (connections from Northern Virginia Metrobuses and the BLUE and YELLOW Metro lines) the 13A bus crosses Memorial Bridge and goes east on Constitution Avenue. Stops at 19th and 17th Streets (eastbound) are two blocks south of DAR. The 13B bus begins at the Pentagon, crosses the 14th Street bridge, connects with other District Metrobus routes at 7th and 10th Streets and runs westbound from points east of DAR on Constitution Avenue eventually returning to the Pentagon. It is not the quickest route from the Pentagon, but the connections east of DAR in downtown are helpful.

During rush hours the X1 bus connects the Kennedy Center area in Northwest with Minnesota Avenue in Northeast passing close to DAR and Union Station enroute.

Afternoons
After 3:00 p.m. catch the westbound 13B bus at the northeast corner of 19th Street and Constitution Avenue (no afternoon stop at 17th Street) and return to the Pentagon Metro Station. Catch the eastbound 13A bus at the southeast corner of 17th Street and Constitution (the corner closest to the Washington Monument).

To points in Northwest Washington, catch the L1 bus on C Street immediately behind DAR Headquarters. It is marked "Chevy Chase Circle," and stops at points enroute.

The 80 bus, which is marked "Fort Totten" and runs throughout the day, stops at 18th and C Streets and continues north up 18th Street to L Street, turns right and continues its route to Fort Totten in Northeast Washington. This bus may be used to reach the Metro stations on the Blue, Orange and Red lines mentioned previously.

2.3
HOURS AND HOLIDAYS

DAR's regular hours are:

Monday–Friday	8:30 a.m. to 4:00 p.m. (Library opens at 8:45 a.m.)
Saturday	Closed
Sunday	1:00 to 5:00 p.m. (All offices except the Library, Seimes Microfilm Center, and the Museum are closed on Sundays.)
Closings:	All Federal Holidays and Sundays preceding Monday holidays. If a holiday falls on a Friday, DAR is also closed the following Sunday. Occasionally, there are other special closings.

DAR is open only to its members during two weeks in mid-April each year for its convention, Continental Congress. Congress is always the week which includes April 19, the anniversary of the Battles of Lexington and Concord. DAR is closed to the public the week before and the week of Congress, as well as the Sunday after Congress adjourns.

Inclement weather:	Generally, DAR closes for bad weather when the Federal Government does. Call before attempting a visit.

Always call to be certain DAR is open before making a visit near a holiday, special event, or in April.

2.4
LUNCH FACILITIES

DAR has a lunchroom on the lower level with drink and snack machines and microwave ovens. Several restaurants are in nearby buildings or up 17th Street near Pennsylvania Avenue. The Department of the Interior Cafeteria, across 18th Street from DAR, is open to the public. Presentation of either a picture ID or a DAR visitor's badge should be sufficient to gain entry to this government building. Visitors in groups may enter both buildings with group badges or sticker badges. During Continental Congress week in April, temporary lunch facilities are available in DAR's lunchroom. Members may enter the Interior Cafeteria that week only by wearing their official ribbon and pins. It can become extremely crowded that week.

2.5
GROUP VISITS

Group visits to DAR are welcomed and encouraged. Individuals may wish to check with local or state genealogical societies regarding possible group visits to Washington, D.C. Many such groups outside the mid-Atlantic region plan research trips to the Nation's Capital on occasion, while those within Virginia, Maryland, Delaware, and Pennsylvania have regular (sometimes monthly) bus trips.

Please follow these guidelines when planning your visit:

● All calls regarding group visits should be made to the DAR Library at 202-879-3229. The National Archives and the Library of Congress's Local History and Genealogy Divisions also appreciate advance notice. Please provide your name and telephone number or that of the group's leader as a contact in the event DAR needs to call someone. Remember that weather conditions in your area may not be the same as in Washington, D.C.

- Schedule all group visits as far in advance as possible to enable the Library to reserve the day you choose or to inform you of conflicts. There is seating for about 100 researchers. The Library maintains a calendar just for group visits. Groups may not visit during the middle of April. Remember that the DAR observes federal holidays, and that there may be some adjustments to our holiday schedule. In short, give yourself plenty of time to adjust to changes which may be necessary.

- Please let the Library know what time you will arrive. The staff will give an orientation, if the group would like one, when all group members are present.

- There are no group fees or reductions for more than one day. If you have a large group it is helpful for the person leading the group to collect the entrance fees from non-DAR members prior to your arrival. Present the collected fees to the Library staff member at the reference desk. This prevents long lines when entering the Library. A check for the total is also acceptable (made payable to "Treasurer General, NSDAR).

- All members of the group must wear some type of name badge identifying them as part of the group. Groups do not sign-in one at a time at the guard desk at the D Street entrance, but members must wear badges. We do request that everyone sign-in at the Library's register for statistical reasons only.

The Library can provide your group with pamphlets and other information sheets in advance to help prepare for the visit.

Should your plans change or you need to cancel your visit, please let the Library know.

2.6
SECURITY AND SAFETY

Visitors to Washington, D.C. should exercise the same caution and awareness they would in any large city. DAR is located in an area with much street and pedestrian traffic. Security personnel in the area surrounding the White House add further vigilance. Basically, be aware of your surroundings. DAR members are urged not to wear their ribbons and pins walking down the street. This is simply a general precaution. The walk to and from the Metro stations is basically a comfortable one.

At DAR, visitors must sign in at the guard desk at the D Street Entrance. They receive a visitor's badge, which they should wear at all times and should return at the end of the day. DAR staff reserve the right to search all bags, purses, and briefcases. DAR is implementing new security measures to protect the collections.

Please watch your step when walking in the Library; step stools are frequently in the aisles. Be careful when standing on step stools. Should you need assistance in reaching an item, please ask the staff to help you.

2.7
DAR HEADQUARTERS FLOORPLAN

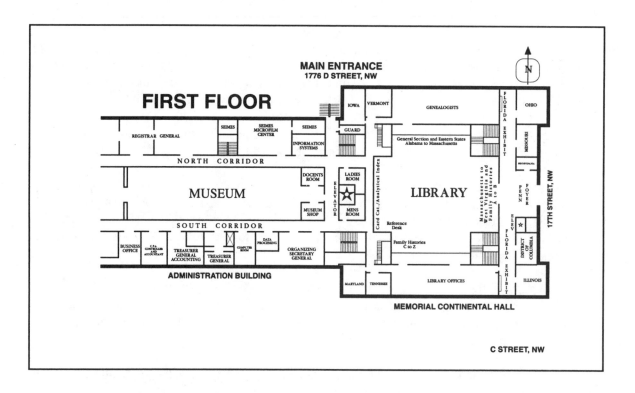

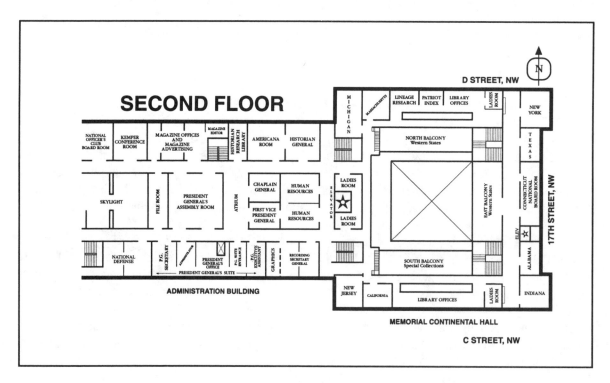

THE DAR LIBRARY

**A view of the setting for the DAR Library in the former
Auditorium of Memorial Continental Hall.**

*Location: Memorial Continental Hall, First Floor,
Reference telephone number: 202–879–3229
(a recording only when the Library is closed)
Acquisitions: 202–879–3250
Serials: 202–879–3228*

In early 1896, DAR established a library in its cramped offices in downtown Washington's commercial district. The primary purposes at the inception were to provide reference material to assist with the verification of membership applications and preservation of historic documents. Not long afterwards, the general public was granted access, thereby expanding the library's purpose to include providing genealogical services to non-members as well as DAR members. In early 1910 the offices and the library moved to Memorial Continental Hall, the National Society's new building. The library moved again to space in Constitution Hall in 1930 but returned to the converted auditorium of Memorial Continental Hall in 1949. This remains its location today.

The DAR Library is a highly specialized collection focusing primarily, but not exclusively, on American genealogy and history. When the Library was established in 1896, the basic collection policy, which remains in place today, emerged:

> ... the field covered by the collection is that part of America represented by local history (state, county, town, and church), genealogies, biographies and vital records. Histories of all kinds relating to the American Revolution, including military and civil records are desired, everything in fact that will assist in throwing light upon the men of the Revolutionary period, including their family lines as well as their service, and connect then with their descendants of the present day.

During the past century, the Library, along with other DAR departments, has grown into one of the major genealogical research centers in the United States. Donations of books, research materials, periodicals, and other sources by Daughters and non-members alike have been the basis for this growth. The result is one of the "must visit" places for genealogists coming to the Nation's Capital.

3.1
USER FEES AND GENERAL GUIDELINES

The Library has been open to the public since the early years of the twentieth century. In 1939 DAR initiated a fee for non-members to support the Library's basic operations, including book purchasing and binding. This remains the case today. The Library charges a daily user fee to non-members of the DAR, SAR, SR, and C.A.R. Members of the latter three groups must present a **current** membership card to receive the fee waver; there are no exceptions to this policy. Fees on Sundays and at lunch time on weekdays are less than the weekday rate. Cash, personal checks, and traveler's checks are accepted, but credit cards are accepted only in the Office of the Corresponding Secretary General. Fees are posted at the Library's entrance, and the staff cannot negotiate their reduction or elimination.

Researchers are welcome to bring their laptop computers. Two-prong adapters may be needed in some outlets. On crowded days, there may be a limited number of outlets available, but the staff will do their best to overcome these problems.

Photography within DAR Headquarters is not permitted. Personal hand-held photocopiers may not be used in any DAR department.

Because it is the only major genealogical research facility open in Washington, D.C. on Sunday afternoons, the DAR Library is usually extremely crowded. Seating is limited. If the staff cannot complete photocopies for researchers, these will be mailed or held for later pick-up.

You will recall that the Librarian General was authorized at the October meeting, to establish a "Wear and Tear Fund," to help pay for the rebinding of books. After due notice was given the patrons of the Library, a charge of 25 [cents] per day was put into effect on November 24th [1939] for nonmembers of this Society, except members of the Children of the American Revolution, Sons of the American Revolution, Sons of the Revolution, and Daughters of the Revolution."

Notice by Adelaide H. Sisson, Librarian General, in her February 1940 Board report in *National Historical Magazine*, March 1940, p. 63.

3.2
SPECIAL FINDING AIDS

3.2.1
THE CATALOGS: CARD, PUBLISHED, COMPUTER

Three forms of the Library's catalog:
card, book, computer.

The Library's catalog has had several different forms over the past century. These all warrant some discussion because most retain their value even today.

3.2.1.1
Card Catalog

Prior to the late 1970s the Library had a very basic dictionary catalog with few subject tracings. There were no call numbers or spine labels on the books to help locate items. The catalog was inter-filed with the Analytical Index. In 1970-1971 the Genealogical Society of Utah microfilmed the entire finding aid. This microfilm has limited usefulness today because of the many subsequent changes and additions. In the mid-1980s the staff carefully and methodically removed the old cata-loging records from the catalog leaving the Analytical Index alone in its place. The old catalog is still maintained in storage for occasional use in reference and cataloging work.

A "reclassification project" in the late 1970s and early 1980s and subsequent cataloging to the pre-sent produced the current card catalog. It is divided into three parts:

author/title: Authors and titles are interfiled in alphabetical order.

family/personal names: Includes not only the major family in the title of a book, but also others treated significantly in the title, contents, or index. The names of individuals who are the subjects of biographies are included in this section.

geographic/general subjects: The Library takes a very geographic approach to subjects. Researchers should consult the catalog using any place name of interest, followed by subject categories. This is the reverse of subject headings in many other libraries. Example: "Morgan County, Ohio–Marriage records", rather than "Marriage records–Ohio–Morgan County." Always start with the geographic or general subject.

The time and expense of producing a card catalog has become excessive in a period when computers can help perform this work. Consequently, the card catalog was "frozen" in spring 1996 and a new computerized on-line public access catalog (OPAC) started in early 1997. Like its predecessor, the card catalog will be retained as a back up to the OPAC. The DAR Library recognizes the present need during this transition period to offer a catalog in several forms.

3.2.1.2
Published Catalogs of Library Holdings

The DAR Library has produced published catalogs of its book holdings three times in this century.

1920:	*Historical and Genealogical Works, National Society Daughters of the American Revolution Library, Memorial Continental Hall.*
1940:	*Catalogue of Genealogical and Historical Works, Library of the National Society Daughters of the American Revolution.*
1982–1992:	*DAR Library Catalog Volume One: Family Histories and Genealogies* (1982) *Supplement to Volume One: Family Histories and Genealogies* (1984) *Volume Two: State and Local Histories and Records* (1986) *Volume Three: Centennial Supplement: Acquisitions 1985-1991* (1992)

The three-volume set, *The DAR Library Catalog*, lists available titles through 1991, and therefore, supersedes all previous catalogs. It is owned by libraries nationwide or may be purchased from the DAR's Corresponding Secretary General. Volume One and its supplement are, however, out-of-print, and limited quantities of Volume 2 and Volume 3 are available. None will be reprinted when stocks are depleted.

The indices to these three volumes essentially condense the library's card catalog. Not only is the printed catalog of value for awareness of the DAR Library's holdings, it can also give researchers useful information that

00001 AASEN — Ausen, Vernon
The descendants of Peder and Siri Aasen/ compiled by Vernon Ausen. Revised edition. — 1986. — 103 p.: ill., geneal. tables, map, ports.; 29 cm. — Typescript. FAMILIES/AASEN/AUSEN

00002 ABBE — Abbe, Sophronia
A genealogical record of the Abbe family of Connecticut/ prepared by Sophronia Abbe. — [19 -?]. — [71] leaves; 20 cm. — Manuscript. FAMILIES/ABBE/ABB

00003 ABBEY —
Memorial of Captain Thomas Abbey: his ancestors and descendants of the Abbey family. 2nd edition. — [S.l.: s.n., s.d.]. — 175 p.: ill., coat of arms, ports.; 26 cm. FAMILIES/ABBEY/ABBEY

00004 ABBOTT — Abbott, Lemuel Abijah
Descendants of George Abbott of Rowley, Mass./ by Lemuel Abijah Abbott. — [S.l.]: Abbott, 1906. — 2 v.: ports.; 24 cm. — Index in v.2. Poor condition; inquire at desk. FAMILIES/ABBOTT/ABBOTT

00005 ABERNETHY — Counts, Gloria Lee
The ancestors and descendants of Asa Andrew and Sceleta Carolina Abernathy Smith/ compiled & edited by Gloria Miller Counts. — North Little: The Compiler, c1984. — v.: ill., coat of arms, facsims., geneal. tables, maps, ports.; 29 cm. — Index. Library holdings: v. 1. FAMILIES/ABERNETHY/COUNTS

00006 ACER — Platter, Virginia Acer
The Acer family/ [Virginia Acer Platter. — S.l.: s.n., 1982-1983]. — 65 leaves: ports.; 29 cm. FAMILIES/ACER/PLATTER

00007 ACHILLES — Smith, Walter Burgess
The Achilles family from New Hampshire 1776-1961/ Walter Burgess Smith. — Washington, D. C.: Holmes Duplicating Co., 1962. — 416 leaves: ill., coats of arms, facsims., ports.; 30 cm. — Index. OV/FAMILIES/ACHILLES/SMITH

Family history titles listed in the
The DAR Library Catalog, Volume 3

a book they should consult actually exists. In other words, the catalog is a bibliography of genealogical publications, some of which may also be found in other libraries. It is a necessary tool which ranks with such publications as *Genealogies in the Library of Congress* and *Compliment to Genealogies in the Library of Congress*. Please note that the numbers next to entries in these catalogs are not call numbers. They are indexing devices solely useful within the catalogs themselves. The "How to Use This Book" section at the beginning of each volume offers guidance.

3.2.1.3
Computerized Catalogs

In early 1997 the card catalogs in the Library and Seimes Microfilm Center were merged into a computerized catalog using existing computerized cataloging records. The new on-line public access catalog (OPAC) speeds listings of new records and alterations to existing ones. Eventually the catalog will be accessible via the Internet.

3.2.2
ANALYTICAL INDEX

The Library's 400-drawer Analytical Index
is a major finding aid.

Since the 1910s, Library staff and volunteers have produced an Analytical Index amounting to over 400 card drawers. This index, typical of similar finding aids in libraries large and small, provides access points to many older county histories and to special book and file collections within the Library. Genealogical Records Committee reports prior to 1970 are indexed here.

The variety of indexing techniques used to create cards makes for some interesting entries. A title noted in 1930 may not really be the title on the book. Creative abbreviations abound. There are many cryptic references to information in this index. The staff will help interpret. Despite these drawbacks, this index is an invaluable finding aid. To locate information cited in the index, one must consult the catalog under either the author or title to determine the proper call words for the book containing the desired reference. Very few of the cards contain call words for books.

An example of a card from the Analytical Index is:

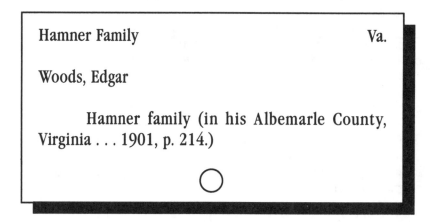

Hamner Family   Va.

Woods, Edgar

        Hamner family (in his Albemarle County,
Virginia . . . 1901, p. 214.)

3.2.3
SPECIAL INDICES

Numerous smaller and separate card indices lead researchers to information on such subjects as all names mentioned in selected Revolutionary War pension applications, the names of some Virginia women during the Revolution, and the library's manuscript collection of genealogical research materials. Other smaller card indices are also available. The staff suspects that several of these have been superseded by newer printed finding aids, but the indices remain available on the slight chance that a morsel of information may have been missed in the new compilations.

Index to Names Appearing in Revolutionary War Pensions

This twenty-three drawer index contains references to the names of individuals which appear in abstracts of **some** Revolutionary War pensions. These abstracts were prepared by DAR staff and volunteers to help prove pending application papers prior to the early 1960s. It is not a complete index of all Revolutionary War pensions. Besides giving an abstract of a pensioner's papers, this index also provides the names of other persons mentioned in the pension which can be valuable when searching for information on individuals living during the late eighteenth and early nineteenth centuries. The 340 volumes of pension abstracts indexed by this finding aid include 233 covering pensions of veterans from around the country; 101 for pensions of New Hampshire veterans; and 6 for pensions of Rhode Island veterans. Additional information on Revolutionary War pensions is in section 13.20.4.15.

Virginia Women in the American Revolution

Ann Waller Reddy, a genealogical researcher in Virginia during the mid-twentieth century, willed her papers and files to the DAR Library upon her death in 1971. The material included this card index containing references to women living during the Revolution who Miss Reddy found in Virginia records and sources. Most of the actual records are not available in the DAR Library. See the next entry for further sources.

Index to the Ann Waller Reddy Collection

Miss Reddy's research papers during her residence in Richmond, Virginia from the 1930s to 1970 comprise this collection. Her lengthy files focus strictly on Virginia families, especially those in eastern and central parts of the state. The index provides access to the major names in each group of files.

Index to New York Bible Records

This is a card index to portions of the New York DAR's set of Genealogical Records Committee Reports. It supplements the printed Master Index to this set and contains some references not found therein.

Index to New York County Records

Same as preceding, except it indexes county records in the set.

Index to Maryland Genealogical Records Committee Reports

This is a partial index to the Maryland DAR's set of reports. In a recent reorganization of this set of books, volume numbers have been reassigned. A chart to convert volume numbers found in the card index to those actually on the book spines is affixed to the shelf near the bound volumes in the Maryland section of the bookstacks. A new, every-name index to the Maryland set largely supersedes this card index.

Index to Miscellaneous Marriage References

This index was compiled many years ago and the staff does not add to it. It contains marriage references arranged first by state and then by surname. We speculate that it was created as part of a defunct project and have no additional information on its sources.

1850 Index, District of Columbia Census

This index was prepared by the District of Columbia DAR and is a useful adjunct to the printed index.

Index to County and Town Records in the DAR Library

Once again, this appears to be the result of a long defunct project. It is arranged by state and then by county or town and provides references to the location of some records in the Library.

Index to Michigan Pioneer and Historical Collections

This index provides access to this important set of forty books on early settlers in Michigan. It is also useful for research in New York, New England, and the Midwest.

Index to the Manuscript Collection

Over the decades, the DAR Library has received various materials which are either too voluminous or too fragile to be added to the regular files. These materials have been gathered into a manuscript collection of research notes and papers from genealogists who bequeathed or donated their work to the DAR. There are frequent additions to the manuscript collection.

3.2.4

INDICES TO LIBRARY MATERIALS ON MICROFILM

In the early 1970s, the Genealogical Society of Utah produced nearly 2,800 microfilm rolls of thousands of one-of-a-kind volumes in the DAR Library. **Printed indices** to much of this material exist, and although these are located in libraries throughout the country, many researchers are unaware of their value and purpose. See the Genealogical Records Committee discussion in Chapter 4 for further details. These four books are *The Vital Record Compendium, The Cemetery Record Compendium, An Index to Some of the Family Records of the Southern States,* and *An Index to Some of the Bibles and Family Records of the United States (excluding the Southern States).*

All four books are sold by Everton Publishers. The microfilms are available at DAR, the Family History Library in Salt Lake City and the Allen County Public Library, Fort Wayne, Indiana.

3.3
THE ARRANGEMENT OF THE DAR LIBRARY

The DAR Library has a unique arrangement, which does not use the Dewey Decimal or Library of Congress classification systems to organize books on the shelf. Instead, a "term classification" system is in place, which utilizes "call words" instead of "call numbers." It is based on the existing arrangement of the books when the entire collection was recataloged in the early 1980s. This layout has a geographical component and subject categories. It is very conducive to browsing and easily adaptable to changing needs and new materials. (Most researchers will find the arrangement very different at first, but many have also commented that they wish other libraries had such a "genealogy-friendly" system that does not rely on numbers.)

There are four major subdivisions of the Library's book collection: General, Families, States & Regions, and Special Collections.

3.3.1
GENERAL SECTION

The General Section contains many subject breakdowns which contain books on general aspects of history and genealogy in the United States. The individual subjects are shelved within the General Section in alphabetical order. Within each subject there are further subdivisions as needed. The following list gives the subject subdivisions within the General Section and some representative examples of further breakdowns. Space limitations on the spine labels necessitate the use of some abbreviations or truncations in the "call words." A diagonal indicates the beginning of a new line, and therefore a new subdivision of a subject. Within each subject and subsection the final line of the "call word" will be the first three letters of the author's last name or of the title if there is no author.

- **Research**
  - Research/Directories
  - Research/Historiography

- **Adoption**

- **African American**

- **Arch** (Architecture)

- **Arch-Lib** (Archives and Libraries)
  - Arch-Lib/LC (Library of Congress)
  - Arch-Lib/LDS (LDS Family History Library and System)
  - Arch-Lib/NARA (National Archives and Records Administration)

- **Bibliogra** (Bibliography)

- **Biography**

- **Cemeteries**

- **Census** (arranged by state, then by census year)

- **Computers** (computer applications for genealogy)

- **Dictionaries** (English and many foreign language dictionaries)

- **Emig** (Emigration and Immigration; arranged in a general section followed by national/ethic groups in alphabetical order and a section of published passenger lists.)

- **Families** (contains collected works on families and general studies on the history of the American family. It is not the same as the "Families" section below.)

- **Genetics**

- **Geography** (contains atlases, gazetters, and postal directories)

- **History** (United States history arranged chronologically)
  - History/1607-1775 (The Colonial Period)
  - History/1775-1783 (The American Revolution)
    - History/1775-1783/African American
    - History/1775-1783/Bibliogra
    - History/1775-1783/Biography
    - History/1775-1783/Claims
    - History/1775-1783/Congress
    - History/1775-1783/F: +a country's name (=foreign involvement in the Revolution by country in alphabetical order)
    - History/1775-1783/Folklore
    - History/1775-1783/Geography
    - History/1775-1783/Jews
    - History/1775-1783/Loyalists
    - History/1775-1783/Military
    - History/1775-1783/Music
    - History/1775-1783/Naval
    - History/1775-1783/Newspapers
    - History/1775-1783/Pensions
    - History/1775-1783/Periodica
    - History/1775-1783/Prisoners
    - History/1775-1783/Records
    - History/1775-1783/Religion
    - History/1775-1783/Spies
    - History/1775-1783/Vital
  - History/1783-1812
  - History/1812-1815 (The War of 1812)
  - History/1815-1861
    - History/1815-1861/Mexican War
  - History/1861-1865 (The American Civil War with subdivisions)
  - History/1865-1917
  - History/1917-1918 (World War I)
  - History/1918-1941
  - History/1941-1945 (World War II)
  - History/1945-

- **Index** (major historical and genealogical indices)

- **Land** (basic studies and sources on United States land record)

- **Law** (general legal studies, dictionaries, and histories)

- **Military** (general studies and histories of the United States military)

- **Names** (books on name studies)

- **Newspapers** (information on United States newspapers)

- **Pensions** (published compilations of pensions for various wars)

- **Periodica** (Periodicals. Major nationally-focused genealogical and historical periodicals filed in alphabetical order by title)

- **Records** (general sources of United States historical records, mostly government publications)

- **Reference** (miscellaneous reference sources)

- **Religion** (general books on the history of religion in the United States followed by subdivisions for specific Christian denominations and Judaism)

- **Vital** (a miscellany of vital records covering the entire United States or major portions)

- **Wills** (some collections of wills from around the United States)

Typical "call words" in the General Section look like this in sequence on book spine labels:

GEN	GEN	GEN	GEN	GEN
ADOPTION	CENSUS	EMIG	HISTORY	PERIODICA
SMI	TEXAS	POLISH	1607-1775	TAG
	1870	KAM	JON	

3.2.2
FAMILIES SECTION

The family histories and genealogies are arranged on the shelf in alphabetical order by the main (or sometimes, first) surname in the title or contents. Cross references in the catalog provide access points for other major surnames covered by each book. A "call word" for a Morrison family history by an author named Smith would look like this in the published catalog or in the OPAC: FAMILIES/MORRISON/SMITH, and like this on the spine label of the book or in the card catalog:

FAMILIES

MORRISON

SMITH

Interpreted, this means the book is in the Families Section in the "M's," in alphabetical order under "Morrison." The third line is the author's last name, if there are multiple books on a surname, they are in alphabetical order by each author within the surname's section.

Family histories owned through 1991 are listed in the published *DAR Library Catalogs, Volumes One and Three*. Hundreds more have arrived since 1991.

The states, regions, and District of Columbia are arranged in alphabetical order.

The states, D.C., and regions **east of the Mississippi River** (except Wisconsin) occupy the majority of the space on the Library's first floor. D.C. and smaller states are in alcoves around the perimeter of the first floor.

"Eastern" regions (Midwest, New England, New Netherland) are on the first floor interfiled in alphabetical order with the states. "The South" region is on the lower south balcony.

The states **west of the Mississippi River** (plus Wisconsin) and "The West" region occupy all space on the upper north and east balconies.

Each state and region has subsections, which in most cases are the same as the subsections of the General Section listed above. Books on specific cities and towns are located in the county in which they are located. Independent cities, such as Baltimore, Maryland and those in Virginia, are located in the counties which surround them. The towns of New England states are arranged in alphabetical order within the county in which they are located. There is some variation, however, in the subsections based on specific unique situations in certain states. The major subdivisions within the states and regions are:

The bookstacks in the
State section of the Library.

- **African American**
- **Architecture**
- **Archives and Libraries**
- **Bibliography**
- **Biography**
- **Counties** (By far this is the largest portion of each state section. Regions do not have a "county" subdivision. The counties are in alphabetical order, and within each county's section the books are arranged in alphabetical order by the first three letters of the author's last name or of the title if there is no author.)
- **Education**
- **Emigration and Immigration**
- **Families**
- **G.R.C.** (the state DAR's Genealogical Records Committee set)
- **Geography**

- History
- Land
- Law
- Military
- Newspapers
- Periodicals
- Records
- Reference
- Regions (publications concerning recognized historic regions of a state)
- Religion
- Vital
- Wills
- Women

Representative call numbers in the Alabama section would look like this on book spines:

ALA	ALA	ALA	ALA	ALA	ALA
ARCH	COUNTIES	HISTORY	LAND	MILITARY	VITAL
BLA	JEFFERSON	GAN	GOL	HAM	GRE
		JON			

The following is a compressed and stylized view of what a researcher sees when facing the Alabama section. The "call words" are shown below the book images for clarity; normally they appear on the book spine labels. Each state and region has a similar arrangment.

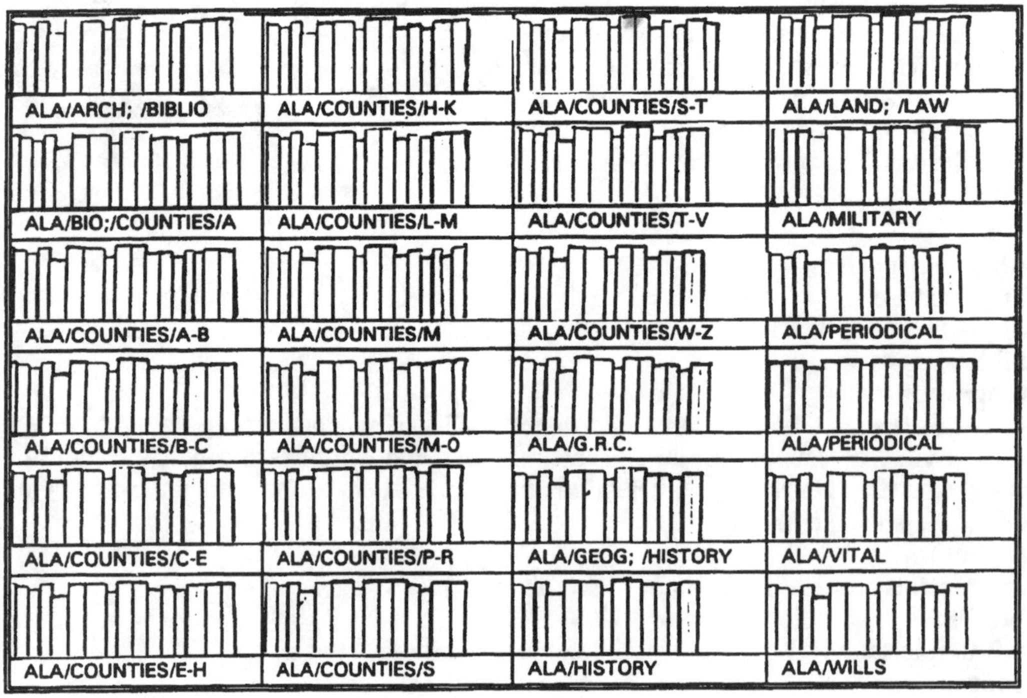

ALA/ARCH; /BIBLIO	ALA/COUNTIES/H-K	ALA/COUNTIES/S-T	ALA/LAND; /LAW
ALA/BIO;/COUNTIES/A	ALA/COUNTIES/L-M	ALA/COUNTIES/T-V	ALA/MILITARY
ALA/COUNTIES/A-B	ALA/COUNTIES/M	ALA/COUNTIES/W-Z	ALA/PERIODICAL
ALA/COUNTIES/B-C	ALA/COUNTIES/M-O	ALA/G.R.C.	ALA/PERIODICAL
ALA/COUNTIES/C-E	ALA/COUNTIES/P-R	ALA/GEOG; /HISTORY	ALA/VITAL
ALA/COUNTIES/E-H	ALA/COUNTIES/S	ALA/HISTORY	ALA/WILLS

The Library maintains several special collections which are housed on the upper south balcony. Each has its own separate subject subdivisions, but these are essentially the same as those in the General Section and the State and Regions Section. These Special Collections are:

A view from the Library's South Balcony.

American Indian Collection is a significant, growing collection of materials on the first peoples of North America focusing on genealogy, history, and culture. The books are arranged by general subject groups, but materials specific to a nation/tribe are organized first by broad Native American cultural areas and then by the nation/tribe name. See section 13.22.

Biography contains studies of prominent historical Americans and collected biography. See section 13.3 for more information.

City Directories number 1,100 volumes from around the United States, mostly from the early twentieth century. See section 13.6.

DAR Publications includes DAR State organization rosters and histories and *The DAR Lineage Books*. See Chapter 12.

Foreign Research is a basic gathering of books to assist researchers with investigations beyond the United States. Refer to section 13.11.

Women's History is a small collection on the history of women in the United States. See sections 13.20.4.6 and 13.29.

W.P.A. Collection contains a large percentage of the publications of the Historical Records Survey of the Works Progress Administration. See section 13.10 for further information.

In addition to these Special Collections housed on the balconies, the Library has other Special Collections and special condition books stored in areas mostly accessible to the staff only. Please ask for assistance in locating materials in the following collections:

American Flag Collection consists of a small set on the history of the American flag.

Lineage Society Collection includes many but not all publications of other lineage societies similar to the DAR, such as the Sons of the American Revolution, the Sons of the Revolution, the Colonial Dames of the XVII Century, and others. See section 13.18 for more information.

"Poor Condition" Books are cataloged books which are brittle or fragile and must be handled with care. Watch for the phrases "Poor condition, ask in office" or "Poor condition, ask at desk" for these books. Please request such books at the reference desk only. In most cases, the staff cannot make photocopies from these volumes.

"Locked Case" Books are cataloged books which are locked in cases because of their age, rarity and value. Researchers must present one form of identification to use these volumes, leave the ID at the reference desk, and return the book to regain their ID. Watch for the initials "L.C." at the beginning of the call words in the catalog.

Oversize Section houses books which will not fit easily on the regular shelves. Their cataloging records note "OV" before the call words.

3.4
FILE COLLECTION

The Library's file collection is a mixture of materials which have come with DAR membership applications (see Chapter 6.9), subsequent donations by DAR members, and items given by the public. Innumerable Bible records, family studies, pamphlets, and research notes are included. Numbering an estimated 250,000 folders, the richness and variety of the collection covers the entire United States and concentrates on the eighteenth, nineteenth, and early twentieth centuries, with significant colonial records as well.

There are no published or in-house guides to the files, which grow by several boxes each month. The simple arrangement in one alphabet within each division of the files by the names of Revolutionary War ancestors or family surnames makes for relatively easy retrieval.

A miscellany of brief sources for each state including pamphlets, short typescripts, handwritten notes, published booklets, extracted journal and newspaper articles and clippings, and copies of original documents comprises the Library's "State File Collection." Cemetery records, military lists, church materials, local histories, and other historically useful materials are represented. Researchers may request staff assistance to browse through a state section for items of interest.

The library staff assists researchers in locating and copying material in the file collection. All files must be ordered and used in the Library office. Most items in the files may be photocopied.

A growing manuscript library of identifiable collections of genealogical research materials is one of the lesser known components of the DAR Library. Each month boxes and folders of notes, documents, unpublished genealogies, and indexes arrive. Examples include the Anne Waller Reddy Collection of Virginia family research performed by a Richmond genealogist in the mid-twentieth century; a two-drawer card file containing data on the Oysterbank family of New England; a largely complete run of *The Hartford Times* (Connecticut) genealogical queries column, 1934-1964; and Lyman Chalkley's original annotated typescript for his three-volume publication *Chronicles of the Scotch-Irish Settlement in Virginia*, first published by the DAR in 1912. The Library's catalog provides access to the manuscript collection. *The National Union Catalog of Manuscript Collections (NUCMC)* set directs researchers to additional manuscript sources beyond DAR holdings.

The Library often receives requests from individuals for information on a relative's research materials which "were given to the DAR." Very rarely does the staff locate such a collection, but sometimes the search is successful. Unfortunately, in the past a register of such manuscript donations was not maintained to help clarify such questions now. A possible solution may be that the relative gave it to the local DAR chapter or state organization. They in turn may have donated it to a local genealogical or historical society. They may have kept the material for their own files. Such materials are unlikely to appear in indices to manuscript collections such as *NUCMC*. Researchers should exhaust all possible leads regarding such donations.

Genealogists of families which live in or passed through Virginia's Shenandoah Valley will all know the name of Lyman Chalkley and his three-volume work *Chronicles of the Scotch-Irish Settlement in Virginia Extracted from the Original Court Records of Augusta County 1745-1800*. Few will realize, however, that this set was originally published by the DAR in 1912, seven years after the National Society purchased the manuscript from Judge Chalkley.

Publication of the *Chronicles* was not without controversy, owing in large part to the fact that the abstracts comprising the book were by no means complete and were very selective. The *Proceedings* for both the 1911 and 1912 DAR Continental Congress contain lengthy discussions on the merits and drawbacks to publishing Chalkley's manuscripts. DAR even commissioned an independent review of the materials. This was performed by one Thomas Forsythe Nelson, was entitled *Report on the Chalkley Manuscripts*, and concluded that while the work was useful, the pervasive gaps therein diminished its publication value.

After much discussion, the DAR decided to publish the material despite its limitations to make some information available from the extensive historical records of Virginia's Augusta County. Chalkley's set has assumed a major place in the historical and genealogical literature of the Shenandoah Valley. It has been reprinted several times. Researchers should be aware that there are many omissions from the original records and should not consider these books the final word from Augusta County's early records. Chalkely's original handwritten volumes and notes are part of the DAR Library's Manuscript Collection.

Some research notes and materials from individuals do exist on the shelves of the Library. In decades past, the staff apparently took such loose papers, bound them together, and added them to the collection as a volume. These materials appear in the catalog now as books.

With a functioning manuscript collection and proper donation procedures in place, the Library welcomes donations of research material. When such collections arrive, they are given a collection name (usually the name of the donor or compiler), accessioned, cataloged with subject tracings, and added to the Manuscript Collection for use.

BALTIMORE DEPARTMENT,

ROYAL INSURANCE COMPANY

(FIRE)

of Liverpool.

M. G. SHAW,
AGENT.

NEW WINDSOR, MD. 188

October 21 1889

My Dear Grandaughter
I will try to write you A full lines but I am suffering
so much with my back that I can scearcely write
but as I doo not know when youill be maried I have
A quilt for you dont know if you are coming up you
and Mr Haden sorry I cant be there but I am not able
to come pleas Let me know if you can come pleas dont
Let him see this I am so nurveous rest all well
my love to all in hast   your poor OLD Granma
S I Shaw

Letter from the Eunice B. Haden Collection,
DAR Library Manuscript Collection Number 95

3.6
RESEARCH SERVICE

The DAR Library offers a research service to members and non-members. The "DAR Library Research Service" information sheet follows. Please consult it for fees and procedures. These may change if necessary and without prior notice.

 National Society Daughters of the American Revolution

DAR LIBRARY ● 1776 D Street, NW ● Washington, DC 20006–5392

DAR Library Research Service

The following options supersede all previous mail order policies.

Photocopy Requests/Search
For books and magazines in the DAR Library collection.
- Photocopying from books and magazines within the limits of copyright law.
- NSDAR members pay a flat fee of $5.00 which includes the first five pages of photocopying. **Please include your membership number in the correspondence.**
- Nonmembers pay a flat fee of $10.00 which includes the first five pages of photocopying
- Send the fee with your inquiry, we will bill you for any photocopying over five pages at the rate of $1.25 for the first page and .30 cents per page thereafter.

File Search
The DAR Library has an extensive file collection relating to Revolutionary War patriots and their descendants, but **we do not have a file for every patriot in the Patriot Index.**
- Finding and photocopying documentation files.
- NSDAR members pay a flat fee of $5.00 which includes the first five pages of photocopying. **Please include your membership number in the correspondence.**
- Nonmembers pay a flat fee of $10.00 which includes the first five pages of photocopying
- Send the fee with your inquiry, we will bill you for any photocopying over five pages at the rate of $1.25 for the first page and .30 cents per page thereafter.
- To comply with state laws, the Library research staff cannot photocopy vital records from state health departments contained in the files, including birth, death, and divorce records.
- Please limit to no more than two patriot files per request.

The Research Service
For questions that require in–depth research.
- NSDAR members pay a fee of $20.00 per hour of research which includes the first five pages of photocopying. **Please include your membership number in the correspondence.**
- Nonmembers pay $25.00 per hour of research which includes the first five pages of photocopying
- Send the fee with your inquiry, we will bill you for any photocopying over five pages at the rate of $1.25 for the first page and .30 cents per page thereafter.
- There is a maximum of four hours of research per request.
- The requestor will be sent a report and informed if additional hours of research are necessary

Write all checks payable to "Treasurer General, NSDAR".

ALL FEES ARE FOR RESEARCH AND ARE NON–REFUNDABLE.
WE DO <u>NOT</u> GUARANTEE THAT MATERIAL WILL BE FOUND.

Revised 12/96   *0297–10000–PS*

3.7
PHOTOCOPIES

The Library staff performs all photocopying to maintain both the copy machines and the materials in the collection. Researchers in person fill out "photocopy order slips" for each book or file containing pages they wish copied. Payment in advance at the reference desk is required. One does not need to bring rolls of coins to make copies at the Library, but small bills are appreciated.

Copyright is a major consideration in the duplication of materials. The DAR Library will not copy entire books or major portions of books for researchers, especially if a book is still under copyright. The staff will assist researchers in an attempt to locate current order information for a book. Researchers may request photocopies by mail from the Library's Research Service. See section 3.6.

On occasion, the staff will not make copies from a book if the copying process will damage the item. Researchers should expect this possibility, and their understanding is appreciated. This is the only reason why copies cannot be made of materials in the Library.

Personal hand-held copiers are not permitted in any of the DAR's departments.

3.8
BOOK AND SERIALS DONATIONS

The Library welcomes donations of genealogical books and other materials from DAR members and the public. Please contact the Acquisitions Librarian to offer items to the Library (202-879-3250). The Serials Librarian processes all donations of newsletters, journals, and other periodicals (202-879-3228). Books and periodicals need not be bound or indexed to be accepted, but binding and indexing are always desirable. The general types of materials acceptable to the Library fall into these broad categories:

- genealogy and family history
- national, state and local history, record abstracts, etc.
- records and histories of religious groups and denominations
- historical and genealogical periodicals, newsletters, journals, yearbooks, etc.
- histories and sources for the period of the American Revolution
- biographies of major figures in American history

One of the unanticipated but none the less desirable results of what I might call the ancestral–patriotic movement is the publication of a variety of fresh, delightful books relating to American history. Personally, I delight in these accessions to our Daughters of the American Revolution Library to such an extent that I have to add many of them to my private library, even though my shelves are filled to overflowing.

Anita Newcomb McGee, First DAR Librarian General,
in her column "Our Library"
American Monthly Magazine, 1897, p. 188-189.

Please do not send poetry, literature, cookbooks, illustrated historical calendars, historical fiction, or children's books. Titles in these subjects do not meet the Library's collection policy.

The Library produces a list of newly **donated** books three times each year in the April, June and December issues of *The DAR Magazine* following the reports of the Librarian General. These lists are arranged by the state from which the book was donated for internal DAR purposes. Lists of newly **purchased** books are too lengthy for inclusion in the magazine.

3.9
FINDING RECENT AND OUT-OF-PRINT BOOKS

Recent books often have order information printed on the back of the title page. The Library staff will help locate order information from this source and our acquisition records. Such standard sources as *Books in Print, Genealogical and Local History Books in Print*, publisher catalogs and the book review sections of major genealogical and historical journals assist with this type of search.

Many, many books in the Library, however, are no longer available for purchase from the author or publisher, especially the family histories and genealogies. For copyright and staffing reasons the Library cannot copy entire books. Incredibly, some ask us to sell the books to them, which is, of course, impossible.

The Library maintains many catalogs of recent publications and receives a number of catalogs from out-of-print/rare book dealers. Directories of these are also available such as the Burns' *A Guide to Used Book Dealers of the Mid-Atlantic*. Some reprint companies specializing in genealogical and local history materials also exist. The staff will help researchers by checking a specific book for possible valid ordering information.

Researchers should also check local yellow page listings under "Books–Used and Rare" for their home city or city in the locality of research interest. These dealers will check their own stock, and many will do searches.

Phone listings on CD-ROM and through the Internet can make this type of long-distance searching easier.

GENEALOGICAL RECORDS COMMITTEE

The New York DAR's Genealogical Records Committee set contains nearly 1,000 volumes.

*I*n 1913 DAR established the Genealogical Research Committee as an internal network to collect genealogical information for the DAR Library. The name changed to Genealogical Records Committee (G.R.C.) in 1932. The main function of this Committee and its state and chapter chairmen is to copy, prepare in proper form, bind and place in the Library information of genealogical value from unpublished sources such as family Bibles, gravestones, court records, etc. A small manual, *Instructions for Copying Source Records and Their Preparation for Library Use*, is available explaining how this work should be performed. Since its inception, the G.R.C. has worked to gather this information with great success.

4.1
G.R.C. REPORTS

Numbering some 14,000 typescript volumes, the *Genealogical Records Committee Reports*, as they are collectively called, comprise one of the most important and unique parts of the DAR Library's holdings. DAR members have gathered and submitted these unpublished compilations of Bible, cemetery, family, vital, county, town, church, and military records since the late 1910s. The pre-1972 books were microfilmed by the Genealogical Society of Utah, but an equal number have arrived since this filming. Because the work of the G.R.C. is on-going, users of the Library should expect to find new material throughout the year. State DAR organizations may also place copies of their reports in a library or libraries in that state. Frequently, these will be the state library, historical society, or a major public library. Sometimes there is a small State DAR library. The DAR Library in Washington is the only research center owning nearly all of the G.R.C. Reports comprising the national set. Approximately 400-500 new books arrive each year. The Library has not been able to determine the locations of all of the state sets unfortunately. See Chapter 12 for a listing of known state DAR libraries and repositories.

The submission of information is simple. Members of the DAR provide previously unpublished genealogical information to their chapter G.R.C. chairman, who passes the properly typed version on to the state chairman. The material submitted may be for any state in the country, not just the state of membership. The state chairman then submits the material collected from her state as one or more volumes to the national office at DAR Headquarters. Most states contribute at least one book of records each year, and several donate many annually.

The varied nature of the contents of G.R.C. reports makes indexing essential. A report from Oregon could conceivably contain records from any other state as well as items from Oregon. Consequently, much material is "buried" in volumes from states where records did not originate. Such is the nature of the genealogical material that any group of genealogists might have in their collection; fewer and fewer people live in the same locality where their ancestors did. Generally speaking, G.R.C. reports from each eastern state tend to contain sources from that state, while the further west one goes the reports contain a greater variety of record origins.

> The work of our Genealogical Records Committee is like the brook, it "goes on forever," and also like the brook it flows through interesting phases of the work and tedious shoals, but finally, gleefully and serenely, flows into the river as the finished volume gets to our National Library of the Daughters of the American Revolution.
>
> Nell Downing Norton, National Vice Chairman,
> Genealogical Records Committee, Central Division,
> in her article "Genealogical Records" in the
> *Daughters of the American Revolution Magazine,*
> December 1946, p. 641.

The size of each state's set of reports varies greatly from the nearly 1,000 New York volumes to a few for Alaska and Hawaii. Some states have prepared published indices to their set of books. Recent every-name indices prepared by DAR members include those for Virginia, Maryland, and West Virginia.

The importance of the G.R.C. Reports for genealogists cannot be overstated. Many privately owned, inaccessible records for families all over the United States have been transcribed. Bible records and cemetery inscriptions are the mainstay of the reports, but just about any kind of record might be found in them. Many cemeteries which were surveyed in the early twentieth century by the DAR no longer exist or the stones are now illegible. Numerous reports contain abstracts of complete county court books such as marriage registers, deed books, and probate records. Church records have been popular sources for abstracts and transcriptions. Every part of the county is not covered in depth, however, but researchers should investigate the possibility that the DAR may have collected exactly what they need. A chapter in one county may have been very active, while one in an adjoining county may not have produced any abstracts.

Access to the information contained in the G.R.C. Reports is through several finding aids. First, the DAR Library's Analytical Index provides entries to many of the reports although indexing of many states' sets stopped in the late 1960s. A few have been brought closer to the present however. This are not an every-name index because of the quantity of books involved. The card citations indicate that information on a specific family or church cemetery, as examples, is located on noted pages of a particular report. The references may be very brief in the early years, not even describing a family's state of residence. More recent indexing includings more descriptive information for each entry to clarify them for researchers.

Please see Chapter 14 for information on the proper bibliographic citation of Genealogical Records Committee Reports.

4.2
LDS MICROFILMS OF G.R.C. REPORTS

In the early 1970s the Genealogical Society of Utah sent a microfilming team to the DAR Library and filmed most of the G.R.C. Reports then in the collection. These films are available for use at the Seimes Microfilm Center, the Family History Library in Salt Lake City and its Family History Centers, and at the Allen County Public Library in Fort Wayne, Indiana. There are nearly 2,800 rolls of microfilm. Each roll contains the pages of several volumes of G.R.C. reports. Since completion of the filming in 1972, thousands more volumes have arrived in the DAR Library. These have not been microfilmed.

Researchers may be familiar with several printed indices to the microfilm of the G.R.C. Reports, but many may not realize that these books actually index a major portion of the DAR Library's collection. Use of these can provide a genealogist with an early start on their visit to the Library. These volumes are:

● John D. and E. Diane Stemmons. *The Cemetery Record Compendium: Comprising a Directory of Cemetery Records and Where They May Be Found.* Logan, Utah: Everton, 1979. Not all cemetery records in this index are for the G.R.C. Reports on microfilm, only those followed by the film numbers to which is appended the note "DAR" [Example: G907987, DAR].

● John D. and E. Diane Stemmons. *The Vital Record Compendium: Comprising a Directory of Vital Records and Where They May Be Located.* Logan, Utah: Everton, 1979. Again, not every listing is for the G.R.C. Reports on microfilm, but many are.

● E. Kay Kirkham. *An Index to Some of the Family Records of the Southern States: 35,000 Microfilm References from the NSDAR Files and Elsewhere.* [Vol. 1]. Logan, Utah: Everton, 1979. The entries are for the G.R.C. microfilms.

● E. Kay Kirkham. *An Index to Some of the Bibles and Family Records of the United States (excluding the Southern States): 45,500 References as Taken from the Microfilm at the Genealogical Society of Utah (NSDAR).* [vol. 2] Logan, Utah: Everton, 1984. The entries are for the G.R.C. microfilms.

The four books listed above are not for sale by the DAR. Inquiries on availability should be sent to Everton Publishers, Inc., P.O. Box 368, Logan, UT 84323-0368.

Genealogists should check these guides to determine if records they need are in DAR collections. Read the introductions to each volume carefully. The only exception in these introductions is the statement that the six-digit film numbers do not apply to the record's location at the DAR. This is incorrect, because a set of the microfilms is in the Seimes Microfilm Center, and the films are arranged by the LDS numbers. Copies from the microfilms may be ordered from the Center.

Reproduction of entire rolls from the DAR's G.R.C. microfilms is restricted by agreement between the Genealogical Society of Utah and the DAR. Requests for such copies must be approved by the DAR Library Director and will be considered on a case-by-case basis. Generally, approval for reproduction of DAR microfilms by GSU will be given only to another library and not to individuals. The DAR itself does not reproduce or loan these microfilms or the original books.

The contents of the G.R.C. microfilms are included in the "Family History Library Catalog" on CD-ROM, part of the *FamilySearch* database, by subjects or by roll numbers. Another older listing of the contents of the G.R.C. microfilms may be available to researchers in libraries around the country:

Ruby Lacy. *DAR Records on Microfilm Available in Salt Lake City Genealogical Society Library*, 4 volumes. Ashland, Oregon: R. Lacy, 1978, 1979.

Vol. 1: Alabama, Arkansas, Illinois, Indiana, Iowa, North Dakota, North Carolina

Vol. 2: Arizona, Connecticut, Delaware, Kentucky, Ohio, Oregon, Pennsylvania, Tennessee

Vol. 3: Colorado, Florida, Louisiana, Maine, Minnesota, Montana, Nebraska, New Hampshire, New Jersey, Rhode Island, Texas, Virginia

Vol. 4: California, District of Columbia & Miscellaneous, Georgia, Idaho, Kansas, Maryland, Massachusetts, Michigan, New York, Oklahoma, South Carolina, Vermont, West Virginia

According to the introduction to these catalogs, they have "been gathered from the reports of the camera operators of the Genealogical Department of the Church of Jesus Christ of Latter Day Saints in Salt Lake City, Utah as they microfilmed the DAR Library collections in 1970-1971." Ten states are not listed in Mrs. Lacy's catalogs; perhaps these were the ones filmed in 1972.

While these catalogs are helpful in that they group together by state all of the randomly assigned film numbers, they naturally repeat the vague and very incomplete title information the film operators noted in their reports. From the viewpoint of the DAR Library, the titles of the books noted in these filming reports usually do not reflect the actual titles of the books as they appear on the title page. Abbreviated titles from the spine of the book may have been used. It is often very difficult and sometimes impossible to match the actual book in the DAR Library with a copy on a reel of microfilm because of these discrepancies.

4.3
THE GRANDPARENT PROJECT

The Grandparent Project began in the late 1950s as a research aid enabling prospective DAR members to link their lineage to those of existing members with shared grandparents. Members were to copy their application papers starting with their grandparents and working back to the Revolutionary ancestor. Because this was a voluntary project among DAR members and because the project started when DAR was nearly seventy years old, many members are not represented in these sources. Consequently, there is not a form for every ancestor listed in the DAR Patriot Index. The Genealogical Records Committee administered the project.

There are a total of 875 volumes of "Grandparent Papers." Whole number volumes 1 (1960) through 670 (1972; Series 12, vol. 57), which comprise the first twelve series of this set, were microfilmed by the LDS Church during its filming project from 1970-1972. Volumes 671 (1973) through 875 (1983) are only in book form. All books must be requested and used in the Genealogical Records Committee Office on the second floor of the Library. While the project itself ended in 1981, papers completed before the termination continued to arrive, so there are volumes dated 1982 and 1983.

The indices to the grandparent papers are located in the DAR Library. There are two indices to the papers, one for the name of Revolutionary War ancestors and one for the names of the grandparents of members who participated in the project. The index to ancestors is complete, but that for grandparents is not. The indices refer to the twelve series and the volume numbers within each series, **NOT** to the sequential whole volume numbers added as a shelving device by the staff.

Please note that changes to records of ancestors' service in the Revolutionary War may have resulted in some ancestors being removed from the *DAR Patriot Index*. To verify service for any Revolutionary War ancestors appearing in the Grandparent Project, please contact the Office of the Registrar General.

The names of the grandparents are only completely indexed for the entire set through part of the letter "H". The names of grandparents in other parts of the alphabet are *partially* indexed. If the line goes through a grandmother, her **maiden name** is used, *not* her married name. Within Series 1-12, the grandparent papers are arranged in alphabetical order by the names of the grandparents within each series. Within volumes 671-875 the papers are arranged in alphabetical order by grandparent's name *within each volume!*

Researchers at DAR may request copies directly through the Genealogical Records Committee Office during their visit to the building. Those seeking access from a distance may write to the Genealogical Records Committee giving the name, birth date, death date, and name of spouse of an individual grandparent or the Revolutionary War ancestor. One may order copies from the Genealogical Records Committee Office for $2.00 per set. All checks should be sent with the request to the appropriate office and be made payable to "Treasurer General NSDAR."

SEIMES MICROFILM CENTER

Location: Administration Building, First Floor, Room 104
Telephone: 202-879-3246

The DAR established the Betty Newkirk Seimes Microfilm Center in 1970, and named it for the then-President General. In April 1978, the 87th DAR Continental Congress made the Microfilm Center a National Committee. A National Chairman is appointed by the President General and each State Regent appoints a State Chairman for this Committee whose chief duty is to promote interest in the Center. The existence and continuing growth of the Center is in conformance with DAR's purpose to collect and preserve documents and records relevant to the individual services of Revolutionary War soldiers and patriots and the lineage of members of proven descent. The Center combined existing microfilm holdings of the Office of the Registrar General and the DAR Library. Since then, the collection has expanded considerably and embraces many valuable research materials. Seimes Microfilm Center works in coorporation with the DAR Library, the Office of the Registrar General, the Lineage Research Committee and the Genealogical Records Committee.

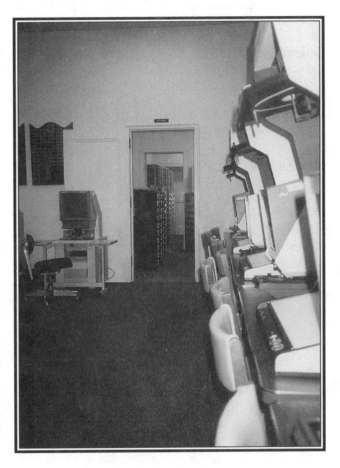

A view in the Seimes Microfilm Center

Visitors should sign-in on entry to the Center, obtain a reader assignment, and explain to the staff what they are researching. Those who are not members of the DAR, SAR, CAR, or SR must present a pass from the Library. The Center is equipped with microfilm and microfiche readers and printers and a CD-ROM computer. Copies may be made from all sources **except** DAR membership applications. These must be ordered in the Registrar General's Clerical Office (Record Copy).

The microform collection has been cataloged. The resulting records are in the OPAC (on-line public access catalog) available for use in the Microfilm Center.

As the DAR's microform library, the Center contains a wide variety of microfilm and microfiche publications and special collections. DAR membership applications, state and federal records pertaining to the American Revolution, federal census records 1840-1900, and many sources from state archives not available elsewhere in Washington form the core of the collection. The major types of sources in the Center are:

DAR Membership Applications: These are on microfilm and microfiche. Researchers should provide the staff with national numbers to view application papers. Order copies in the Office of the Registrar General.

Federal census records, 1840-1900 including the 1880 and 1900 Soundex. See the "Census Research" section in Chapter 12 for more information. Selected lists for the 1790 through 1830 censuses are available on CD-ROM. Printed census indices are in the DAR Library.

Genealogical Records Committee Reports on microfilm: Nearly 2,800 rolls of unique DAR volumes were produced by the Genealogical Society of Utah in 1970-1972. These films are in the Center along with printed indices. See Chapter 4.2 for details.

Special Collections: Most of these sets of microfilm or microfiche contain state and local records. For additional listings see Chapter 13.27.

- Draper Manuscript Collection
- Index to pre-1870 Vermont vital records
- South Carolina Combined Alphabetical Index and other South Carolina probate and land records
- Spanish Land Grants in Florida
- Illinois Name Index to Early Records and Index to Illinois County Histories
- Kentucky county tax lists (pre-1850)
- Maryland Prerogative Court Wills 1639-1777
- Massachusetts Vital and Town Records on microfiche
- Missouri county records (indices to deeds, wills, marriages for most counties; 400 reels)
- New Jersey county ratables, 1778-1832
- North Carolina records of Revolutionary War accounts and Warrants and Surveys, Western Territory (Tennessee) 1778-1791
- New Hampshire indices to vital records to 1900
- Ohio Civil War Regimental Histories and Reunions
- Ohio County History Surname Index
- Tennessee Index to Land Grants, 1775-1905

Federal Revolutionary War records: Major microfilm publications relating to the American Revolution from the National Archives are available in the Center. Many similar sources from state archives are also available or planned for purchase.

- *Compiled Service Records of American Naval Personnel ... Quartermaster General and the Commissary General ... During the Revolutionary War, NARA RG-93, M-880*
- *Compiled Service Records of soldiers who served in the American Army during the Revolutionary War, NARA RG-93, M-881*
- *General Index to Compiled Service Records of Revolutionary War Soldiers, NARA RG-93, M-860*
- *Miscellaneous Numbered Records ... 1775-1783, NARA RG-93, M-847 Special Index to Numbered Records...1775-1783, NARA RG-93, M-847*

- *Papers of the Continental Congress, NARA RG-360, M-247*
- *Records of the Continental Loan Office, 1777-1791, NARA RG 53, M-247*
- *Revolutionary War Pension and Bounty Land Warrant Application Files, NARA RG-15, M-804*
- *Ledgers of Payments to U.S. Pensioners Under Acts of 1818 through 1858, NARA RG-217, T-718*

These are just a few examples of valuable sources available in the Microfilm Center. The holdings in general compliment those in the DAR Library. A continuing effort to acquire further materials from state archives promises to enrich the collection with sources not available in any other research center in Washington, D.C.

The number of staff members in the Center is small, therefore, they cannot perform genealogical research. Please contact the DAR Library's Research Service for this assistance. Orders for photocopies from sources in microform, however, may be made directly to the Center in writing.

A valuable addition to the library during the past three years have been the microfilming of the state census records from 1850 through 1880. Thirty-one states have completed this project. We had hoped to have the number finished during this regime. We have just received a letter from the Acting Chief, Information and Publications, Bureau of the U.S. Census, telling us that because of the requirements of the armed forces "In order to avoid the possibility of rationing films you are strongly urged to phtograph nothing but your most important work. The photographing of old records and similar documents should be postponed for the duration." Therefore it is with regret we annound that we shall discontinue microfilming the census records until such time as we can obtain films.

from, Report of the Librarian General, April 1945, *National Historical Magazine*, June 1945, p. 407.

OFFICE OF THE REGISTRAR GENERAL

*T*he Registrar General's office is comprised of several sections and committee offices: the Genealogy Department, the Clerical Department, the Record Copy Office, the Patriot Index National Committee, and the Lineage Research National Committee Office. The Seimes Microfilm Center has been under the joint supervision of the Registrar General and the Librarian General since 1970. Some of the activities of these sections is pertinent to general genealogical research, while others are specifically internal.

Basically, the Registrar General oversees the processing and approval of membership applications and the attendant materials that process produces. These materials represent a significant portion of the DAR's unique research sources. Genealogists should understand the arrangement, benefits, and limitations of these sources to make the most of their content.

6.1
THE GENEALOGY DEPARTMENT

The staff genealogists work specifically on the verification of application papers for pending members of the DAR and supplemental applications for members. Prospective members make their contacts with this office through the chapter and state registrars. Anyone interested in initiating the membership process should contact the DAR's Membership Services office or a local DAR chapter. The work of the Genealogy Department is vital to the continued admission of new members to the National Society. The office itself does not provide genealogical research or reference assistance to individuals either by phone, by mail, or in person. General researchers should not contact the Genealogy Department with these objectives in mind.

From a general research standpoint, however, the importance of the Genealogy Department is its production of verified membership applications. These become available to researchers and potential DAR members shortly after the application has been approved. The application papers, the supporting documentation which accompanies them and related finding aids are some of the DAR's most basic and important research sources.

6.2
LINEAGE RESEARCH NATIONAL COMMITTEE

The Lineage Research office, established in 1961, assists prospective members who have been referred by a State Lineage Research Chairman. The staff does not provide assistance to the public or help with supplemental applications for members.

For those who are seeking membership in the DAR, the national office will assist in the following three categories:

- Locating a line to a Revolutionary War Patriot
- Locating documentation for DAR applications which now require additional proof.
- Locating another ancestor as a substitute when necessary.

Details on the Committee's work may be found in the DAR publication "Application Papers: Instructions for Their Preparation" (September 1995, page 17).

The Committee also assembles a "Lineage Research Kit" of information brochures, research aids and forms relating to genealogy. This may be purchased through the Office of the Corresponding Secretary General.

6.3
THE REGISTRAR GENERAL CLERICAL DEPARTMENT
AND RECORD COPY OFFICE

Location: Administration Building, First Floor, Room 108
Telephone: 202-879-3247

The R.G. Clerical Department is often a researcher's first stop at DAR Headquarters. The staff maintain the actual ancestor card file of "The DAR Patriot Index" (see section 6.4) and serve as the public contact point for access to membership applications and supplementals through the index. Visitors to the Clerical Office may request information on a specific ancestor in person. The staff will also respond to requests for information from the index in writing and by telephone. Information provided by telephone will be limited, however, to verification of the fact that an individual is an established ancestor. National numbers will not be given over the telephone. Please do not request information by fax. All inquiries are answered in order of receipt.

To gain access to membership applications on microfilm, researchers must have the national numbers of a DAR member. They obtain these in the Clerical Office by completing the following form for the staff to use in checking the card index.

ANCESTOR'S NAME

WIFE'S NAME

DATE OF BIRTH

DATE OF DEATH

STATE OF SERVICE

CHILD, IF KNOWN

It is very important to provide as much information as possible to help the staff identify the correct ancestor. Copies of *The DAR Patriot Index, Centennial Edition* are available on the research table in this office or in libraries nationwide to help begin the search. Earlier editions are not valid. One important piece of information is the name of a specific child through which a researcher seeks a lineage. Researchers may request three national numbers at a time and may request more later. If one is only seeking information on a patriot's Revolutionary War service, please state that.

Prior to the late 1980s, when the practice was abolished, some members closed their applications to viewing for personal reasons. Consequently, there are some applications which may not be examined. The staff will state if the only paper on a particular ancestor is closed, but they cannot provide additional information on that paper until the member dies, resigns or personally lifts the restriction.

This office also maintains a 317-drawer card index of the national numbers of DAR members. The cards are in numerical order and list each member's ancestor(s) associated with her original and any supplemental applications. The index helps tie together these papers which are filed in different locations and reproduced on different microfilms or microfiche based on the date they were received.

After receiving a national number, researchers must go to the Seimes Microfilm Center to view the films. See Chapter 5 for more information on the Center.

Copies of applications (record copy) must be ordered, however, through the Clerical Office using the proper form. As of this writing, the cost for a copy of one set of application papers (four pages) is $5.00. Checks should be made payable to "Treasurer General, NSDAR." Mail order should be sent to "Record Copy," Office of the Registrar General, 1776 D St., N.W., Washington, D.C. 20006-5392.

Orders placed in person prior to 12:30 p.m. each day may be ready by 2:00 p.m. Those placed later will be ready the following day or may be mailed on request. Only six record copy orders may be placed at a time in person. There is no limit on the number which may be ordered by mail. Pre-payment is required.

Some restrictions apply on obtaining copies of DAR membership applications. Please see the order forms on the next two pages for details.

RECEIPT NO. _____

N S D A R
OFFICE OF THE REGISTRAR GENERAL
Record Copy Department

<u>WALK IN</u>

Date: _____

<u>ONLY</u> those who fall into one of the categories listed below (as written in the Executive Board Ruling 1967), may receive copies of applications of <u>**ACTIVE**</u> members:

_____ a. Members of the NSDAR (Give your DAR Number)
_____ b. Prospective members of the NSDAR (Give Chapter name)
_____ c. Genealogist of the N.S.C.A.R.
_____ d. Official Registrar/Genealogist of the S.A.R.
_____ e. Official Registrar of the S.R.

<u>**PLEASE CHECK CATEGORY ABOVE.**</u>   **FEE PER COPY: $5.00**

Number of Copies Ordered: _____ Amount $ Paid: _____ CASH _____ CHECK

NAME OF ANCESTOR OR MEMBER   **NSDAR NUMBER**

1. _____   _____

2. _____   _____

3. _____   _____

4. _____   _____

5. _____   _____

6. _____   _____

REQUESTOR'S NAME AND ADDRESS:

_____

_____

_____
City & State   Zip Code

National Society Daughters of the American Revolution
Administration Building, 1776 D Street, NW
Washington, DC 20006–5392

RECORD COPY DEPARTMENT, Office of the Registrar General

REQUEST FORM
COPY OF ANCESTOR AND/OR MEMBER'S APPLICATION

INSTRUCTIONS: 1. Complete ONLY the section applicable. If you wish a copy of a specific ancestor record filed by a member, use the DAR Member's Application section ONLY. **2.** If you want the record of a specific ancestor and do not have the name of the member, use the Revolutionary War Ancestor portion ONLY. **3.** GIVE ALL KNOWN DATA FOR THE ANCESTOR AND LIST ANY VARIANT SPELLINGS FOR THE SURNAME. **4.** Clearly indicate if you will accept a paper thru a child other than the child listed. **5.** USE A SEPARATE FORM FOR EACH RECORD REQUESTED. (Form may be copied.) **6.** PRINT or TYPE all sections. Your name, address and chapter name must be LEGIBLE. **7.** Check for the NONREFUNDABLE search/copy fee in the amount of **$5.00 per record** requested must be made payable to the Treasurer General NSDAR. Fee must be paid in advance.

DO NOT USE THIS FORM FOR ANY REQUESTS EXCEPT RECORD COPY

REVOLUTIONARY WAR ANCESTOR ONLY

FULL Name of Revolutionary Ancestor _____ Date of Birth _____

Date of Death _____ Name of Wife/Wives _____
(Card index does NOT GIVE child's mothers name in multiple marriages)

State from which ancestor served/resided during Revolution _____

Name of Child thru whom descent is claimed _____

IF line thru this child is not established or is "closed", will you accept a paper thru another listed child?

YES _____ NO_____

DAR MEMBER'S APPLICATION ONLY

FULL name of member whose paper is requested:

_____
(First)   (Middle)   (Maiden)   (Married)

(**Note:** If married more than once, give all married names)

NSDAR National Number _____ Living _____ Deceased _____
(If Known)   (Year)

Name of DAR Chapter and State _____

REVOLUTIONARY ANCESTOR(S) credited to above member _____

Note: By 1967 Executive Committee Ruling, **ONLY** those who fall in to one of the following categories may receive copies of application papers of <u>active</u> DAR members:
  a. Member of NSDAR (give NSDAR membership number or Chapter name)
  b. Prospective member of NSDAR (give name of DAR Chapter invited to join)
  c. Genealogist for the N.S.C.A.R.
  d. Registrar General/Genealogist or official genealogist N.S.S.A.R.
  e. Registrar of the S.R.
  Papers of inactive and deceased members are available to the general public.

NAME AND ADDRESS OF PERSON REQUESTING COPY:

_____ Eligibility Category _____

_____

_____ Zip _____

Chapter Name _____ National Number _____

Date of Order _____

NOTE: Form may be photocopied for additional ancestor and/or member records requested.
Please allow 4 to 6 weeks for processing.

(0796–5000–PS)

6.4
THE DAR PATRIOT INDEX

"The DAR Patriot Index" is a resource well known to many genealogists in its published form, but it is actually more than just a set of books. Basically, it is a listing of the established Revolutionary War ancestors of DAR members but not a list of all participants in the American Revolution.

The actual "DAR Patriot Index" is a large file of 4" x 6" ancestor cards, which the Registrar General's staff maintains. In recent years the staff have entered the information on the ancestor cards into a computerized database, *The Ancestral Retrieval System*. Neither the card index and the computerized system are open to manual investigation by researchers, but the office staff will assist researchers. The index is kept very current by the addition of new cards, new entries on existing cards and additions to the computer database shortly after new ancestors are verified by an application paper or a supplemental application. The appearance of a patriot's name in the index indicates that there has been at least one application or supplemental application since 1890 establishing that ancestor's service.

Each ancestor card provides space (although every space is not always completed) for the following basic information on established Revolutionary soldiers or patriots:

- birth and death dates and places

- place(s) of residence

- name(s) of spouse(s)

- place(s) of residence

- children through which DAR lineages have been established and associated national numbers needed to consult application papers

- type of Revolutionary War service and place or state

- notations by the staff explaining details about the ancestor and related application papers, such as "data in," "corrected copy," "future applicants must complete," or "Tory."

The "Patriot Index" has been condensed several times into the published *DAR Patriot Index*. The first was in 1966. It was followed by three paperback supplements between 1969 and 1976. The three supplements, plus additions and corrections were incorporated into volume 2 in 1979. A 1982 supplement followed. Finally, volume three was published in 1986. The subtitle of volume 3 is *An Index to the Spouses of the DAR Patriots*. **Please note that all of these volumes are superceded and contain records which have since been corrected or deleted.** The 1986 volume may still have some usefulness because it indexes the spouses of many valid Patriots. Use it with caution, however.

The latest edition of *The DAR Patriot Index* was published in April 1994. This three-volume "Centennial Edition" has a spine date and a title page date of 1990, but it contains names of established ancestors of DAR members through December 1993. Updates to listings in the published index show newly established ancestors and appear six times each year in *The DAR Magazine*'s column "New Ancestors." The listing of Revolutionary ancestors by DAR members changes constantly, and researchers may maintain awareness of these updates to keep apace of new information.

6.5
THE LINEAGE BOOKS OF THE
DAUGHTERS OF THE AMERICAN REVOLUTION

From 1890 to 1939 the National Society Daughters of the American Revolution published 166 volumes containing the lineages of accepted members through national number 160,000 (admitted in April 1921). The set is available in many large libraries around the country having been used by the DAR to exchange with other libraries for their publications. It is often the genealogist's first contact with DAR records, which, unfortunately, can lead to problems in further research and documentation of genealogies.

DAR recommends that researchers **USE GREAT CAUTION** when studying the *Lineage Books*. The staff genealogists of DAR no longer accept lineages cited in the *Lineage Books* as suitable proof for applications by potential new members. The set is useful only for clues to a lineage. The lineages contained in these books are quite old and deserve careful scrutiny. Consequently, there have been at least seventy-six years during which many new sources have become available to researchers. Over 600,000 applications for membership in DAR have been approved since the last published lineage from 1921.

Thousands of corrections have been made to the records in this set during this period. These corrections *have not* been published in supplemental volumes to the *Lineage Books*, and are therefore available only in the Office of the Registrar General. Corrections are, however, periodically published in the *DAR Magazine* in a condensed form. There is no complete published index to these, although The *DAR Patriot Index*, of course, updates the established ancestors' names. The corrected lineages themselves are not published in the magazine, however. Additionally, some older lineages listed in the set, may never have had another applicant associated with them to help identify errors and make corrections. All lineages, whether they be those in the *Lineage Books* or those submitted subsequently to them, should be verified with the Registrar General's office. Documented corrections may be sent to the Corrections Genealogist; see this section below.

Although there are major limitations to the validity of information in the *Lineage Books*, researchers may find valuable clues hidden in the pages of this set of 166 volumes. A four-volume set of indexes was published between 1916 and 1940. In 1980 and several times since then, the Genealogical Publishing Company of Baltimore, Maryland has reprinted this set as *Index to the Rolls of Honor in the Lineage Books of the National Society of the Daughters of the American Revolution*. This set of books covers volumes 1-160, but not the last six volumes. Copies must be ordered directly from the Genealogical Publishing Company. Volumes 161 to 166 have been indexed in a separate publication: Ethel McNabb. *Index of the Rolls of Honor (Ancestor's Index) in the Lineage Books of the National Society of the Daughters of the American Revolution, Volumes 161-166* [S.l.: s.n.], 1965. This volume is not presently available from a publisher to our knowledge.

All volumes of the *Lineage Books* have been out-of-print for many years. They will not be reprinted in either book form or microform. No copies are available for purchase from any office at DAR.

In any event, researchers should use this entire set with the greatest of caution. Some information is correct. Other information is not. The DAR Library has shelved its set of *Lineage Books* away from the main collection, but library users can certainly use the books if they so desire. Anyone inquiring as to their location is warned of the limitations and is referred to the Registrar General's office for current information. Librarians and researchers elsewhere must be aware of the limitations of this set of books.

The [DAR] ... deserves great credit for pioneering in developing an interest in family history. At that time [1890] we were comparatively close to the Revolutionary patriots we wished to honor, the last of whom had died in 1868 at the age of over 104 years— these men and women who, who in the period 1775-1783, contributed physically or materially to the success of the struggle for independence, or established themselves as loyal to the American cause.

Daughters and granddaughters of these patriots were living in 1890, and it was easy for them to remember, or, with the aid of family Bibles and tradition, to say who these parents and grandparents were. Genealogy as a science or profession had not been extensively developed. At the very beginning we asked of an applicant for membership in the Society only the names of here line and some service attributed to the patriot ancestor. What a loss that we did not require the birth, death and marriage dates, with reference as to where these occurred! The members could at that time so easily have supplied much that it now requires a great deal of research to find. If these had been given, it would have brought out the fact that the memory and tradition were often mistaken, and that for a father and son, brothers were sometimes given on these undated papers and accepted in good faith without proof. Sometimes a collateral relation, such as a uncle or nephew, would be claimed.

No attempt was made to check the line with new records coming in. Also no attempt was made to identify an ancestor with the service claimed. When the service was checked by a pension, it frequently happened that the pension record itself was not obtained, but reference was made to a list of pensioners in which the soldiers name appeared, with no data to identify him as the one having the service claimed in the pension.

Comments by Eleanor B. Cooch,
Registrar General, 1941-1944,
in her article "Papers Without Proofs and Lineage Books" in
National Historical Magazine, April 1944, p. 206.

6.6
DAR MEMBERSHIP APPLICATIONS AND RELATED SOURCES

6.6.1
APPLICATION PAPERS

The result of the work of the staff genealogists is the verified application papers. The originals are stored in the building for safekeeping in acid-free boxes, and research copies are available in microform in the Seimes Microfilm Center. Researchers who know the national number associated with a paper should go directly to the Microfilm Center to view the application. If one knows the name of a DAR member and would like to view her application paper but does not have the national number, please request assistance in the Office of the Organizing Secretary General [see Chapter 8]. If one knows the name of a Revolutionary War ancestor and wishes to identify which applications are associated with the ancestor, please request assistance in the Registrar General's Clerical Office.

Since the beginning, DAR application papers have been four pages in length. There have been various revisions to the content and detail of the papers over the years, usually to request more information for accuracy and clarity in the lineage. Generally, the structure of the papers is:

Page 1: identifies the applicant, her ancestor, and clerical information regarding the stages of the application through the final approval date.

Page 2: outlines the lineage of the applicant to the Revolutionary War patriot. Since 1890 spaces for such information as birth, marriage, and death dates, locations, and similar details were added.

Page 3: lists the documentation or sources proving the lineage. Staff genealogists make notations here which have varied over the years. Some state "data returned" or "data in file case," explaining the probable location of supporting documentation. Page 3 of the current application also has a section for listing the children of the patriot.

Page 4: lists the service that qualifies the ancestor as a Revolutionary War patriot.

A free and helpful booklet, *Application Papers: Instructions for Their Preparation*, describes an application in explicit detail and offers guidelines for its completion. Details on acceptable proof and acceptable Revolutionary War service are included. It is a very helpful discussion of applications for anyone completing an application or for researchers who study accepted applications. Every chapter registrar should own a copy as well. Copies are available from the Corresponding Secretary General.

Two other booklets provide additional instruction on completing application papers and insight to the information they contain. *Is That Service Right?* and *Is That Lineage Right?* examine specific problems one may encounter and offer solutions. Both booklets are available for purchase from the Corresponding Secretary General.

Please see Chapter 14 for information on the proper bibliographic citation of DAR Membership Applications.

6.6.2
"SHORT-FORM" APPLICATIONS

Beginning in 1964 the DAR used "short-form" applications to allow applicants to "piggy-back" onto applications of their close relatives within four generations. Because they build on earlier papers and because recent documentation relating to individuals alive after 1910 is not open to research, proof for short forms is very limited.

6.6.3
SUPPLEMENTAL APPLICATIONS

Many Daughters have proven and recorded their lineage to more than one Revolutionary War patriot by submitting "Supplemental Applications." In the very early days these may have accompanied the original application. Now they are submitted later. Many of these early supplementals were not microfilmed. This causes research problems. Generally, a notation on the first application paper will state that there are additional papers on file. The national number index in the Clerical office will also reveal their existence and lead to the location of the originals.

To solve this problem, the Registrar General's Office created "*Add Volumes*" to contain supplementals. The first *Add Volume* starts in 1897. Supplemental papers are assigned the member's national number plus an *Add Volume* number, and these appear on the ancestor cards in the Patriot Index. They are filed within the appropriate *Add Volume* by the national number. Presently, each Add Volume contains 200 supplemental applications beginning with the lowest national number in that batch. Not every members submits these additional papers. Those who submit them do so whenever they chose. Consequently the numbering within each *Add Volume* skips many national numbers. Supplementals are microfilmed or microfiched and available in the Microfilm Center.

Please see Chapter 14 for information on the proper bibliographic citation of DAR Supplemental Application Papers.

6.6.4
MICROFORMS OF APPLICATION PAPERS

Reproduction of applications and supplementals began in 1961. All microforms are in the Seimes Microfilm Center. The older microfilm has some arrangement and legibility problems and is gradually being replaced with microfiche. Presently, these microforms total 2,210 reels of microfilm and seven, three-section drawers of microfiche. This material is only at DAR and is not available on inter-library loan through any facility.

6.6.5
CLOSED AND QUESTIONED LINEAGES

The staff genealogists may close lines or require new documentation if an error in the lineage or Revolutionary War service is discovered. Contact the Corrections Genealogist for information. Refer to section 6.5 on the *DAR Lineage Books*, which definitely fall into the category of questionable sources.

APPLICATION FOR MEMBERSHIP

TO

The National Society

OF THE

DAUGHTERS OF THE AMERICAN REVOLUTION,

WASHINGTON, D. C.

State, *District of Columbia*

City, *Washington*

Name of Chapter, *Mary Washington*

National Number, _____   Chapter Number, *200*

(Miss ~~or Mrs.~~) *Mary Custis Lee*

Wife of _____

Address *Washington, D. C.*

DESCENDANT OF

Major General Henry Lee "Light Horse Harry"; Lieut. Col. Henry Lee, Martha Dandridge Custis Washington

Application examined and approved *April 30th*, 190*1*

Elizabeth Blair Lee
Chapter Regent.

Mary P Brown
Chapter Secretary.

Violet Blair Janin
Chapter Registrar.

Examined and approved _____, 190___
Registrar General.

Accepted by the National Board of Management _____, 190___
Recording Secretary General.

Application and duplicate received by Registrar General _____, 190___

Fees paid to Treasurer General _____, 190___

When the applicant derives eligibility of membership by descent from more than one ancestor, and desires to take advantage thereof, separate applications to be marked "Supplemental application," and numbered like the original, should be made in each case. Applications must be made in duplicate, and should be sworn to before an officer authorized to administer an oath and having a seal.

Do not encroach on this margin, which is needed for binding.

APPLICATION FOR MEMBERSHIP.

To be filled out and after being properly endorsed by the local chapter, forwarded to the Registrar General of the National Society, 902 F Street, Washington, D. C.

When approved by the National Officers, one copy will be returned to the Registrar of the Chapter, and the other will be filed with the National Society.

TO THE BOARD OF MANAGERS OF THE

DAUGHTERS OF THE AMERICAN REVOLUTION.

I Mary Custis Lee being of the age of eighteen years and upwards, hereby apply for membership in this Society by right of lineal descent in the following line from Major General Henry Lee (Light Horse Harry) who was born in "Leesylvania", Va. on the 29th day of Jan. 17 58 and died in Cumberland Island, Ga. on the 25th day of March, 1 818 and who served in the War of the Revolution.

I was born in the Homestead of Arlington County of Fairfax State of Virginia

I am the daughter of General Robert Edward Lee and Mary Randolph Custis , his wife;

the said General Robert E. Lee was the Son of Maj. Gen. Henry Lee 2nd and Anne Hill Carter , his wife;

the said Maj. Gen. Henry Lee was the Son of Lieut. Col. Henry Lee and Lucy Grymes , his wife;

the said Lieut.Col. Henry Lee was the Son of Colonel Henry Lee and Mary Bland , his wife;

the said Colonel Henry Lee was the Son of Richard Lee and Lettice Corbin , his wife;

the said Richard Lee was the Son of Col. Henry Lee and , his wife;

and he, the said Major General Henry Lee is the ancestor who assisted in establishing American Independence, while acting in the capacity of Major General in the Revolutionary Army.

Nominated and recommended by the undersigned, a member of the Society.

Virginia Miller nat. no. 161
Vice Regent, Mary
Washington Chapter DAR.
Washington D. C.

Signature of applicant.

Mary Custis Lee

Residence

Washington D C
& Virginia

Any woman may be eligible for membership who is of the age of eighteen years, and who is descended from a man or woman who, with unfailing loyalty, rendered material aid to the cause of Independence ; from a recognized patriot, a soldier or sailor or a civil officer in one of the several Colonies or States, or of the United Colonies or States ; *provided that the applicant be acceptable to the Society.*

Give below a reference, by volume and page, to the documentary or other authority upon which you found your record. Where reference is made to unpublished or inaccessible records, the applicant must file duplicate certified copies of same. Statements based upon tradition cannot be considered.

ANCESTOR'S SERVICE.

My ancestor's services in assisting in the establishment of American Independence during the War of the Revolution were as follows:

Henry Lee ("Light Horse Harry") Captain of a Company of Virginia Dragoons, June 18th 1776. Company attached to and formed part of 1st Continental Dragoons, March 31st, 1777.

By act of Congress April 7th, 1778, Henry Lee was promoted to rank of Major Commandant. By the act of September 24th 1779 a vote of Congress was tendered by Congress to Major Lee for bravery and ability shown at Paulus Hook, and a gold medal was ordered to be presented to him Oct. 21st 1778. His Battalion was designated Lee's Partican Corps ; Lieut. Col. of same Nov. 6th 1780, and served to close of the war. Engaged in battles of Paulus Hook, Camden, Guilford, Hobkirks Hill, Siege of ninety six and others.

Henry Lee was born at Leesylvania near Dumfrees, Prince William Co., Va. Jan. 29th 1756 died at Cumberland Island Ga. March 25th 1818. Married twice 1st wife, his cousin, Matilda Lee 2nd wife Anne Hill Carter Married 1793.

His father Lieut. Col. Henry Lee settled in Prince William Co., Leesylvania near Dumfrees. Member of Provincial Convention 1774-75-76 and in State Senate 1780, as County Lieutenant for Prince William Co., and was active during the Revolutionary war born 1729 died 1787. Supplemental papers filed as a descendant of Martha Dandridge widow of Daniel Parke Custis and wife of George Washington (as a Revolutionary Heroine.)

(Signature of Applicant) *Mary Custis Lee*

The following is a memorandum of the authority for the foregoing statement:

Heitman's Historical Register page 260.

Appleton's Cyclopedia of American Biography, page 667.

" Lee of Virginia " page 329. (Genealogy) by

Edmund J. Lee   Light Horse Harry.

NATIONAL NUMBER ._____   CHAPTER NO. . ___

THE NATIONAL SOCIETY

of the

Daughters of the
American Revolution,

WASHINGTON, D.C.

APPLICATION FOR MEMBERSHIP

Name of Chapter *Mary Washington*
City *Washington*
State *District of Columbia*

Application filed *My 6 - 1901.*
Approved by Registrar *May 8 - 1901.*
Elected and papers signed *May 1 - 1901*
Sent to Registrar General *May 1 - 1901*
Accepted by the National Board of Management ___

Certificate of membership issued by Registrar General ___

Notified ___
Resigned ___
Deceased ___

[The blanks below must be filled by applicant]

A DESCENDANT OF

Maj. Gen Henry Lee

or

Mary Custis Lee

The following form of acknowledgment is recommended

Deponent further says that the said *Maj. Gen Henry Lee* (name of ancestor from whom eligibility is derived), is the ancestor mentioned in the aforegoing application, and that the statements herein before set forth are true to the best of her knowledge and belief.

(Signature of Deponent) *Mary Custis Lee*
Washington U.C.

Subscribed and sworn to before me at

Washington, DC this *1st*

day of *May* A.D. *1901.*

William A. Smith,
Notary Public.

[SEAL]

Do not encroach on this margin, which is needed for binding.

The officer before whom this verification is made must affix his official seal.

APPLICATION FOR MEMBERSHIP TO THE NATIONAL SOCIETY
OF THE
DAUGHTERS OF THE AMERICAN REVOLUTION
WASHINGTON, DC

State _____

City _____

Name of Chapter _____

Computer Code Number _____

National Number _____

(Miss or Mrs.) _____
       (First Name)   (Middle and Maiden Name)   (Last Name)

Wife ❑   Widow ❑   Divorced ❑ _____
                              (Husband)

Residence _____
     (Number)   (Street)   (City)   (State)   (Zip Code)

Print or type name exactly as you wish it to appear on DAR Certificate.

_____

Revolutionary Ancestor _____

As chapter officers, the undersigned have examined the completed application of the above applicant.

_____
                              Chapter Regent

_____
                              Chapter Registrar

_____ , 19 _____

Application, duplicate, and Fees received by the Registrar General _____

Signatures checked by the Registrar General _____

Application verified and approved _____

_____
                              Registrar General

Accepted by the National Board of Management _____ , 19 _____

_____
                              Recording Secretary General

Endorsement for membership at large:

_____
State Regent

★ Endorsement of member for member:

_____   _____
Member   *National Number*

Nominated and recommended by the two undersigned members of the Society in good standing, to whom the applicant is personally known. Endorsers must be of same chapter; if joining At Large, of the same State.

ENDORSED IN HANDWRITING BY

DAR National Number _____   DAR National Number _____

Name _____   Name _____

Residence _____   Residence _____

Chapter _____   Chapter _____

When filled out and properly endorsed, the application must be forwarded to the Treasurer General, NSDAR, 1776 D Street, NW, Washington, DC 20006-5392, with the necessary fee and dues. When approved by the National Board, one copy will be returned to the Registrar of the Chapter or to the individual, *if joining At Large*, and the other will be filed with the National Society. The application, information thereon, and supplemental data become the property of the National Society.

September 1996   *(0996-25000-OP)*

LINEAGE

1. _____ being duly sworn
(Full Name of Applicant)

I was born on _____ at _____
(1) married on _____ at _____
to _____ born on _____
at _____ died or divorced _____
(2) married on _____ at _____
to _____ born on _____
at _____ died or divorced _____

I am the daughter of

2. _____ born _____ at _____
died at _____ on _____ and his (first or) wife
_____ born _____ at _____
died at _____ on _____ Married – Date _____
Place _____

3. The said _____ was the child of
_____ born _____ at _____
died at _____ on _____ and his (first or) wife
_____ born _____ at _____
died at _____ on _____ Married – Date _____
Place _____

4. The said _____ was the child of
_____ born _____ at _____
died at _____ on _____ and his (first or) wife
_____ born _____ at _____
died at _____ on _____ Married – Date _____
Place _____

5. The said _____ was the child of
_____ born _____ at _____
died at _____ on _____ and his (first or) wife
_____ born _____ at _____
died at _____ on _____ Married – Date _____
Place _____

6. The said _____ was the child of
_____ born _____ at _____
died at _____ on _____ and his (first or) wife
_____ born _____ at _____
died at _____ on _____ Married – Date _____
Place _____

7. The said _____ was the child of
_____ born _____ at _____
died at _____ on _____ and his (first or) wife
_____ born _____ at _____
died at _____ on _____ Married – Date _____
Place _____

8. The said _____ was the child of
_____ born _____ at _____
died at _____ on _____ and his (first or) wife
_____ born _____ at _____
died at _____ on _____ Married – Date _____
Place _____

9. The said _____ was the child of
_____ born _____ at _____
died at _____ on _____ and his (first or) wife
_____ born _____ at _____
died at _____ on _____ Married – Date _____
Place _____

10. The said _____ was the child of
_____ born _____ at _____
died at _____ on _____ and his (first or) wife
_____ born _____ at _____
died at _____ on _____ Married – Date _____
Place _____

11. The said _____ was the child of
_____ born _____ at _____
died at _____ on _____ and his (first or) wife
_____ born _____ at _____
died at _____ on _____ Married – Date _____
Place _____

12. The said _____ was the child of
_____ born _____ at _____
died at _____ on _____ and his (first or) wife
_____ born _____ at _____
died at _____ on _____ Married – Date _____
Place _____

SAMPLE

REFERENCES FOR LINEAGE

Give below proof for EACH statement of Birth, marriage, Death dates and places and connections between generations from the applicant through the generation of the Revolutionary ancestor. Published authorities should be cited by title, author, date of publication, volume and page. Send ONE certified, attested copy OR photocopy of unpublished data. Give *National Numbers* and relationships of any *close relatives* credited with this ancestor.

1st. Gen.

2nd Gen.

3rd Gen.

4th Gen.

5th Gen.

6th Gen.

7th Gen.

8th Gen.

9th Gen.

10th Gen.

11th Gen.

12th Gen.

SAMPLE

My Revolutionary ancestor was married

(1) to _____ at _____ , 1 _____

(2) to _____ at _____ , 1 _____

(3) to _____ at _____ , 1 _____

CHILDREN OF REVOLUTIONARY ANCESTOR

As proven by:

NAMES	DATES OF BIRTH — PLACE	TO WHOM MARRIED, NOTING IF MARRIED MORE THAN ONCE
_____	_____	_____
_____	_____	_____
_____	_____	_____
_____	_____	_____
_____	_____	_____
_____	_____	_____
_____	_____	_____
_____	_____	_____
_____	_____	_____
_____	_____	_____
_____	_____	_____

ANCESTOR'S SERVICES

The said _____ who resided

during the American Revolution at _____ assisted in establishing

American Independence, while acting in the capacity of _____

_____

My ancestor's services during the Revolutionary War were as follows:

SAMPLE

˙Give references by volume and page to the documentary or other authorities for MILITARY RECORD: *Where reference is made to unpublished or inaccessible records of service, the applicant must file the official copy.*

ELIGIBILITY CLAUSE

"Any woman is eligible for membership in the National Society of the Daughters of the American Revolution who is not less than eighteen years of age, and who is descended from a man or woman who, with unfailing loyalty to the cause of American Independence, served as a sailor, or as a soldier or civil officer in one of the several Colonies or States, or in the United Colonies or States, or as a recognized patriot, or rendered material aid thereto; provided the applicant is personally acceptable to the Society." (Constitution, Article III, Section 1.)

Date of marriage may be substituted for dates of birth and death where such date proves the soldier to have been living during the Revolution and of a suitable age for service.

The following form of acknowledgement is required:

Applicant further says that the said _____ (name of ancestor from whom eligibility is derived) is the ancestor mentioned in the foregoing application, and that the statements hereinafter set forth are true to the best of her knowledge and belief.

This applicant also pledges allegiance to the United States of America and agrees to support its Constitution. This applies to applicants for membership within the United States of America and its territories.

Signature of Applicant _____
                      (First Name)   *(Middle and Maiden Name)*   *(Last Name)*

Subscribed and sworn to before me at _____
                                        (City)   *(State)*

this _____ *day of* _____ *A. D.* _____

(SEAL)

                                            (Signature of Notary **OR** *Attest of Chapter Regent* **and** *Registrar)*

                                            My Commission Expires: _____

6.7
THE CORRECTIONS GENEALOGIST

For an organization as old as the DAR and with as many application papers as it holds, there is always the potential for errors and for corrections. Many of the older DAR application papers and supplementals do not have much supporting proof. There are often mistakes in these. The Registrar General's staff includes a "Corrections Genealogist," whose responsibility is to handle lineage and service which are in error or suspected to be in error. The DAR is interested in receiving **documented** information on any lineage or service which falls into these categories. Many records have been corrected over the years, and doubtless there are others which still need attention. To bring a correction to the DAR's attention or to inquire about corrections, please contact: The Corrections Genealogist, Office of the Registrar General, DAR, 1776 D St., N.W., Washington, D.C. 20006-5392.

6.8
ETHNIC AND MINORITY GENEALOGIST

A senior genealogist at DAR serves as a specialist identifying Revolutionary War service for minority (African American and Native American) participants. The National Society has had an ongoing publishing project since 1988 to produce lists of these individuals and commentary on their service. Each bears the title *Minority Military Service 1775-1783* and the name(s) of a state or states covered.

6.9
SUPPORTING DOCUMENTATION FOR APPLICATIONS

Along with the application papers themselves, prospective members submit supporting documentation to back up the lineage and service in the paper. All of this material becomes the property of the DAR on receipt.

The documentation submitted with the application is evaluated by the Genealogy Department. The current policy is to place check marks on the application when information is verified by a document. Older applications may also be used to verify the information, and a notation to that national number should appear. When the Genealogy Department completes its work, the file is microfiched for department use only, post-1910 personal information and vital records are destroyed, and the remaining historical documentation is transferred to the DAR Library for addition to the file collection. The types of materials which are usually retained are pages or sections from published family histories not in the Library, deeds, wills, Bible records, photographs or transcriptions of tombstones, research notes, and other pertinent sources.

While membership applications are prepared on acid-free, rag-content forms, the documentation will likely not be archivally sound. Some may fade and become difficult to read.

Where are the supporting documents which were submitted with membership applications to prove the lineage? The *surviving* files of material are available for research in the DAR Library, which houses it in two sections. The first covers documentation files which came with applications prior to and including the DAR's October Board of 1958 (National Numbers 1 to 462457); the second covers those subsequent to that date. The files in each section are arranged by the names of the Revolutionary ancestors, *NOT* by national number or members' names.

Several years ago the Registrar General's office had a project to remove the remaining pieces of documentation from the original applications, place them in files, and add them to the Library's file collection. They completed extractions from the following volumes of original application papers:

- volume 5, # 819-# 1000 (October 1891) through volume 368, # 73601-# 73800 (June 1909)
- volume 3333, # 487001-# 487200 (February 1962) to the present

In addition, assorted other applications and some supplementals have been checked.

For documentation for an application between 1909 and 1962, there is the possibility that material may still be with the original papers. The Library staff will check this for the patron. Please do not request this information in the R. G. Clerical Office. There are **many** applications which **do** have a few pages of documentation with them still. When the staff finds items with the orginial applications, they remove it, attach a cover sheet, and add it to the pre-1958 files in the Library office.

There are many gaps in the supporting documentation. With over 776,000 members since 1890, in theory, there should be an equal number of files of material to back-up the application papers. This is not, however, even close to the actual number of files which exist. At this writing, the Library has 1,230 linear feet of documentation files–over twice the height of the Washington Monument! The Library staff estimates this to translate into about 250,000 files. Consequently, only about 30% of applications have supporting files.

Why are there gaps? In the early years of the National Society, the amount of proof required to support an application was small in comparison to what is needed today. The availability of historical sources was also much less than now. In the days before photocopy machines, originals sent in with the application were often returned because there were no other copies. Some carbon copies and handwritten transcriptions were retained. Once photocopying became widespread in the 1960s less material was returned. Not until the late 1970s was proof for the first three generations beginning with the applicant herself required with the application. Consequently, many early papers do not have any proof to support them beyond what is written in on the paper itself. Vague references to "bible records, cemetery records, and family papers" may be the only clues which will appear. This is not to say that there is no proof available for early applications, but there is not a great deal. The Library staff will check for any file and report whether or not one was found.

More documentation files exist for applications in the middle and late twentieth century, but again, there are gaps. During some periods, the proof papers were returned to the member after her application was approved. The material was returned because of storage limitations, lack of staff for processing, and the reasons mentioned previously. This practice has not been followed since 1984. There also may be no file because a member joined on a "short-form" application, "piggy-backing" onto an established application paper. The necessary documentation would not be available in the research files because it relates to recent generations. DAR staff has removed documents which are directly associated with the member or her immediate family and which post-date 1910. This information is not available for research purposes for privacy reasons.

During the past ten years, the Library staff have taken the remaining files covering 1958 to the present and arranged them. Volunteers have played a major part in this process.

Researchers must consider the possibility that an older application has been updated or superceded by a newer one, so there is the chance that files could appear in both sections of the files. Often, there is no file under an ancestor's name in either section of the files.

The contents of a file may relate to any individual in any generation of a member's lineage. There may not be much material clarifying the Revolutionary service of an ancestor, but then, there may be considerable proof. Each file is different, but Bible records and other vital records do predominate.

One may request a search for a particular file if they are visiting the Library and may obtain copies of older material included in the files. Mail inquiries are accepted, but the volume of such requests results in long delays before the staff can process such orders. Please direct all inquiries regarding the files to the DAR Library.

Outside of the Library and DAR Headquarters researchers may wish to contact the DAR member herself concerning the documentation from her application. Addresses are available in the Office of the Organizing Secretary General. There is no guarantee that you will receive a response, but many members will likely be glad to provide assistance to someone investigating a shared family connection.

There is also a slight possibility that some older documentation may be retained by chapter registrar's with the chapter's copies of members application papers. One may determine the name of a member's chapter in the Office of the Organizing Secretary General and obtain the registrar's name and address. Please bear in mind, however, that the registrars of the 3,000 DAR chapters are volunteers and are very busy. There is no guarantee that the registrar will be able to help you or even respond to your inquiry. Despite these limitations, contacting a chapter registrar may be the only way to obtain valuable information.

The supporting documentation for membership applications represents a large, unique research collection in the DAR Library. Its processing by staff and careful use by reseachers, will insure the preservation of valuable information for future genealogists.

Please see Chapter 14 for information on the proper bibliographic citation of documentation supporting DAR Membership Applications.

OFFICE OF THE HISTORIAN GENERAL

Location: Administration Building, Second Floor, Room 206
Telephone number: 202–879–3256

*B*esides having responsibility for the National Society's official archives, for the "Special Collection Relating to the History of the NSDAR" and for various historical activities, the Office of the Historian General maintains the Americana Collection of approximately 4,000 accessions and several other sources useful for genealogical research. In addition, a small collection of books established in 1967, the Historical Research Library, is available.

DEPARTMENT HISTORIAN OF THE GENERAL

7.1
AMERICANA COLLECTION

The Americana Collection had it beginnings in 1940 at the time of the celebration of the DAR's fiftieth anniversary "as a repository of manuscripts and imprints pertaining primarily to Colonial America, the American Revolution, and the Early Republic." Its collections focus on the period prior to 1860 with some exceptions. Manuscripts of many types are preserved here, including Bible records, letters, diaries, court papers, historic vital records, and land records. Printed sources include books, almanacs, pamphlets, school books, and photographs. The "genealogical card index" provides access to information about accessions received prior to circa 1970, and researchers will find references to church records, deeds (mostly from New England), ledgers and account books, vital records for entire families, and many personal names associated with documents. The staff in this department has compiled in-house inventories of accessioned collections or individual items from the periods of the American Revolution and the Civil War.

A brochure is available on the collection, which says the following regarding access to materials:

> The contents of this collection are available for public inspection and for research. Requests for photocopies of material in the collection are handled by the Office of the

Historian General. That office reserves the right to evaluate each request and to deny permission, in certain instances, such as when originial copies are too fragile, bound in volumes, or restricted material. Exhibits are mounted in special display cases in the Americana Room and are changed periodically. Individuals and groups are welcome. Tours can be arranged by prior consultation with the staff of the Historian General's Office.

7.2
LOCATED AND MARKED GRAVES
OF REVOLUTIONARY WAR SOLDIERS AND PATRIOTS

**Revolutionary marker placed on grave of Joseph Harrison
by the Edward Bumcombe Chapter**
Photo from the DAR Magazine, August 1929

An activity which has been foremost in the historic preservation efforts of DAR members since the early years of the National Society is the locating and marking of the graves of Revolutionary soldiers and patriots, their spouses and their daughters. Surveys and transcriptions of cemetery records in general have occupied the time of many Daughters and the Library contains many volumes of these records. The Office of the Historian General, however, maintains several card files, or indices, of reported "located" and "marked" graves. Please be aware of the fact that not all of the "reported" graves have been documented; errors do exist in these listings. The inclusion of a name in one of these sources does not serve as proof of Revolutionary War service. Use these indices for clues.

Index of Reported Located Graves of Revolutionary War Soldiers and Patriots
This index is a finding aid to the located graves which have been reported by DAR members and others since the late 1890s. It provides access to those listings published in the Reports to the Secretary of the Smithsonian from 1898 to 1974 (see below), as well as to others which have been listed since then. A few cards include photographs of the tombstones. Listings of located graves which appeared in the *Smithsonian Reports* were also collected, indexed, and published in a four volumes, privately printed, non–DAR sponsored work by Patricia Law Hatcher, *Abstract of Graves of Revolutionary Patriots*, Dallas, Texas: Pioneer Heritage Press, 1987-1988. The DAR published lists in pamphlet form in the mid to late 1970s noting additional reported located graves. This pamphlet is entitled *Located Graves of Soldiers and Patriots of the American Revolution, March 1, 1974–March 1, 1976*. Some further lists appeared in *The DAR Magazine* in the years immediately after 1978. There have been no subsequent publications other than those in the magazine.

Index of Reported Marked Graves of Revolutionary War Soldiers and Patriots
The DAR Magazine provides researchers with frequent references to grave marking ceremonies by DAR chapters. No comprehensive index to these activities exists; however, any information concerning the date of placement and dedication of a marker may provide clues about when an article may have appeared in *The DAR Magazine* describing the event. Some of these entries include photographs of the ceremony. The Office of the Historian General generally does not have information concerning the proof of these locations and markings.

Index of Reported Marked Graves of Wives and Daughters of Revolutionary War Patriots and Soldiers

Index of Reported Marked Graves of Signers of the Declaration of Independence

Index of Reported Marked Graves of DAR Members
This multi-drawer card index gives useful information relating to marked graves of deceased DAR members. It is not comprehensive, however, and only includes those marked until the mid-1990s, when this function was transferred to the Office of the Organizing Secretary General.

Index of Reported Marked Graves of Real Daughters
This index notes the graves of DAR members who were actually daughters of Revolutionary War participants. See section 7.4 for more information.

Index of Reported Historical Markers Placed by DAR Chapters (arranged by state)

7.3
DAR REPORTS TO THE SECRETARY
OF THE SMITHSONIAN INSTITUTION

One requirement made of the DAR in its 1896 incorporation by the United States Congress was an annual report to the Secretary of the Smithsonian Insitution. The first was a "catch-up" seven-year report and covered the years 1890-1897 and was published in 1899. After their submission, the reports became government documents, were submitted to the United States Senate by the Smithsonian along with annual reports of many other organizations, and included in the U.S. Serial Set. Each DAR Report is therefore available in any library which owns the Serial Set. A complete set is available in the Office of the Historian General and a partial set is in the Library.

Besides the lists of graves of Revolutionary soldiers and patriots just mentioned, the Reports contain many other sources of genealogical interest. A few have been published as separate volumes, but most are not well known. The following details the contents of these reports.

Report, v. 1, 1890-1897 (1899), Serial #. This report does not contain historical records.

Report, v. 2, 1897-1898 (1900), Serial #4044, v.16
    Appendix B: Graves Identified by Dorothy Quincy Hancock Chapter, Bernardstown, Massachusetts
    Appendix D: Roster of women nurses enlisted for Spanish-American War by DAR Hospital Corps

Report, v. 3, 1898–1900 (1901),

 Appendix C: The Ancient Burying Ground of Hartford (Names on the gravestones standing in 1835)

 Appendix D: Unpublished list of Massachusetts citizens who loaned money to the government during the Revolution

 Appendix E: Georgia Soldiers of the Line-Revolutionary War (from papers in the Office of the Secretary of State of Georgia)

 Appendix F: Alphabetical list of Georgia Revolutionary Soldiers of all ranks and names including Continental, Militia, Provincials, Minute Men, Rangers, Partisans, Mariners, Sons of Liberty, Independents, etc.

 Appendix G: Soldiers of the American Revolution and Pioneers of Broome County, New York

 Appendix H: List of Historic Spots in Lower Merion (Montgomery County, Pennsylvania)

Report, v. 4, 1900–1901 (1902),

 Appendix A: Some Rolls of Connecticut Soldiers

 Appendix B: List of Revolutionary Soldiers Graves, Worcester, Massachusetts

 Appendix C: Historical Collections of General Frelinghuysen Chapter, Somerville, New Jersey

 Appendix D: Entry from the Account Book kept by Capt. David Tarbox, Hebron, Connecticut

 Appendix E: Partial List of Delaware's Revolutionary Soldiers

 Appendix F: List of Historic Spots in Blockley, Pennsylvania

 Appendix G: Roll of General Sumters Regiment of South Carolina

 Appendix H: Record of Revolutionary Ancestors of Members of Ascutney Chapter, Windsor, Vermont

Report, v. 5, 1901–1902 (1903),

 Appendix B: List of Revolutionary Soldiers, compiled by Capt. B. F. Johnson, Additional to List Published Under Appendix E in our Third Report, with Corrections of that List.

 Appendix C: Revolutionary Soldiers Buried in the Vicinity of Attleboro, Massachusetts

 Appendix D: Revolutionary Soldiers Buried at Hookset, New York

 Appendix E: List of Recruits from the Cape May Battalion and Revolutionary Soldiers of Cape May County, New Jersey

 Appendix F: Revolutionary Ancestors of members of the Knickerbocker Chapter, New York

 Appendix G: Revolutionary Soldiers Buried in Jefferson County, New York

 Appendix H: Revolutionary Soldiers Buried in Lake and Geauga Counties, Ohio

 Appendix I: Revolutionary Soldiers Graves, Located by Ox-Bow Chapter, Vermont

Report, v. 6, 1902–1903 (1904),

 Appendix A: Revolutionary Soldiers Buried in Derby, Connecticut

 Appendix B: Revolutionary Soldiers Buried in Massachusetts

 Appendix C: Records of Revolutionary Soldiers Furnished by General William Floyd Chapter

 Appendix D: List of Revolutionary Soldiers from Seneca County, N.Y.

Report, v. 7, 1903–1904 (1905) to Report, v. 9, 1905–1906 (1907). These reports do not contain grave listings or other records.

Report, v. 10, 1906-1907 (1908) to Report, v. 15, 1910-1911 (1912). These reports contain grave listings.

Report, v. 16, 1912-1913 (1914),
    Appendix B: List of Real Daughters
    Appendix C: Classified List of [Graves of] Revolutionary Soldiers

Report, v. 17, 1913-1914 (1915),
    Appendix: Pierce's Register [Subsequently reprinted as a separate volume by other publishers.]

Report, v. 18, 1914-1915 (1916) to Report, v. 20, 1916-1917 (1918). These reports contain grave listings.

Report, v. 21, 1917-1918 (1919),
    Appendix: A Pension List of Revolutionary Soldiers from Connecticut

Most of the remaining reports contain grave listings which have all been published and indexed as noted above.

Please see Chapter 14 for information on the proper bibliographic citation of these DAR reports to the Smithsonian.

7.4
"REAL DAUGHTERS"

All DAR members are called "Daughters." Those members who were the actual daughters of Revolutionary War soldiers and patriots were known as "Real Daughters." More than 700 women enjoyed this distinction. The Office of the Historian General has the finding aid listed above as "Index of Reported Marked Graves of Real Daughters" as well as a photograph collection of some of these interesting women and a few files of additional information. Issues of *The DAR Magazine*, especially those published prior to the 1940s, also contain useful vignettes of Real Daughters, generally complete with likenesses of the women under discussion. The Historian General's Office has a listing of those Real Daughters who were honored by an article in *The DAR Magazine*. See section 13.8 for additional information on this subject.

Georgia's Real Daughter Sisters
Left — Mrs. Mary Pool Newson
Right — Miss Sarah Pool
Photo from the DAR Magazine, August 1929

THE HISTORICAL RESEARCH LIBRARY

The Office of the Historian General has a small Historical Research Library containing a variety of materials on American history and historical subjects and individuals. Many biographies of famous figures in American history, especially George Washington, are housed here. There is some duplication with the DAR Library's biography collection. Studies in women's history and the presidency are other areas of concentration.

An excellent and complete collection of the state guides in the "American Guides Series" is part of this library. They are the work of the Federal Works Agency of the Work Projects Administration and date from the late 1930s and early 1940s.

Some useful bibliographic sources for American imprints are in this collection as well. Shaw and Shoemaker's *American Bibliography: A Preliminary Checklist 1801–1834* (with indices), Jones and Leypoldts' *The American Catalog: Author and Title Entries of Books in Print and for Sale 1876–1910*, and similar compilations provide good information on this subject.

OFFICE OF THE
ORGANIZING SECRETARY GENERAL

Location: Administration Building, First Floor
Telephone: 202-879-3223

The Office of the Organizing Secretary General maintains records relating to chapter organization, historical and current membership materials, national numbers of all members since 1890 and addresses of active members.

8.1
MEMBERSHIP RECORDS

Each woman who has become a DAR member receives a national number. Since 1890 there have been over 776,000 members, and the national numbers are assigned by the Office of the Registrar General in sequence as the member is admitted. To gain access to open application papers of members, one must obtain the national number of the member in the Office of the Organizing Secretary General before visiting Seimes Microfilm Center to view the application paper.

Several important microfiche and computerized indices are available in this office. The staff checks these sources for information requested by researchers in person or by mail. Concise questions may be answered by telephone. There is some overlap between the indices due to the time involved in implementing new systems during different periods. Generally, these finding aids assist in locating national numbers of members and information on their length of membership and date of death/resignation. The indices are:

- **Index of active and inactive members since 1969** (microfiche). It continues to about 1984.

- **Index of inactive members to 1979** (microfiche).

- **Computerized index of active (and some inactive) members since 1969**. Because a great many active DAR members joined prior to 1969, the computerized records include them.

- **Index of marriages of DAR members to 1969**. Name changes for members are important in tracing information about their membership records.

- **Index of members-at-large to 1969**. The members-at-large are also included in the other pre-1969 indices mentioned above.

This office also maintains a file on the former and current National, State and Chapter Officers of the DAR. If an ancestor or relative were an officer, information on her activities may be available.

8.2
ADDRESSES

The Organizing office **will** give the address of an active member or the address of the current chapter regent of the last known chapter of a deceased or inactive member for **possible** referral by that regent to a relative of the member or the former member herself.

The office will not give the last known address of a deceased or inactive member. There is a possibility that living former members or families of deceased members do not wish to receive correspondence relating to the member's genealogical materials. Consequently, this policy seeks to preserve their privacy.

Although the Organizing office prepares mailing lists for the National Society's use, **DAR does not distribute these lists to any organization or individual.**

8.3
WAS SHE A DAR MEMBER?

This question is a frequent one received by several offices at DAR. The staff of the Organizing office will check their records to attempt an answer. Frequently, however, there is some family memory that a woman was a member of a lineage society, and researchers assume this to be the DAR because it is the largest and most well known of these groups. Actual membership in such groups as the Daughters of the Revolution, the United Daughters of the Confederacy, the Colonial Dames, and other groups is often the basis for these inquiries. Although it may not always be possible, researchers should try to verify which organization an individual joined before contacting any lineage society including the DAR.

Some applications for DAR membership are not approved. A woman may have gone through the application process and had her paper returned for additional proof or clarification. She may never have completed the work and resubmitted the paper. As a result, there may be a memory among family members that this happened. The DAR does not maintain records of individuals whose membership application was not successful.

Name changes and other variations on a person's name can prevent the Organizing staff from determining whether a woman was a DAR member or not. Please provide as complete information as possible in your inquiry to help overcome these stumbling blocks to research. State and city of residence at the time of membership, or more than one if relocations occured, are additional important facts the staff needs to know. The city and state play an important part in determining whether there is a DAR chapter in that location. If a DAR chapter exists or existed in a particular location, the Organizing staff can research and verify whether a member paid her national dues through a specific chapter.

Older membership records may be incomplete owing to extensive use of the cards in the past, some possible misfilings or records which may have "disappeared" over the decades.

Other sources for membership records include state and chapter historical rosters and histories produced by the state DAR organizations and local chapters. The Office of the Organizing Secretary General does not maintain these publications. Most state histories and historical rosters are available through either the Library or the Office of the Historian General. Chapter publications are, however, usually only available from the chapter and are not considered public information. A collection of these is not maintained at DAR headquarters with the small exception of a few in the custody of the Historian General.

Membership card for former First Lady Mamie Eisenhower

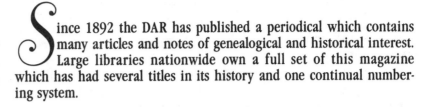

THE DAR MAGAZINE

S ince 1892 the DAR has published a periodical which contains many articles and notes of genealogical and historical interest. Large libraries nationwide own a full set of this magazine which has had several titles in its history and one continual numbering system.

- *The American Monthly Magazine*, v. 1 (July 1892)–v. 42 (June 1913)
- *Daughters of the American Revolution Magazine*, v. 43 (July 1913)–v. 72 (December 1938)
- *The National Historical Magazine*, v. 73 (1939)–v. 79 (1945)
- *The Daughters of the American Revolution Magazine*, v. 80 (1946) to the present
  [**Note:** Until v. 51 (July–December 1917) a volume comprised half a year or six issues.]

Several regular features of *The DAR Magazine* are especially useful to genealogists. Although genealogical information has appeared in the publication since 1892, the "Genealogical Department" column began in 1900 and ran until June 1957 with that title and as "Genealogical Source Material" from July 1957 to July 1961. This column contained record abstracts and articles addressing particular research areas and methodology. Afterwards, the succeeding column has tended to be mostly genealogical queries. The columns' title was changed to "More Genealogy" beginning in April 1984. Researchers should be aware that there are no correspondence files relating to any queries published in *The DAR Magazine*.

In recent years, the staff of the Genealogical Records Committee (G.R.C.) has abstracted genealogical information from documentation files in the DAR Library on specific surnames. These abstracts are published in the "More Genealogy" column. They appear as time permits and abstracts are available.

Any researcher may submit a query for publication. Guidelines for submission appear at the beginning of each column in each issue of the magazine. Send queries directly to the Genealogical Records Committee at DAR's address.

The *DAR Patriot Index* is discussed in detail in the section on the Office of the Registrar General, but additions and corrections to this publication appear regularly in *The DAR Magazine*. Lists of "New

Ancestors" registered by members through applications or supplement applications approved by the staff genealogists are printed in the magazine three issues after the month in which the new applications are approved at the DAR's National Board of Management meetings (February, April, June, October, and December). Corrections to the *Patriot Index* are compiled semi-annually and published on a space-available basis. More detailed information on new ancestors and corrections is available from the Office of the Registrar General.

Three times a year, in the April, June and December issues of the magazine, lists of new books donated to the DAR Library appear after the Librarian General's report in the section entitled "Minutes: National Board of Management." These lengthy lists can provide tips on newly published books, and researchers may inquire of the DAR Library how to obtain a particular book from a publisher. In 1989 the lists of purchased books, which had been included earlier, were discontinued because of the space they consumed in the magazine.

The DAR Library's newsletter, *Continental Columns*, is printed four times a year in *The DAR Magazine*. The newsletter began in 1993, had a hiatus in 1996, and returned in 1997. It provides current information on new materials and sources at the DAR Library and other research offices at DAR.

Please see Chapter 14 for information on the proper citation of articles in *The DAR Magazine*.

9.1
INDICES TO THE DAR MAGAZINE

No single index provides access to *The DAR Magazine*. Indexing is provided by several publications, but all of these are out of print. The quality and depth of coverage in these finding aids vary considerably, but researchers should consult them instead of attempting to use the magazines alone. Use of these indices, especially the annual ones is tedious, and DAR staff is unable to undertake detailed searches because of these limitations. A master index is in the planning stages. The currently available indices in book form are:

● Elizabeth Benton Chapter, NSDAR. *Genealogical Guide: Master Index of Genealogy in the Daughters of the American Revolution Magazine, v. 1–84 (1892–1950)*. Washington, D.C.: DAR, 1951.

● Elizabeth Benton Chapter, NSDAR. *Supplement to Genealogical Guide: Master Index of Genealogy in the Daughters of the American Revolution Magazine, v. 85–89 (1950–1955)*. Washington, D.C.: DAR, 1956.

These two publications were reprinted as one book as *Genealogical Guide: Master Index of Genealogy in the Daughters of the American Revolution Magazine, volumes 1–84 (1892–1950) with Supplement, volumes 85–89 (1950–1955). Combined Edition*. Baltimore: Genealogical Publishing Company, 1994. This edition also contains a introduction which explains the benefits and limitations of the indices.

● Mary Emery, Ervil Norton, and Ruth Gee. *Index to Genealogical Records in the 1956 DAR Magazines, v. 90*. [S.l.]: Seminole Chapter, NSDAR, 1957.

● Martha Porter Miller. *Index to the Genealogical Department of the Daughters of the American Revolution Magazine, v. 91 (1957)*. Washington, D.C.: M. P. Miller, 1958.

- Martha Potter Miller. *Index to the Genealogical Department of the Daughters of the American Revolution Magazine, v. 92 (1958)*. Washington, D.C.: M. P. Miller, 1961.

- John Frederick Dorman. *Index to the Genealogical Department of the Daughters of the American Revolution Magazine, v. 93 (1959)–v. 101 (1967)*. 9 annual volumes. Washington, D.C.: J. F. Dorman, 1961-1968.

The preceeding entries represent a consistant run of indices to The DAR Magazine through 1967. Subsequent volumes have not been indexed in these forms. Several other indices to parts of *The DAR Magazine* also are available:

- Mrs. Balfour N. Clark. *An Index to Genealogical Data in the Daughters of the American Revolution Magazine 1926-1946*. Corsicana, Texas: James Blair Chapter, DAR, 1947.

- Mary Knight Crane. *A Condensed Index to the Genealogical Material, Marriage and American Revolutionary War Records Contained in the Daughters of the American Revolution Magazine, v. 1 to 55 Inclusive* [1892-1921]. Erie, Pennsylvania: M. K. Crane, 1922.

- Louise H. Rainey. *Index: American Monthly Magazine, Daughters of the American Revolution Magazine*. New York: L. H. Rainey, 1938. This index appears to cite articles beginning with v. 17 (1900) and ending with v. 71 (1937).

- Katie-Prince W. Esker. *The Genealogical Department: Source Records from the DAR Magazine 1947-1950*. Baltimore: Genealogical Publishing Company, 1975.

- Lorena Wildman. *Genealogical Guide to the Daughters of the American Revolution Magazine volume[s] 95-99 (1961-1965)*. Spokane, Washington: Eastern Washington Genealogical Society, 1981.

- Ellen Smith Long. *Partially Annotated Index of Articles of Bicentennial Interest Published in the Daughters of the American Revolution Magazine 1956-1975*. Waycross, Georgia: E.S. Long, 1976.

- Barbara Schull Wolfe. *Federal and State Records, DAR Magazine from Beginning to May 1976, with Supplement to 1982*. Indianapolis: Ye Olde Genealogie Shoppe, 1984.

- Mrs. Frank R. Mettlach. *Listing of Historical Articles in the Daughters of the American Revolution Magazine 1892-1970*. Washington, D.C.: DAR, 1970.

Other published indices to genealogical periodicals have included the DAR's publication.

- *Genealogical Periodical Annual Index, v. 1 (1962)* to the present. Bowie, Maryland: Heritage Books, 1962- .

- Michael B. Clegg and Curt B. Witcher, editors. *Periodical Source Index (PERSI)*. Fort Wayne, Indiana: Allen County Public Library Foundation, 1987- .

- Kip Sperry. *Index to Genealogical Periodical Literature, 1960-1977*. Detroit: Gale, 1979. Gale Genealogy and Local History Series, v. 9.

★   *Chapter 10*

OFFICE OF THE CURATOR GENERAL
DAR MUSEUM

Location: Administration Building, Third Floor, Room 303
Telephone: 202-879-3288

 he DAR Museum is a collection of early American decorative and fine arts and crafts. While not a genealogical department like many others at DAR it does have, nonetheless, a genealogical presence because of the composition of the collections, the general atmosphere in which they reside in the building, and the simple fact that it belongs to the DAR.

Among the Museum's treasures are a small number of family record needlework pieces, which are excellent examples of this highly personal artform. Additionally, some family histories have accompanied other donations to the Museum and are kept on file with the object records. These provide a family context in which to view the items. Questions regarding these sources should be directed to the Museum Registrars in the Office of the Curator General.

Over the years the DAR Museum has mounted many exhibits which have focused on women's history, the American Revolution, genealogy and related subjects. Descriptive checklists or catalogs were prepared for some of these and are available in the Museum Office and the DAR Library. Background information for these exhibits may also be available from the Office of the Curator General. Among these exhibits were:

- *Lafayette in America* (1979)

- *The Jewish Community in Early America: 1654-1830* (1980-1981)

- *When You See This, Remember Me: Early American Samplers* (1982)

- *Old Line Traditions: Maryland Women and Their Quilts* (1985)

- *Childhood Lessons: Educating Through Toys, Dolls and Books of the 19th Century* (1988-1987)

- *First Flowerings: Early Virginia Quilts* (1987)

- *For My Little Ones* (1988)

- *Family Record: Genealogical Watercolors and Needlework* (1989)

- *Magnificent Intentions: Decorative Arts of the District of Columbia, 1791-1861* (1991-1992)

- *Souvenirs from the Voyage of Life* (1992-1993)

- *True Love and a Happy Home: Cultural Expectations and Feminine Experiences in Victorian America* (1993)

- *George Washington: The Man Behind the Image* (1994-1995)

- *Classical Quilts* (1995)

- *American Women, American Fashion: Costume from the DAR Museum Collection* (1996)

- *Bound for the West: Women and Their Families on the Western Trails, 1840-1880* (1996-1997)

Sampler made by Emily Tarr, 1835, of Georgetown, Maine.
Photograph by Helga Photo Studio

In 1989, the DAR Museum presented an exhibit "Family Record: Genealogical Watercolors and Needlework" and published a catalog with the same title written by Gloria Seaman Allen, then-Director and Chief Curator. The exhibit and the catalog, which is now out of print, offered excellent examples of this art work gathered from many collections and annotated entries with descriptive commentary. A sample from the exhibit follows and is representative of the Museum's holdings and of some of the items in the Historian General's Americana Collection.

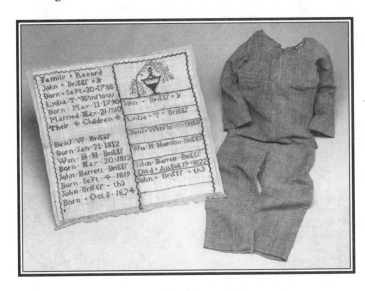

Child's suit made by Lydia Winslow Briggs, 1822, of Sumner, Maine, and needlework family record, attributed to Lydia Briggs, 1822.
Photograph by Mark Gulezian

The Museum Reference Library is a small collection of books on pertinent subjects. Among these are titles on American artisans, clockmakers, pewterers, gunsmiths, furniture makers, and painters. Books on ceramics, silver, brassware, glassware, textiles, quilts, folk art, needlework, costume and toys combine with others on U.S. history, Women's studies, architecture, intererior decoration and antiques to provide general background for the Museum's areas of specialization. Genealogists researching individuals in such fields *may* gain insight from the materials in this library.

OFFICE OF THE CORRESPONDING SECRETARY GENERAL

Location: Administration Building, Lower Level, Room LL3
Telephone: 202-879-3218

This office functions as the DAR's "book shop" and sells all DAR publications including:

- *The DAR Patriot Index*

- *DAR Library Catalog, Volumes 2 and 3*

- *Is That Lineage Right?*

- *Is That Service Right?*

- *"A Century of Service:" The Story of the DAR*

- *Women in the American Revolution*

- *Minority Military Service 1775-1783 (series)*

- *Daughters Overseas: A History of Units Overseas*

Request a copy of "DAR Publications and Supplies" for a full and current listing of these materials. DAR publications are only available for purchase from the National Society's Corresponding Secretary General.

The Lineage Research Kit, prepared by that Committee and available from the Corresponding Office, contains various collected guides for basic genealogical research. Basic genealogical charts and pedigree charts are also for sale here.

Corresponding also distributes various free information sheets including the following on DAR or related to genealogical research:

- *Application Papers: Instructions for Their Preparation* (1995)

- *All About the DAR* (formerly DAR in Action)

- *DAR Policies*

- *DAR Fact Sheet* (1996)

Chapter 12

PUBLICATIONS AND SOURCES
OF THE STATE DARS AND CHAPTERS

*M*ost of the State DAR societies or organizations have produced various publications of research value. Historical rosters and organization histories predominate, although some states and chapters have published volumes of record abstracts and historical sources. Please note that lineages published in these state books are not necessarily acceptable to DAR staff genealogists in support of membership applications.

Addresses of State and Chapter officers may be obtained in the Office of the Organizing Secretary General. Refer to section 8.2.

The most significant state-produced compilations are the Genealogical Records Committee reports discussed in detail in Chapter 4. The DAR Library staff has attempted several times in recent years to determine the locations of the state copies of these reports. The results of these surveys have been mixed. The following libraries or research facilities have been identified by DAR state librarians as having holdings of DAR materials. These do not include membership applications, but rather, G.R.C. reports, some state publications, and other historical and genealogical materials collected by Daughters in each state. Collections will vary in size and content, but only a few are considered large. Addresses for the public institutions mentioned in the following list are found in such publications as *The American Library Directory*.

12.1
STATE DAR COLLECTIONS AND LIBRARIES

Alabama
No separate DAR state library

Alaska
No separate DAR state library

Arkansas
DAR materials are housed in the Little Rock Public Library, and some are also in public libraries in Jonesboro, Fort Smith, Pine Bluff, Fayetteville, and Texarkana.

Arizona
No DAR state library. Some DAR materials are in the Tucson Genealogical Library, Arizona State Genealogy Library in Phoenix, and Sun City Genealogy Library.

California
California DAR Library, 201 West Bennett Avenue, Glendora, CA 91740. This library was established in 1988. Other materials are in the California State Library in Sacramento; its branch in San Francisco, the Sutro Library; and the Genealogy Department of the Los Angeles Public Library.

Colorado

No separate DAR state library. Denver Public Library holds DAR Collection.

Connecticut

No separate DAR state library

Delaware

No separate DAR state library

District of Columbia

The D.C. DAR has a small library in its headquarters in Northwest Washington, but District Daughters have supported the DAR Library since its founding in 1896.

Florida

The Florida State DAR Collection is housed in the Orange County Library System, Genealogical Department, 10 North Rosalind, Orlando, FL 32801. There is also a DAR collection at the University of West Florida Library, Pensacola.

Other libraries with some DAR materials are Polk County Historical and Genealogical Society Library in Bartow; Palm Beach County Genealogical Society Library in West Palm Beach; Miami-Dade Public Library, Genealogy Collection in Miami; Bay County Public Library, Genealogy Collection, Panama City; and Tampa Public Library.

Georgia

The Georgia Genealogical Records Committee Reports are available in their entirety at the Georgia Department of Archives and History, Atlanta, and a partial set of these compilations is owned by the Georgia Historical Society in Savannah.

Hawaii

Aloha Chapter House and Memorial Library, 1914 Makihi Heights Drive, Honolulu is the state's main genealogical facility.

Idaho

Idaho State Genealogical Library, 325 State Street, Boise.

Illinois

DAR Southern Illinois Genealogical Library, Centralia Public Library, Centralia

Indiana

No separate state DAR library. Some materials are in the Allen County Public Library in Fort Wayne and the Indiana State Library, Genealogy Division in Indianapolis.

Iowa

No separate state DAR library. Some materials are in the Iowa State Genealogical Library, Iowa City; the Iowa Historical Center, Des Moines; and the Iowa Genealogical Society Library, Des Moines.

Kansas

Kansas DAR Library, Dodge City Recreation Center, Vine & G Streets, Dodge City

Kentucky

The John Fox Jr. Library, Duncan Tavern in Paris and the Kentucky Historical Society in Frankfort own some DAR materials.

Louisiana

Annie Laurie Moody LSDAR Collection, East Baton Rouge Public Library. Some material is also in the Louisiana State Library, Baton Rouge.

Maine

No separate DAR state library. The Maine State Library in Augusta and the Bangor Public Library own some DAR materials.

Maryland

The Maryland DAR State House in Baltimore holds some materials but is not open to the public, and some items are in the Maryland Historical Society, Baltimore.

Massachusetts

The Massachusetts DAR's collection was removed from the New England Historic Genealogical Society several years ago and placed in the Haverhill Public Library, Haverhill.

Michigan

The Michigan DAR has placed its compilations in the Burton Historical Collection of Detroit Public Library and in the Library of Michigan in Lansing.

Minnesota

DAR materials are in the Minnesota Historical Center in St. Paul, the Minneapolis Public Library, St. Paul Public Library, and Duluth Public Library.

Missouri

The Missouri State DAR Library Collection is housed at Missouri University Library in Columbia. Some materials are also in the Mid-Continent Public Library in Independence and the Springfield Public Library.

Mississippi

The Mississippi State DAR Library Collection is housed in the Eudora Welty Library in Jackson.

Montana

No separate DAR state library

Nebraska

Edith Abbot Memorial Library in Grand Island houses the Lue R. Spencer State DAR Collection.

Nevada

No separate DAR state library

New Hampshire

No separate DAR state library

New Jersey

The New Jersey DAR Collection is housed at the Special Collections Department of the Alexander Library at Rutgers University, New Brunswick. Some materials are also in the New Jersey State Library, Trenton.

New Mexico

Some materials are in the Special Collections of the Albuquerque Public Library.

New York

Collections are housed in the New York Public Library in New York City, and the New York State Library in Albany.

North Carolina

Some materials are in the North Carolina Department of Archvies and History in Raleigh.

North Dakota

Collections are in the North Dakota State Archives in Bismarck

Ohio

Collections are in the Ohio Historical Society in Columbus.

Oklahoma

The Oklahoma DAR Collection is in the Oklahoma Historical Society, Oklahoma City.

Oregon

The Caples House Museum in Columbia City is the Oregon DAR's state library. Other materials have been placed in the Genealogical Forum of Oregon Library in Portland, the Oregon Historical Society in Portland, and the Oregon State Library in Salem.

Pennsylvania

Some materials have been placed in the Genealogy/Local History Section of the Pennsylvania State Library in Harrisburg.

Rhode Island

Some materials are in the library of the Rhode Island Historical Society in Providence.

South Carolina

The South Carolina DAR Collection is housed at Camden Archives in Camden. Some materials are also in the South Carolina Department of Archives and History in Columbia and the South Carolina Historical Society in Charleston.

South Dakota

Some materials are in the South Dakota State Archives in Pierre.

Tennessee

Some materials are in the Tennessee State Library and Archives in Nashville.

Texas

Some materials are in the Clayton Library Center for Genealogical Research, Houston Public Library. Other local libraries receive materials from chapters.

Utah
No separate state DAR library

Vermont
Materials are placed in the Vermont Historical Society's Library in Montpelier.

Virginia
Some materials are in the Library of Virginia in Richmond.

Washington
The Washington State Society DAR's collection is housed in the Yakima Valley Genealogical Society Library in Yakima. Other materials are available in the Spokane Public Library, the Seattle Public Library, and the Washington State Library in Olympia.

West Virginia
Various materials have been placed in the West Virginia and Regional History Collection at West Virginia University in Morgantown, Marshall University Library in Huntington, the West Virginia Department of Archives and History in Charleston, and the West Virginia Room of the Waldmore Library in Clarksburg.

Wisconsin
No separate DAR state library

Wyoming
Materials are in the Wyoming State Library in Cheyenne.

12.2
SELECTED STATE DAR PUBLICATIONS

Many of the DAR State Organizations/Societies have published rosters and histories which may contain information useful to genealogists researching Daughters in their family histories. Please remember that the records in these volumes may not always coincide with the information which the National Society now considers to be accurate. Like the *DAR Lineage Books* and other similar publications, corrections and additions may have occured since publication.

Alabama (Alabama Society of the National Society Daughters of the American Revolution)
- *Alabama DAR Chronological History 1894-1970* (1970)
- *Membership Roll and Register of Ancestors, Volume 1 (1949); Volume 2 (1961); Volume 3* (1970)
- *Roster of Revolutionary Soldiers and Patriots in Alabama* (1979)

Alaska (Alaska Daughters of the American Revolution)
- No rosters or histories are in the DAR Library or DAR Archives.

Arizona (Arizona Society Daughters of the American Revolution)
- *Arizona State History of the Daughters of the American Revolution* (1930)
- *Arizona Daughters of the American Revolution, Territorial Days to 1990* (1990)
- *History of the Arizona State Society DAR 1930-1980* (1980)

Arkansas (Arkansas State Society National Society Daughters of the American Revolution)
- *Roster of the Arkansas Society and Register of Ancestors, 1893-1968* (1968)
- *First Supplement to the Roster of the Arkansas Society* (1978)
- *Second Supplement to the Roster of the Arkansas Society* (1988)
- *History of the Arkansas State Society DAR* (1931)

California (California State Society of the National Society Daughters of the American Revolution)
- *California DAR Ancestry Guide* (1976)
- *California History of the DAR, 1891-1938, Volume I* (1939)
- *California History of the DAR, 1938-1968, Volume II* (1969)
- *California History of the DAR, 1968-1980, Volume III* (1981)
- *Deeds Not Dreams: One Hundred Years of Service by California Daughters* (1991)
- *California's Seventy-five Historic Years, DAR 1891-1966* (1966)

Colorado (Colorado Daughters of the American Revolution)
- *Colorado DAR Member and Ancestor Index* (1981)
- *Colorado DAR Member and Ancestor Index and Supplement to October 10, 1984* (1987)
- *Supplement to the Colorado DAR Member and Ancestor Index, 1979-1984* (1987)
- *History of the DAR of Colorado, 1894-1941* (1941); *1953-1971* (1971); *1971-1987* (1987)

Connecticut (Connecticut Daughters of the American Revolution, Inc.)
- *Chapter Sketches, Connecticut DAR: Patriots' Daughters* (1904)
- *Connecticut State History of the DAR* (1929)
- *A Glance Back: Connecticut DAR Historical Directory, Vol. 1* (1969)
- *Honoring NSDAR: Connecticut Members and Their Revolutionary Patriot Ancestors* (1995)

Delaware (The Delaware State Society Daughters of the American Revolution)
- *Roster and Ancestral Roll Delaware DAR* (1940)

District of Columbia (District of Columbia Daughters of the American Revolution)
- *State History District of Columbia DAR, 3 volumes* (1934)
- *Diamond Jubilee Chapter Histories District of Columbia Society Daughters of the American Revolution, 1892-1966* (1966)

Florida (Florida State Society, National Society Daughters of the American Revolution)
- *Florida State Society NSDAR Historic Chapter Names 1895-1995* (1995)
- *History 1892-1933 Daughters of the American Revolution of Florida, Volume 1* (1933)
- *History 1933-1946 Daughters of the American Revolution of Florida, Volume 2* (1946)
- *History 1946-1958 Daughters of the American Revolution of Florida, Volume 3* (1958)
- *History and Roster Florida State Society of the DAR, Volume 4* (1968)
- *History and Roster Florida State Society of the DAR, Volume 5* (1978)
- *History and Roster Florida State Society of the DAR, Volume 6* (1988)
- *Florida State Society National Society Daughters of the American Revolution: Historic Chapter Names 1895-1995* (1995)

Georgia (Georgia State Society of the National Society Daughters of the American Revolution)
- *Membership Roll and Register of Ancestors of the Georgia State Society NSDAR* (1946, 1956, 1966, 1976, 1986)
- *Histories of Revolutionary Soldiers Contributed by Georgia Chapters, 26 volumes*
- *Revolutionary Soldiers Buried In Georgia*
- *Chapter Histories DAR of Georgia 1891–1931* (1931)
- *History of the Georgia State Society DAR 1899–1981* (1982)

Hawaii (Hawaii State Society, National Society Daughters of the American Revolution)
- *History of the DAR in the Hawaiian Islands* (1928)

Idaho (Idaho Daughters of the American Revolution)
- *History and Register 1904–1934 Idaho State Society DAR* (1934)
- *History 1963–1987 Idaho State Society DAR* (1987)
- *Idaho DAR State and Chapter History* (1931)
- Ancestor Index, Idaho State Daughters of the American Revolution (n.d.)

Illinois (Daughters of the American Revolution of Illinois)
- *Illinois State History of the Daughters of the American Revolution* (1929)
- *Illinois State History of the Daughters of the American Revolution* (1969)
- *Illinois State Directory of Members and Ancestors DAR* (1957)
- *Supplement to Illinois Ancestral Directory Members and Ancestors DAR* (1962)
- *Bicentennial Supplement to Illinois Ancestral Directory of Members and Ancestors DAR* (1976)

Indiana (Daughters of the American Revolution of Indiana)
- *Roster of Soldiers and Patriots of the American Revolution Buried in Indiana, Volume 1* (1938)
- *Roster of Soldiers and Patriots of the American Revolution Buried in Indiana, Volume 2* (1938)
- *Roster of Soldiers and Patriots of the American Revolution Buried in Indiana, Volume 3* (1981)
- *A Roster of Revolutionary Ancestors of the Indiana Daughters of the American Revolution, Volumes 1 & 2* (1976)
- *History of the Daughters of the American Revolution in Indiana* (1984; 4th edition)

Iowa (Iowa Society Daughters of the American Revolution)
- *Revolutionary War Soldiers and Patriots Buried in Iowa* (1978)
- *Biographies of State and Chapter Regents of the Iowa Society DAR* (1930)

Kansas (Kansas Society Daughters of the American Revolution)
- *Roster, Kansas Society Daughters of the American Revolution* (1970)
- *History of the Kansas Society Daughters of the American Revolution, 1894–1938* (1938)
- *Kansas State Society of the NSDAR History 1944–1986* (1986)

Kentucky (The Kentucky Society, Daughters of the American Revolution)
- *Graves of Revolutionary Soldiers, Their Wives and Children, Buried in Kentucky* (1943)
- *Ancestor Roster of the Kentucky Society DAR* (1986)
- *History of the DAR in Kentucky 1890–1929* (1929)
- *History of the Kentucky Society DAR* (1969)

Louisiana (Louisiana Society of the National Society Daughters of the American Revolution)
- *Revolutionary Ancestors of the Louisiana Society of the NSDAR 1895-1989* (1991)
- *Roster Louisiana State Society DAR* (1954)
- *History of the Chapters of the Louisiana Society DAR* (1951)

Maine (Maine State Organization, National Society Daughters of the American Revolution)
- *Ancestral Roll and Chapter Roster* (1975, 1987)
- *Index to Miscellaneous Records* (1987)
- *History of the Maine Society DAR* (1946)
- *Ancestral Roll, Maine DAR, and the List of Maine Soldiers at Valley Forge 1777-1778* (1948)

Maryland (Maryland State Society Daughters of the American Revolution)
- *Directory of Maryland State Society Daughters of the American Revolution and Their Revolutionary War Ancestors 1892-1965* (1966)
- *Directory of Maryland State Society Daughters of the American Revolution and Their Revolutionary War Ancestors 1965-1980* (1979)
- *History of the Maryland State Society DAR 1892-1933; 1933-1943* (1933, 1943)

Massachusetts (Massachusetts Daughters of the American Revolution)
- *State History of the Massachusetts Daughters of the American Revolution* (1932)
- *State History of the Massachusetts Daughters of the American Revolution 1932-1941* (1941)
- *History of Massachusetts Daughters of the American Revolution 1932-1959* (1959)
- *Massachusetts Real Daughters* (1914)
- *Massachusetts State Directory of Members and Ancestors* (1974)

Michigan (Daughters of the American Revolution of Michigan)
- *Historical and Genealogical Record of the Michigan Daughters of the American Revolution*: Volume 1 and 2, 1893-1930 (1930); Volume 3, 1930-1940 (1940); Volume 4, 1940-1952 (1952); Volume 5, 1952-1964 (1964); Volume 6, 1964-1976 (1977); Volume 7, 1976-1988 (1990)

Minnesota (Minnesota Society, Daughters of the American Revolution)
- *Highlights in the History of the Minnesota State Society of the NSDAR, 1891-1991* (1994)
- *History of the DAR Chapters of Minnesota* (1928)

Mississippi (The Mississippi Society of the National Society of the Daughters of the American Revolution)
- *Mississippi Daughters and Their Ancestors* (1965, 1979)
- *Historical Directory of the DAR in Mississippi* (1933)
- *Chapters of the Mississippi Society, DAR* (1968)
- *Mississippi: Her People, Places and Legends* (DAR history; 1977)

Missouri (Missouri State Society of the National Society, Daughters of the American Revolution)
- *Missouri State History of the DAR* (1929)
- *Missouri State History and Directory of the Daughters of the American Revolution, Bicentennial Edition* (1976)
- *Revolutionary Soldiers Buried in Missouri* (1906)
- *Centennial Jubilee History of Missouri DAR Chapters* (1990)

Montana (Montana Society, Daughters of the American Revolution)
- *State Centennial History, Montana State Society DAR 1894-1994* (1994)
- *History of the DAR in Montana 1894-1940* (1940)
- *Montana Society DAR History 1940-1960* (1960)
- *State History Montana Society DAR 1960-1970; 1970-1980* (1970, 1980)

Nebraska (National Society Daughters of the American Revolution in Nebraska)
- *Nebraska State History of the Daughters of the American Revolution* (1928)
- *DAR Nebraska Ancestor Index* (1994)
- *DAR Nebraska Ancestor Directory* (1994)
- *History of Nebraska Chapter Names* (1978)

Nevada (Nevada State Society, Daughters of the American Revolution)
- No rosters or state history are in the DAR Library or the DAR Archives

New Hampshire (New Hampshire State Organization of the National Society of the Daughters of the American Revolution)
- *New Hampshire State History of the DAR* (1930)
- *Supplement to the New Hampshire History of the DAR 1930-1940* (1940)
- *Second Supplement to the New Hampshire History of the DAR 1940-1970* (1970)
- *A Brief History of the New Hampshire Society DAR* (1985)
- *New Hampshire Directory of Members and Ancestors* (1964)
- *New Hampshire Directory of Members and Ancestors, Supplement* (1976)

New Jersey (New Jersey State Society of the National Society of the Daughters of the American Revolution)
- *State History of the New Jersey DAR* (1929)
- *New Jersey State Society History DAR 1891-1974* (1974)
- *History of Chapter Names of the New Jersey State Society of the Daughters of the American Revolution 1891-1985* (1985)

New Mexico (New Mexico State Organization, Daughters of the American Revolution)
- *New Mexico DAR Lineage Book* (1976)
- *Members of the New Mexico State Organization NSDAR* (1995)
- *History of the New Mexico State Organization NSDAR*, 3 volumes, 1971, 1987.

New York (New York State Organization, National Society Daughters of the American Revolution)
- *History of the New York State Conference DAR: Its Officers and Chapters with National Officers from New York and Roster of Real Daughters [volume 1]* (1923)
- *History of the DAR of New York State 1923-1938, volume 2* (1938)
- *History of the DAR of New York State 1938-1953, volume 3* (1953)
- *History of the DAR of New York State 1953-1974, volume 4* (1974)
- *Historic Chapter Names 1890-1987* (1987)

North Carolina (National Society Daughters of the American Revolution in North Carolina)
- *Genealogical Register Members and Revolutionary Ancestors 1890-1981* (1981)
- *Fifty Years of Service: History of the NSDAR of North Carolina* (1950)
- *North Carolina DAR Genealogical Register* (1947)

North Dakota (North Dakota State Society of the National Society Daughters of the American Revolution)
- *History of the North Dakota Daughters of the American Revolution 1915-1976* (1980)

Ohio (The Ohio Society of the Daughters of the American Revolution)
- *Ohio State History of the DAR, volume 1* (1928)
- *Ohio State History of the DAR, volume 2* (1946)
- *Ohio State History of the DAR, volume 3* (1978
- *Master Index Ohio Society Daughters of the American Revolution, Genealogical and Historical Records, Volume 1* (1985)
- *Official Roster of the Soldiers of the American Revolution Who Lived in the State of Ohio,* 3 volumes (1959)

Oklahoma (Oklahoma State Society of the National Society Daughters of the American Revolution)
- *History of the Oklahoma Society DAR 1894-1939* (1939)
- *Oklahoma Society NSDAR Roster, 1909-1959 (1976)*

Oregon (Oregon State Society of the National Society Daughters of the American Revolution)
- *Oregon State Roster of Ancestors, Daughters of the American Revolution (1963)*
- *Oregon State Roster of Ancestors, Daughters of the American Revolution, First Supplement* (1978)
- *Oregon Daughters of the American Revolution* (1989)
- *History of the Oregon Society DAR* (1931)

Pennsylvania (The Pennsylvania State Society Daughters of the American Revolution)
- *The Pennsylvania Society of the DAR 1894-1930* (1930)
- *Pennsylvania State History of the DAR* (1947)
- *Pennsylvania State History of the DAR* (1976)
- *Pennsylvania State History of the DAR* (1990)

Rhode Island (Rhode Island State Society, Daughters of the American Revolution)
- *Revolutionary War Records and Biographical Sketches of the Ancestors of Rhode Island Daughters of the American Revolution,* 3 volumes (1964)
- *State History of the Rhode Island DAR* (1930)
- *State History of the Rhode Island DAR 1930-1938* (1938)

South Carolina (South Carolina State Society of the National Society of the Daughters of the American Revolution
- *Membership Roster and Ancestral Index, 1954-1986* (1988)
- *Roster and Ancestral Roll, South Carolina DAR* (1939, 1954)
- *History of the South Carolina DAR,* 3 volumes (1937, 1946, 1976)

South Dakota (South Dakota State Organization Daughters of the American Revolution)
- No rosters or state history are in the DAR Library or DAR Archives.

Tennessee (Tennessee Society Daughters of the American Revolution)
- *Membership Roster and Soldiers, The Tennessee Society of the Daughters of the American Revolution, 1895-1961, Volume 1* (1961)
- *Membership Roster and Soldiers, The Tennessee Society of the Daughters of the American Revolution, 1960-1970, Volume 2* (1970)
- *Membership Roster and Soldiers, The Tennessee Society of the Daughters of the American Revolution, 1970-1984, Volume 3* (1985)
- *Roster of Soldiers and Patriots of the American Revolution Buried in Tennessee* (1974)
- *History of the Tennessee Society DAR 1892-1990* (1991)
- *Tennessee State History DAR* (1930)

Texas (Texas Society National Society, Daughters of the American Revolution)
- *History of the Texas Society NSDAR* (1975)
- *Alamo Heroes and Their Revolutionary Ancestors* (1976)
- *Directory of the Texas Society of the NSDAR* (1990)
- *Texas State History of the DAR* (1929; reprint 1987)
- *Texas Society DAR Roster of Revolutionary Ancestors*, 4 volumes (1976)
- *History of the Texas Society NSDAR* (1976)

Utah (Utah Society Daughters of the American Revolution)
- *Who's Who in the Utah DAR* (1976)

Vermont (Vermont State Society Daughters of the American Revolution)
- *Vermont State Conference DAR 1892-1930* (1985)
- *Vermont DAR State History Book (1931-1985)* (1985)

Virginia (Virginia Daughters of the American Revolution)
- *Roster of the Virginia Daughters of the American Revolution (Revised) 1890-1958* (1959)
- *History of the Virginia State Society DAR* (1930)
- *History of the Virginia Daughters of the American Revolution 1891-1987* (1987)
- *History of Chapter Names, Virginia DAR* (1964), and *Supplement* (1967)

Washington (Washington State Society of the National Society, Daughters of the American Revolution)
- *History and Directory of the Washington State Society NSDAR*, 6 volumes (1924-1987)

West Virginia (West Virginia Society, Daughters of the American Revolution)
- *West Virginia State History DAR* (1928)
- *West Virginia Daughters and Their Revolutionary Patriot Ancestors* (1981)
- *West Virginia State History DAR 1928-1982* (1982)

Wisconsin (Wisconsin Society Daughters of the American Revolution)
- *Wisconsin Society DAR in Review 1892-1971* (1971)
- *Wisconsin Society DAR in Review 1971-1989* (1989)
- *State History DAR Wisconsin 1892-1937* (1937)
- *Revolutionary War Ancestors, Members Numbers,* and *Supplements 1891-1964* (1964)

Wyoming (The Wyoming Society Daughters of the American Revolution)
- *Wyoming DAR Member and Ancestor Index* (1985)
- *History of the DAR of Wyoming 1894-1946* (1946)

12.3
DAR CHAPTERS AND THEIR PUBLICATIONS

Many of the over 3,000 DAR chapters have published their own histories and rosters of members and their ancestors. These can be useful, once again, if a relative or direct forebear were a very active member of a chapter, biographical information may appear. Not all of these chapter histories are available in DAR collections. Addresses of chapters are available from the Office of the Organizing Secretary General.

12.4
UNITS OVERSEAS

Members of the DAR have long lived beyond the borders of the United States. During various periods in the past, DAR chapters have existed in such varied locations as Havanna, Cuba; Shanghai, China; and Manila, Philippines. Today, Daughters have organized chapters in Great Britain, France, Mexico, Australia, and Canada. The history of these foreign connections has been told by Virginia C. Russell in the DAR's publication, *Daughters Overseas: A History of Units Overseas*. Information on DAR members who were active in the older chapters overseas during the early twentieth century may also be found in articles in *The DAR Magazine* and in materials in the Office of the Historian General.

GUIDE TO SUBJECT RESEARCH IN DAR COLLECTIONS

*B*ecause of the varied and separated nature of many of the research collections at DAR, a subject approach to these sources beyond the department chapters is necessary. The broad categories of research in this chapter highlight the holdings of the DAR and how they relate to American genealogical research in general.

13.1
AFRICAN AMERICAN RESEARCH

During the past twenty years there has been an explosion of publishing in African American studies. Examinations of African American genealogical research have also increased in number. The DAR Library has developed a strong, growing collection of basic and detailed printed sources on this subject.

In the Library's General/African American section are many research manuals and guidebooks, histories of Americans of African descent, slavery and abolition studies, examinations of the "Great Migration" in the early twentieth century, and general reference materials. These offer researchers with a starting point and with ideas for further investigation. Blockson's *Black Genealogy*, Byers' *African American Genealogical Source Book*, Johnson and Cooper's *A Student's Guide to African American Genealogy,* and Streets' *Slave Genealogy: A Research Guide with Case Studies* are just a few of these items. *Roots* by Alex Haley, who undertook some of his research in the DAR Library, is also available in this section. Important periodicals, such as *The Journal of the Afro-American Historical and Genealogical Society, and The Journal of Negro History* offer much useful material.

At the beginning of the state sections are subsections for collected materials on each state for African American history and genealogy. One excellent example is Dr. Barnetta White's landmark publication *Somebody Knows My Name: Marriages of Freed People in North Carolina, County by County.* Within

One of the great stimuli to the popularity of genealogical research in the late twentieth century was the publication in 1976 of Alex Haley's account of his family history, *Roots*. The subsequent televising in early 1977 of the miniseries reached an enormous audience. Coinciding with the Bicentennial of the Independence of the United States, these events combined to spark the imagination of the American public and to spur many into seeking their own family origins and the roles these ancestors played in the nation's development. The DAR Library recorded a fifty percent increase in visitors in 1976-1977 over the previous year as a result. Interest has not waned in the past two decades.

In the mid-1960s and early 1970s Haley frequented the three major genealogical research centers in Washington, D.C. as he began his investigations. A few long-time staff members recall his visits to the DAR Library. In 1984, speaking to the DAR's Continental Congress, Haley remembered:

> *It was in the course of this that I would come to work at the DAR Library. There is one particular thing a lot of people don't realize and that is that the DAR Library is special in terms of black genealogical research.*

Haley continued with a discussion of the presence of old plantation records and inventories which contain the names of many Southern slaves, and that if one is "blessed and lucky" their ancestors may appear in such records in the DAR Library.

the county holdings researchers will find an increasing number of new publications such as published registers of free blacks in Virginia, Maryland, and the District of Columbia and community histories. African Americans appear throughout county histories and record abstracts, but researchers will be frustrated on occasion by older compilations of records which only list whites. Fortunately, recent abstractors are attempting to fill in these gaps. The Library's collection of District of Columbia marriage records is an example of such older and newer coverage.

Family histories, a significant portion of the Library's book collection, offer researchers of African American families many opportunities. Representative examples of studies specifically on black families include Fears' *Slave Ancestral Research: It's Something Else* and *Slave Ancestral Research in Seven Steps with in the Jackson-Moore Family History and Genealogy...*, Jupiter's *Agustina of Spanish West Florida and Her Descendants...*, Madden's *We Were Always Free, The Quander United Tricentennial Celebration, 1684-1984*, Redford's *Somerset Homecoming*, Sutton's *The Nickins Family, Non-Slave African American Patriots*, and Warner's *Free Men in an Age of Servitude: Three Generations of a Black Family*. Donations of African American family histories or notification of their publication are appreciated.

Family histories and genealogies of white families are also very important to African American researchers for the information they may reveal on the slave owners, their records, and their migrations. There are many such studies in the Library.

The Library's collection of census indices and the attendant microfilms in Seimes Microfilm Center are other useful sources. Among these indices are those for the 1850 and some 1860 slave schedules of the federal censuses. Although the actual schedules are only available locally at the National Archives and despite the fact that the indices only index the slave owner and not the slaves by name, these are important records. Some special compilations, such as Nitchman's *Blacks in Ohio, 1880* are based on census records.

An increasing number of excellent studies relating to the records of blacks in America's wars are natural inclusions for DAR collections, particularly those concerning the American Revolution. In addition to other studies on the latter subject, the DAR has had a project for many years to document minority service in the Revolution. The results to date are the following booklets compiled by Senior Genealogist, Elisabeth Whitman Schmidt. Rita Souther wrote the historical text for the Rhode Island volume, and Hazel Fuller Kreinheder penned the same for the Connecticut and Massachusetts booklets.

- *Minority Military Service, Connecticut, 1775-1783.* (1988)
- *Minority Military Service, Maine, 1775-1783.* (1990)
- *Minority Military Service, Massachusetts, 1775-1783.* (1989)
- *Minority Military Service, New Hampshire/Vermont, 1775-1783.* (1991)
- *Minority Military Service, North Carolina, 1775-1783.* (1996)
- *Minority Military Service, Rhode Island, 1775-1783.* (1988)
- *Minority Military Service, South Carolina and Georgia, 1775-1783.* (1997)
- *Minority Military Service, Virginia, 1775-1783.* (1995)

Heinegg's *Free African Americans in North Carolina and Virginia*, Green's *Black Courage*, Moebs' *Black Soldiers, Black Sailors, Black Ink: Research Guide on African-Americans in U.S. Military History*, Schubert's *On the Trail of the Buffalo Soldier: Biographies of African Americans in the U.S. Army, 1866-1917*, and Wilson's *Black Phalanx: African American Soldiers in the War of Independence, the War of 1812 and the Civil War* are examples of further military studies.

The Library's "Women's History" section also includes various historical studies and collected biographies of African American women and their roles in American history. In late 1995 and early 1996 the DAR Museum presented an exhibit "Talking Radicalism in a Greenhouse: Women Writers and Women's Rights." The exhibit contained much relating to women's rights and to the abolition movement. A descriptive checklist of the exhibit items is available from the DAR Museum Office.

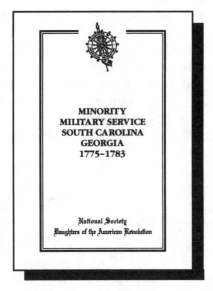

MINORITY
MILITARY SERVICE
SOUTH CAROLINA
GEORGIA
1775-1783

National Society
Daughters of the American Revolution

13.2
BIBLE RECORDS

Family births, marriages and deaths recorded in Bibles are the staple of genealogical research. DAR collections abound with Bible records from across the United States and from all periods. The gathering of these essential sources has been and remains an important part of the DAR's commitment to the preservation of historical materials.

The Library welcomes donations of Bible records. Donors may make copies onto acid-free paper including the title page of the Bible. Details such as the Bible's publication date, current ownership, and other identifying facts linking the sources to a given family in a specific place are extremely important.

There are numerous Bibles in DAR collections. The DAR Museum and the Office of the Historian General collect Bibles for their artistic or printing value, and the Library accepts donations of entire Bibles to insure preservation of the family register pages they include.

Researchers may search for Bible records in the following locations:

● throughout the Library's book collection accessible through the Analytical Index and the catalog in published family histories

● in the Genealogical Records Committee reports, including the LDS microfilms of the pre-1972 reports in the Library's file collection under family surnames or names of Revolutionary War ancestors of DAR members

● in the Library's manuscript collection under specific surnames

● in the Historian General's Americana Collection

● in indices to genealogical periodicals which contain innumerable Bible record transcriptions

---

On a cautionary note, there are always problems with transcriptions of any kind, and those of Bible records are no exception. Illegibility of originals and improper corrections to original spellings and punctuation are common. In addition to casual mistakes, typographical errors, and inadvertant omissions, researchers may encounter the occasional serious problem. Falsified or altered records can appear, unfortunately. See the following recent article for an example of a questionable Bible record in a *Genealogical Record Committee Report:* Warren L. Forsythe, "Resolving conflict between records: a spurious Moseley Bible," *National Genealogical Society Quarterly,* 84:3 (September 1996), 182-199. Always take what is in print and seek to verify information with as many other sources as possible.

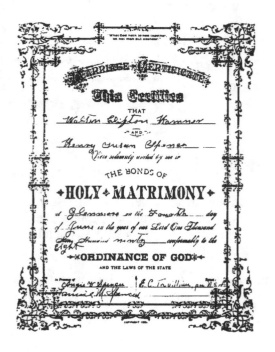
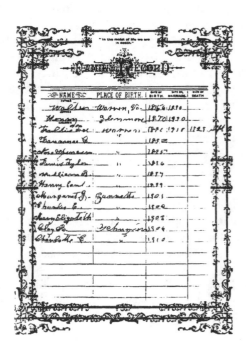

Pages from the Hamner Family Bible, Buckingham County, Virginia in possession of Eric G. Grundset.

13.3
BIOGRAPHICAL RESEARCH

Genealogy is very closely related to biography, and many genealogists attempt to create accurate biographies of their ancestors as part of their research. Because of the closeness of these two studies, the Library maintains many biographical materials.

The Biography Special Collection on the upper south balcony contains numerous biographies, autobiographies, diaries, and collected papers of historically prominent Americans, particularly from the period of the American Revolution. Most biographies contain sections on the family and sometimes the genealogy of the subject. Genealogists would do well to consider the possibility that if their ancestor were a neighbor of a well-known individual, then that ancestor may have had contacts with the neighbor and consequently appear in his or her papers. Important clues to one's own family history may appear in some unrelated person's papers, and if that person were Adams, Washington, or Jefferson, it makes the resulting genealogy even more interesting.

Collected biographies constitute an important part of the Library's biography collection. *The Genealogy and Biography Master Index* provides access to many lengthy and many brief biographies and related genealogical information. Biography guides and indices direct researchers to still other potential sources. Standard sets such as *The Dictionary of American Biography, The Encyclopedia of American Biography, volumes 1-54 (1917-1933)* and *The Encyclopedia of American Biography, New Series, volumes 1-40 (1934-1970)* offer considerable information. Large, but incomplete, runs of *Who's Who in America* and *Who Was Who in America* are familiar sources.

One major finding aid for both biography and genealogy is the Godfrey Memorial Library's monumental publication *The American Genealogical-Biographical Index to American Genealogical, Biographical, and Local History Materials*. In 187 volumes (through early 1997) and nearly through the alphabet, the *AGBI* gives researchers access to hundreds of studies and sources. The Library owns the majority of the items indexed.

Within each state section is a Biography subsection containing collected biographies for each state. These vary in quality, reliability, age, and numbers. Many historical organizations are producing biographical dictionaries for their respective states, and the Library acquires these as they appear. Rosters of state legislators, governors, jurists, attorneys, and other prominent individuals are numerous. Biographies also constitute major portions of state, county and local histories produced during the nineteenth and twentieth centuries, sources which fill the shelves of the Library.

The Historical Research Library of the Office of the Historian General also contains many biographies of famous Americans. Refer to section 7.5.

13.4
CEMETERY RECORDS

Among the major materials represented throughout DAR collections are cemetery records. Cemetery surveys have been one of the DAR's primary volunteer activities from the early years of the National Society, and the resulting volumes of transcriptions number in the thousands. Most have entered the DAR Library through the Genealogical Records Committee, which collected many of them before urbanization and suburbanization began to obliterate smaller family cemeteries near cities.

The DAR's survey of local cemeteries has varied in depth and coverage depending on the activities of individual members and local chapters. In some counties work has been extensive and long-term; in others, either spotty, short-term, or non-existant. Many surveys compiled years ago have never been updated and reviewed. Others have been brought up-to-date through the efforts of DAR members and chapters or local historical and genealogical societies. The Library has acquired hundreds of volumes of cemetery records from these local groups around the country.

In the General/Cemeteries section are useful sources such as national directories of cemeteries and undertakers and studies on epitaphs, funeral customs, and tombstone art, including the publications of the Association for Gravestone Studies.

Because of the many forms in which cemetery records appear, researchers must take a broad approach in their search in DAR collections and consider several areas of the building in their quest for these sources. In every instance (unless otherwise noted), check the names of counties, towns, villages, or churches where a cemetery may be located, the names of family cemeteries, and the names of specific cemeteries. Major sources at DAR for cemetery research include:

- The Library's catalog and analytical index under the name of the cemetery, church, town, or county followed by "Cemetery records."
- The Library's state file collection
- LDS microfilms of DAR materials (prior to 1972) and other sources using *The Cemetery Record Compendium*.... See Chapter 5.
- The *Periodical Source Index* and *Genealogical Periodical Annual Index* listing hundreds of cemetery transcriptions in genealogical and historical periodicals and journals
- Seimes Microfilm Center, which has numerous cemetery records in microform.
- The Office of the Historian General's card indices to located and marked graves of Revolutionary soldiers, members, etc. See section 7.2.

13.5
CENSUS

DAR owns census records in various formats, but most are either in books or on microforms. These sources are located in several places.

13.5.1
FEDERAL CENSUS RECORDS

With the proximity of the National Archives and space considerations in mind, the Seimes Microfilm Center has not acquired all federal census records on microfilm. It does, however, hold a significant portion of these records. DAR does not own the non-population or special census schedules with the exception of some mortality schedules (see section 13.5.4). The following list details these holdings.

1790: Published books in the DAR Library

1800: Published indices for this census in the DAR Library usually include not only the heads of families but also the numbers of household members by age group and gender. Microfilm of a few small states or portions of a few states is available.

> The 33rd Congress of the National Society ... adopted a Resolution requesting an appropriation by the Government for the restoration and preservation of the Early Census schedules of the population of the United States. This request has been granted so no further solicitation of the support of your Members of Congress for this particular measure is necessary.
>
> The project was approved, funds were allotted for this purpose and work is now in progress covering all of the items requested—the restoration of the 19 damaged volumes, the photostating of the schedules of 1800, 1810 and 1820, for use in place of the originals which are to be withdrawn from further use.
>
> Our special thanks are due President Roosevelt, the Civil Works Administration, and those of the Census Bureau whose approval made this result possible. The National Society Daughters of the American Revolution is to be congratulated upon their achievement of this project which is in conformity to the foundation principles of our Organization.
>
> From Lue R. Spencer's article
> "A D.A.R. Achievement,"
> *DAR Magazine*, February 1934, p. 100.

1810: Published indices for this census in the DAR Library usually include not only the heads of families but also household members by age group and gender. Microfilm of a few small states or portions of a few states is available.

1820: Microfilm of a few small states or portions of a few states.

1830: Microfilm of a few small states or portions of a few states.

1840: Microfilm for the entire country is available.

1850: Microfilm for the entire country is available.

1860: Microfilm for the entire country is available.

1870: Microfilm for the entire country is available.

1880: Microfilm for the entire country is available including the Soundex.

1890: Indexes for the Special Census of Widows and Veterans are available for some states. An index for the few surviving population schedules is available in the Library.

1900: Microfilm for the entire country is available including the Soundex.

1910: Only Maryland, Nevada, and North Dakota are available. Consult the rest at the National Archives.

1920: Only Indiana population schedules and index are available. Consult the rest at the National Archives.

13.5.2
INDICES FOR FEDERAL CENSUS RECORDS

The Library owns indices to nearly all of the federal censuses for the years 1790 through 1870. There are a few exceptions for the 1870 census which were either never published, are unavailable, or are in production. Most of these indices are in the Library's "General" section in the census subsection arranged by state and year. A few microfiche indices for some states also are available in the Microfilm Center.

Because of the varying quality of these indices, researchers are encouraged to use an index first, and if a name is not found but a county is known, read through the entire census for that county. Census takers did, however, miss many families and individuals, while some people avoided these government agents. All genealogical research guides offer sound advice on census research.

The Microfilm Center also owns a "national" census index produced on microfiche by Accelerated Indexing Systems (AIS) (1983 edition). AIS produced this index by merging and sorting the data from the state indices it had published into one large alphabet for the various census years. The index is comprised of several "searches" which focus in the following manner: Search 1 (Colonial & United States 1600-1819); Search 2 (1820-1829); Search 3 (1830-1839); Search 4 (1840-1849); Search 5 (Southern States 1850-1860); Search 6 (Northeastern and Northern States 1850); Search 7 (Midwestern and Western States 1850-1906); Search 7A (United States 1850-1906); Search 8 (United States Mortality Schedules, 1850-1885). Because of the production of many census indices since this edition appeared in 1983, this national index is more comprehensive for the earlier years covered than for the later ones. Many of the later years will only be covered by the printed indices available by state. Some early AIS census indices actually provide access to early tax and other lists and not census records specifically. These are included in this national census index. AIS provided a guide to this microfiche index entitled *American Genealogical Computer Catalogue (AGCC)* in 1983. Another helpful guide is the LDS-produced *Accelerated Indexing Systems, Inc. Microfiche Indexes*, which is its Genealogical Library Instructional Materials, Series F, No. 1: Branch Genealogical Libraries: Instructional Materials. Both offer insight into the use of this microfiche index.

13.5.3
TRANSCRIPTIONS OF FEDERAL CENSUS RECORDS

Scattered throughout the entire book collection in the DAR Library are transcriptions of federal census records for counties across the United States. These volumes will be located, for the most part, in the "State" section, then the county subsection. They will be available for some counties and not for others. Often if the Library's collection on a given county is weak, it will acquire these transcriptions to fill the gap. Some transcriptions of census records will also appear in genealogical periodicals and in the Genealogical Records Committee Reports. Indices to these types of publications must be consulted to locate this information.

13.5.4
FEDERAL MORTALITY SCHEDULES AND POPULATION SCHEDULES
FORMERLY IN DAR CUSTODY

During the twentieth century, DAR has taken on the role of temporary custodian for a number of volumes of original records, once the property of the Bureau of the Census. In the years before the establishment of the National Archives, the Bureau distributed various schedules from several federal censuses to repositories in the appropriate states. On two occasions, the DAR accepted volumes for which the Bureau did not find homes.

From 1919 to 1930 DAR housed 134 volumes of agricultural, industrial, social, and manufacturing schedules for Colorado, the District of Columbia, Georgia, Kentucky, Louisiana, Montana, Nevada, Virginia, and Wyoming. Not every type of schedule was held for each state however. The Library transferred these volumes to Duke University, Durham, North Carolina in 1930. The records are listed in *Guide to the Cataloged Collections in the Manuscript Department of the William R. Perkins Library*, Duke University, edited by Richard C. Davis and Linda Angle Miller, pages 589-590.

In the late 1930s the Bureau of the Census deposited volumes of mortality schedules with the DAR, which maintained them until 1980 when they were transferred to the National Archives for preservation and microfilming. These records now constitute National Archives Microfilm Publication T655. The actual records involved were: Arizona, 1870, 1880; Colorado, 1870, 1880; District of Columbia, 1850, 1860, 1870, 1880; Georgia, 1850, 1860, 1870, 1880; Kentucky, 1850, 1860, 1870, 1880; Louisiana 1850, 1860, 1870, 1880; and Tennessee, 1850, 1860, 1870, 1880. The Library owns indices to all of these records except for Colorado and 1880 Tennessee. These indices were prepared by various DAR members around the country.

The first edition of Val D. Greenwood's *Researcher's Guide to American Genealogy* (1973) correctly showed DAR as the custodian of these mortality schedules. The second edition (1990) of this volume notes the transfer to the National Archives. The Library still receives inquiries concerning these schedules as well as others which it never owned. Greenwood's list provides an accurate guide to the location of these and other mortality schedules.

The DAR again served as the temporary custodian for census records in 1956, but in this instance the volumes originated with the National Archives. After microfilming and attempting to find suitable locations in the states for the federal copy of the 1880 census population schedules, the Archives deposited 167 volumes with the DAR. These sources were maintained in the DAR Library until 1980. At that time the DAR decided to find repositories in each state involved to accept these deteriorating volumes. Although the records of this transfer are incomplete, the following list specifies the number of transferred books and their present locations:

- **ARIZONA** (1), Arizona Department of Library, Archives and Public Records, Phoenix.

- **CONNECTICUT** (10), Connecticut State Library, State Archives, Hartford.

- **IDAHO** (1), Idaho State Historical Society, Boise

- **IOWA** (33), State Historical Society of Iowa, Des Moines.

- **KANSAS** (21), Kansas DAR Library, 700 Avenue G, Box 103, Dodge City, KS 67801

- **MISSISSIPPI** (23), location not known. The Mississippi Department of Archives and History does not own these volumes.

- **MISSOURI** (45), Missouri State Archives, Jefferson City.

- **NEW HAMPSHIRE** (3), New Hampshire Archives, Concord.

- **NEBRASKA** (10), Edith Abbott Memorial Library, Grand Island.

- **NEW MEXICO** (3), location not known. The New Mexico Records Center and Archives states they do not own these volumes.

- **RHODE ISLAND** (6), Rhode Island Historical Society, Providence.

- **UTAH** (3), Utah State Archives and Records Services, Salt Lake City.

Although the 1880 population schedules are available on microfilm, the potential for illegible spots on the films makes the existance of the original volumes important. Several of the state agencies indicated that they also own the state copies of these schedules. Researchers may wish to compare the two copies, looking for discrepancies in transcriptions and perhaps omissions.

The 1980 transfers of the 1880 population schedules and the various mortality schedules mark the end of DAR's involvement in the retention and preservation of such federal records. The Library's research service will check the indices to the mortality schedules on written request. The Library does not, however, own many printed indices for the 1880 population schedules with the exception of those for a few states and some for individual counties.

Periodically, new indices to mortality schedules which were never owned by the DAR are published, and the Library adds these to the census index collection.

13.5.5
STATE CENSUS RECORDS

DAR owns a limited selection of state census records and accompanying indices to a few of them. Most notable in book form are Ann Smith Lainhart's transcriptions of the 1855 and 1865 Massachusetts state censuses for many towns; miscellaneous counties' schedules for some New York state censuses in printed volumes; the 1852 California state census in book form; and microfilm of surviving schedules for twenty-five Michigan counties for 1894. Examples of other published versions include the 1771 Vermont census, the 1784–1787 North Carolina census, and the 1885 Florida census. There are also various books dubbed "state censuses" which are, in fact, contructed from surviving tax lists. Examples of this include the 1740, 1760, 1782–1785 and 1787 "censuses" for Virginia. More state census records will be added in coming years.

13.6
CITY DIRECTORIES

In March 1987 the DAR Library received a donation of nearly 1,100 city directories from around the United States from the Bureau of the Census. These volumes are concentrated around the years 1910, 1920, 1930 and 1940, because they were once used by the Bureau to conduct age searches for individuals in the federal censuses for those years. Anyone who has conducted genealogical research in urban areas will testify to the value of city directories in helping to pinpoint the place of residence for individuals and families. They also frequently list occupations. The Library was fortunate to acquire these volumes because they added an additional dimension to the collection by providing sources for the twentieth century, a period lightly covered in the holdings.

THE

WASHINGTON DIRECTORY,

SHOWING THE

NAME, OCCUPATION, AND RESIDENCE

OF EACH

Head of a Family & Person in Business

TOGETHER WITH

OTHER USEFUL INFORMATION

- - - - - - -

CITY OF WASHINGTON

PRINTED AND PUBLISHED BY S. A. ELLIOT

Eleventh street w. near Pennsylvania Avenue

....

1827

THE

WASHINGTON DIRECTORY.

———

☞ *For explanation of abbreviations, see Preface.*

RESIDENTS.

ABBOT, John, clk in third auditor's office; dw Georgetown
Abbot, Joseph, hackman, n w corner Pn and 13w
Achman, Mrs. widow, Bn btw 19 and 20w
Acken, William, shipwright, corner 9e and Ms N Yard
Adams, John Quincy, President of the United States, at the President's mansion
Adams, Mrs. widow, 14e near Eastern Branch
Adams, Rebecca, widow, Bn btw 3 and 4e Capitol Hill
Adams, Margaret, widow, Ds btw 3 and 4e
Adams, Joseph, carpenter, 13½w btw C and Ds
Adams, Thomas, chairmaker, s side Pen av btw 12 and 13w
Adams, George, collector 5th and 6th wards, 8e btw K & Ls
Adams, George, police officer, corner 4e and Ls
Adams, John, bricklayer, Gn btw 17 and 18w
Addison, Thomas B. clk in general post office; dw Georgetown
Addison, W. D. clk in general post office; dw Pr. George's county, Md.
Agg, John, writer, Mrs. M'Cauley's, Pen av
Aiken, Prudence, widow, n side Cn btw 4½ and 6w
Alexander, Charles, upholsterer, n side Pen av btw 12 & 13w

The directories represent cities large and small across the country. They range in size from six-inch thick tomes covering New York, Chicago, Boston and Los Angeles to smaller compilations for such smaller urban areas as Grand Junction, Colorado (1912-13); Park Ridge, Illinois (1922-23); Columbia, Pennsylvania (1909), and Charlottesville, Virginia (1912-13). The condition of the volumes varies considerably. Some are very tattered and crumbling, and use is therefore restricted. Others are in excellent condition. Still others are bound photocopies of the original directory. All contain a wealth of information.

An important collection of Boston city directories from 1789 to 1868 is on microfiche in the Microfilm Center.

Many libraries own city directories for their locality and state, and some have holdings covering the entire United States. Researchers should investigate these important sources to learn more about their families and ancestors. The Library welcomes donations of city directories from anywhere in the United States for any time period.

13.7
COLONIAL RESEARCH SOURCES

Located on the east coast as it is, the Library naturally has excellent holdings of materials for the original colonies on the Atlantic seaboard. Additionally, because many DAR members also have belonged to the great "colonial" lineage societies, they had a heightened awareness of colonial publications and family histories. Consequently, many have have contributed these materials to the DAR Library over the past century. Early in its history the Library assumed a focus beyond the Revolutionary period as a result of the broad interests of members.

Published and microfilmed colonial records and local histories combined with continuing acquisitions of recent publications for this period make the colonial research materials in the library extensive and extremely popular. Published collected sets of the records of colonial governments for most of the colonies provide valuable sources, and major microform collections of additional records offer further avenues for research.

Immigration to the colonies during the seventeenth and eighteenth centuries has been the subject of numerous studies, many of which are discussed in greater detail in section 13.14. These represent a significant portion of the published passenger records in any library.

Colonial wars are the subjects of numerous publications in the Library's collections. Despite major record loss in some states for the colonial period, historians and genealogists have produced considerable literature to document these conflicts. Refer to section 13.20.1 for more information.

Many printed family histories and genealogies extend into the colonial period. The published lineage books and other compilations of some lineage societies with a colonial focus, such as the Colonial Dames of America, the National Society Daughters of the American Colonists, and the Society of Colonial Wars, are partially available for clues. Sources and publications related to the popular quest for descent from the first settlers in Virginia and Massachusetts are a surprising find for many researchers at DAR.

One point which is often forgotten, probably because it is so obvious, is that all Revolutionary War ancestors of DAR members were born in the colonial period and for this reason, the application papers themselves contain tens of thousands of connections to colonial families. Although not required and not encouraged, researchers will occasionally encounter lineages on older DAR membership applications extending a generation or two prior to the Revolutionary ancestor.

13.8
"DAUGHTERS" AS RESEARCH SUBJECTS

If an ancestor or relative were a member of the DAR, there will be some information on her at DAR Headquarters. The first step in researching a DAR member would be to obtain a copy of her membership application, any supplemental applications she may have filed, and any supporting proof for these papers.

Obtaining the member's national number is a crucial step in the research process. Request these in the Office of the Organizing Secretary General with submission of the member's name or in the Office of the Registrar General with submission of the ancestor's name. With the national number in hand, a visit to the Seimes Microfilm Center will enable researchers to view the application paper in microform. Copies of deceased or inactive members applications may be ordered in the Office of the Registrar General. The surviving supporting documentation from applications is housed in the Library's file collection. All of these sources should provide some basic information on the member.

DAR members who were national officers will likely have generated a variety of records or listings to help flesh out a biography. The Organizing Secretary General's Office maintains a file of information on national officers. Many national officers' photographs appear in issues of *The DAR Magazine* during their terms in office. Biographical sketches often accompany magazine entries during DAR election years. Photographs and other biographical information may appear also in various DAR publications in the Office of the Historian General.

Information on state DAR officers may appear in various state publications such as state DAR histories and historical rosters which often include biographical sketches of State Regents and officers. State yearbooks and other publications, if available, may also assist with this research. State Historians may also be able to help provide information on historic state officers.

The Office of the Historian General (until 1994) and the Office of the Organizing Secretary General (after 1994) maintain records of marked graves of many deceased DAR members. Contact either of those offices for information on their holdings.

13.8.1
"REAL DAUGHTERS" AND "REAL GRANDDAUGHTERS"

Members of the DAR who were the actual daughters and granddaughters of Revolutionary War soldiers and patriots were known as "Real Daughters" and "Real Granddaughters." Besides their membership applications, which would only show a generation or two, a variety of information is available on these women. The Office of the Historian General maintains several files of material on women in these categories as well as a card file of marked graves of some Real Daughters. In the early years of the twentieth century, *The DAR Magazine* published biographical articles on Real Daughters, and a card index in the Magazine Office provides citations to these sketches. A list of Real Daughters is available in the Registrar General's Clerical Office, the Office of the Historian General, and the Library. Please see section 7.4 for more advice on researching Real Daughters.

13.9
FAMILY HISTORIES AND GENEALOGIES

About 40,000 volumes of published and unpublished family histories comprise a significant part of the collection. Most are listed in *The DAR Library Catalog, Volumes One and Three*. They cover all periods in American history and many have sections tracing the family back to its previous home across the ocean.

Genealogical compilations vary considerably in format and reliability. Some are detailed and well documented, while others are someone's rough notes and charts bound together with little proof included. The Library accepts all offers for these materials with the idea that every book may provide clues and proof of a lineage. Preservation of *any* genealogical information is another consideration. The Library receives new family histories daily from DAR members and non–members alike and welcomes all such donations. To donate a book to the Library, please contact the Acquisitions Librarian for procedures.

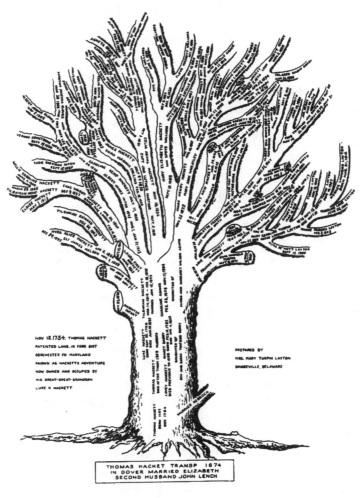

A Hackett Family Tree
From the DAR Magazine, April 1931, p. 222

Collected family histories are a common format. Many include the words "encyclopedia" or "compendium." These are located in the General, State and Foreign sections of the bookstacks depending on their subject focus. One such gathering is unique to the DAR Library: the "turquoise set." This includes numerous, brief genealogies and histories which were once housed in the Library's file collection because they would not wear well on open shelves. The staff removed them, arranged them alphabetically by surnames, and bound them into fifty-eight volumes. All are cataloged and accessible through the catalog.

An important and often difficult-to-locate source for genealogy is the family newsletter. Thousands must circulate, but few find their way into libraries. The Library owns many historical and currently published family newsletters and journals. These are bound and placed in the Family Section. The latest issues are in the files of the Serials section of the Library office. Associated with these newsletters are many family associations. The Library has directories and lists of many of these to help researchers.

Biographies of prominent individuals usually contain considerable information on that person's family, descendants and ancestors. Reseachers suspecting a connection to the well-known should consult biographies for clues.

Gaining access to family histories and genealogies is always a challenge. Many individual books do not have indices, a fact which greatly limits their usefulness. The Library catalogers will make up to ten subject tracings for major surnames mentioned in each book they process. These tracings appear in the catalog and provide considerable cross referencing to hidden surnames. Aside from the Library catalog itself, various indices to family histories and genealogies guide researchers to the location of more hidden material. The Library's Analytical Index serves this purpose, along with such published guides as *The American Genealogical-Biographical Index* and *The Periodical Source Index*.

Most family compilations are printed in limited quantities. The Library is fortunate to have so many of these. Researchers frequently request ordering information, which is often not available. If the book were donated by a DAR member, one may request that member's address from the Organizing Secretary General's Office in hopes that the member may provide ordering information. The Library maintains information on out-of-print and rare bookdealers and on some companies specializing in photocopy reprints of old genealogies. A long standing policy, based on concern for copyright protection and on limited staffing, prevents the Library from making copies of entire books.

A frequently overlooked source for details of family history are architectural histories, pictorial books of houses and buildings in states or counties, and similar publications. After all, families lived in houses and the history of those families is part of the history of the house. These compilations of architectural information may be found in several locations in the DAR Library. "Architecture" books are near the beginning of most state sections. There are many studies of historic buildings in the county sections as well and in the Museum Reference Library.

In addition to books, the Library's files contain innumerable brief typescript studies and pamphlets. Many of these are unavailable elsewhere. A collection of a few hundred genealogical charts and "family trees" is also available. In Seimes Microfilm Center, researchers will discover nearly 400 reels of microfilm containing copies of family genealogies and histories. Some of these are duplicates of volumes in the Library; others are not. All microforms are cataloged.

13.10
FEDERAL GOVERNMENT RECORDS

What Might Have Been

DAR began a campaign shortly after the turn of the century urging its members to contact their elected officials in the United States Congress for the purpose of gaining support for the creation of a national archives. During the course of this effort, which lasted off and on until the late 1920s, various sites were considered by the federal government for the proposed building. One was in the block between E and F, 18th and 19th Streets, N.W., the present location of the General Services Administration. If only this site had been selected–it is a short two-blocks from DAR Headquarters! The actual site of the National Archives is now eight long blocks by foot from DAR–"you can't get there from here" by public transportation very easily.

Census, passenger lists, land registers, pension records and other federal records which have been published are plentiful in DAR collections. These sources are discussed in other sections of this chapter.

Numerous published finding aids to the holdings of the National Archives point the way to research just eight blocks down Constitution Avenue at Archives I or in College Park, Maryland, at Archives II. Less obvious are valuable materials available in the Library such as *The Territorial Papers of the United States* in twenty-six volumes concerning the governments of territories which became states and *The Official Records of the War of the Rebellion* examining the Civil War.

13.10.1
THE U.S. SERIAL SET

Another very useful publication which opens the door to voluminous federal sources is *The U.S. Serial Set Index* which is a finding aid to federal government publications since the 1780s. The Library owns this index through 1889 and portions of the *American State Papers* series. Although the entire Serial Set is not available at DAR, a largely complete collection is owned by the

Department of the Interior's Natural Resources Library next door to DAR. This library is open to the public with presentation of a photo ID and makes the Serial Set easily accessible.

13.10.2
W.P.A. PUBLICATIONS

The DAR Library owns about 1,000 volumes of the publications of the Historical Records Survey of the Works Progress Administration (later the Work Projects Administration). Because of the DAR's involvement at the local level in supporting the work of the W.P.A. during its lifetime from 1935 to 1942, the W.P.A. donated many of its publications to the DAR Library. In the Washington area, only the National Archive's Library, now at Archives II in College Park, Maryland, has a larger collection of W.P.A publications.

The majority of the published volumes is in the series "Inventory of the County Archives," These inventories of county records list local records found in courthouses in the states at the time the survey was completed. Not all counties in every state have a published inventory. Even if a county of interest is not available, researchers may wish to review an inventory for another county as a representative example of the types of records which should be in any county in that state. Many of the publications have useful introductions and discussions of records and record-keeping practices.

Portions of other W.P.A series are available in the Library's special "W.P.A. Collection." These include inventories of federal records in the states, calendars of manuscript collections, guides to the records of religious bodies, and indices to a few newspapers. All are of potential value to genealogists and should not be overlooked.

Separate from the special collection of W.P.A materials, researchers will also encounter many transcriptions of records at the county level prepared by the W.P.A.'s Historical Records Survey. Several state sections—particularly Florida, Michigan, Tennessee, and West Virginia—include numerous such volumes. Once again, because of the DAR's local support for W.P.A projects, the DAR Library received many of these transcriptions which are very similar to the DAR's own Genealogical Records Committee reports.

In the Historical Research Library, maintained by the Office of the Historian General, is a set of the Federal Works Agency of the Work Projects Administration's series of state guides in the "American Guide Series." See section 7.5 for more information.

13.11
FOREIGN RESEARCH

DAR collections focus largely on American sources and families, but because research often takes genealogists beyond American shores the Library maintains a basic selection of research guidebooks, dictionaries, atlases, indices, and historical sources designed to lead researchers to other materials and research centers. As new guides are published for different countries, the Library acquires them.

Among the holdings in this section are materials on the following countries and regions:

Africa — Basic histories of West African kingdoms, nations and peoples, particularly Liberia and Sierra Leone, combined with the African American research materials (see section 13.1) offer introductory sources for researchers of African descent.

Australia — Basic information sources are available.

Bermuda — Important record abstracts from the seventeenth to nineteenth centuries are available.

Canada — In terms of organization, the Canadian section of the DAR Library follows the pattern of the United States section. The bulk of the Canadian collection is arranged by "province" and by county or other subdivision within the province. Here the researcher will find province histories such as *New Brunswick, A History: 1784-1867* by W.S. MacNutt and vital records such as Reid's *Marriage Notices of Ontario* and Hale's *Early New Brunswick Probate Records*.

Because the United States has a history of relations with eastern Canada dating back to colonial days, the heaviest concentration of books is for the eastern provinces such as Ontario, Quebec, Prince Edward Island, Nova Scotia, and New Brunswick. At the end of the Revolution, a number of American Loyalists settled in these eastern provinces of Canada and the Library has a number of books on the topic (see section 13.20.4.15). All Canadian provinces are represented in the collection, however.

Highlighting the Canadian section is an extremely useful series of books published by The Genealogical Research Library of Toronto. These books are *The Atlantic Canadians 1600-1900, The Central Canadians 1600-1900, The Western Canadians 1600-1900* and *The French Canadians 1600-1900*. Each title contains three volumes listing over 500,000 names. The books provide the user with an alphabetical list of every adult male and single female householder known to be living in Canada between those years. A variety of sources were consulted to compile these books including land records, city and town directories, early Canadian census records, marriage records and cemetery records. Additional information for the entries includes place of residence and occupation.

In addition to *The French Canadians 1600-1900*, the Library has several specialized works on French Canadian families. These include the *Dictionnaire Genealogique des Familles du Quebec des Origines a 1730*, and Tanguay's multivolume *Dictionnaire Genealogique des Familles Canadiennes*, both of which lists individuals alphabetically by surname and include such details as birthdate, marriages and children. The serial publications *Lost in Canada?* and *Our French-Canadian Ancestors* have lengthy narrative articles on lives of individual ancestors with citations to sources.

England — A mixed collection of English materials is owned by the Library. Research manuals, collected family studies, and archival guides predominate. A largely complete set of the *Publications of the Harleian Society*, containing many abstracts from church registers, is a source which adds some depth generally not found in the Library's foreign books.

The 1983 edition of the *Domesday Book* is also available. This multivolume compilation of the 1086 Norman census of England's population and property is a unique resource for medieval England.

A few genealogical periodicals, notably *The Genealogist, The Genealogist Magazine*, and *Family Tree Magazine*, have been donated to the Library in recent years and provide useful articles on English methodology, sources, and specific families. Some of the standard works on English royal and noble lineages are also available, including some editions of *Burke's Landed Gentry* and related publications.

Emigration from England during the colonial era is the subject of numerous volumes in the "General/Emigration & Immigration" section. The work of Peter Wilson Coldham, such as *The Complete Book of Emigrants* and *The Complete Book of Emigrants in Bondage*, document English migrants to the American colonies and are popular, standard studies. Many others offer similar lists and histories of this crucial influx of settlers. Published materials for the post-Revolution period are limited for English immigrant research however.

Innumerable American family histories and genealogies and compiled studies carry lineages back to England, and these are plentiful in the Library's collections. Many works on the Chesapeake and New England colonies examine English connections and family origins of those American "cradle" regions. In the Library's section on the American Revolution, researchers will find a growing literature on the English involvement in the war with the rebellious colonies.

France — Basic information sources for French research are available. Specific studies on French Huguenot immigrants to the American colonies highlight this well-known group, particularly sources for Huguenots in Virginia and South Carolina. Records and histories for Acadian immigration, for French refugees from Santo Domingo, and for French Canadian research round out the French-related holdings in the Library. See also the discussion of French military involvement in the American Revolution in section 13.20.4.11

Germany — Sources for German and German-American research pervade the DAR Library. Standard, published historical sources for immigrants into the American colonies and the resulting records of their settlements, churches, and families in Pennsylvania and other middle colonies/states abound. More recent publications by Burgert, Jones and others on the origins and settlements of German immigrants offer valuable information. The popular series *Germans to America* lists passenger arrivals after 1850.

A copy of Siebmacher's *Wappenbuch* is available. This is a multi-volume study of heraldry and names with a history of publication dating to the seventeenth century.

Genealogical periodicals *German Genealogical Digest, Publications of the Pennsylvania German Society, The Germanna Record, The Report of the Society for the History of Germans in Maryland, Der Kurier*, and *The Palatine Immigrant* expand the Library's coverage.

For information on the Hessians during the American Revolution refer to section 13.20.4.14.

Ireland — Irish immigrants to America during the colonial perioid are often hidden by the similarities of their names to those of other migrants from the British Isles, but they were here. While some studies document and examine these early arrivals, most recent material for Irish immigration focuses on the departures during the Great Famine of the 1840s. The Library offers various histories and published passenger lists for this period including Glazier and Tepper's *The Famine Immigrants 1846–1851* (7 volumes) and Harris and O'Keefe's *The Search for Missing Friends: Irish Immigrant Advertisements Placed in the Boston Pilot* (1831- ; 5 volumes to date). Collected family histories and research manuals for Ireland provide additional opportunities for understanding the Irish research process.

Italy — Basic information sources for Italian research in the Library include the series *Italians to America*, the journal *POINT: Pursuing Our Italian Names Together*, and various local studies.

Latin America — A number of new guides to Hispanic genealogical research have appeared in recent years, and the DAR Library has acquired these to give proper referral to researchers. These include:

Byers' *Hispanic American Genealogical Sourcebook*; Platt's *Hispanic Surnames and Family History*; and Ryskamp's *Tracing Your Hispanic Heritage*.

There are also numerous sources on Hispanic families in the Southwestern states, Louisiana, and Florida in the appropriate state section. These range from collected genealogies, histories, and record abstracts. Spanish Land Grants in Florida are available on microfilm in the Seimes Microfilm Center. Spanish participation in support of the American Revolution is also the subject of various studies in the Library. See also the discussion of Spanish involvement in the Revolution in section 13.20.4.12.

Netherlands — Basic Dutch information sources, major nineteenth-century immigration indices, and considerable materials in the New Netherland, New York, and New Jersey sections of the Library comprise the majority of the resources relating to the Dutch in North America in DAR collections.

Poland — Basic information sources are available along with some local sources on major Polish-American communities.

Russia — Basic information sources are available for nineteenth and early twentieth century Russian immigration to the United States. Some sources on the history of Russian America are in the West Region section of the Library.

Scandinavia — Very basic Scandinavian research guides cover the Nordic countries. Information on specific groups of immigrants or individuals to North American is more extensive and may be found in county and community histories for areas where they settled.

Sweden is best represented in the Library's collections primarily because of its size and the centuries old connections with North American settlement. Among the major sources for Swedish research are the *Swedish American Genealogist*, printed immigration indices, and histories and sources relating to Swedish and Finnish settlers of New Sweden in the mid-seventeenth century.

Scotland — Scots immigrants have come to America since the seventeenth century but are often difficult to trace because of Anglicized names and poor to nonexistent migration records. Various researchers have worked to illuminate the role of the Scots in early America, and the Library maintains a good collection on this subject. The work of David Dobson has been significant in filling in gaps in the historical record and includes such titles as *Directory of Scottish Settlers* (7 volumes), *Directory of Scots Banished to the American Colonies 1650-1775*, *Scots on the Chesapeake 1607-1830*, and *Scots in the Carolinas*. Others have produced similar studies, and there are several which focus specifically on Scottish settlers in specific states, such as Haw's *Scots in the Old Dominion*, Meyer's *Highland Scots of North Carolina 1732-1776*, and Steen's *New Aberdeen or the Scotch Settlement of Monmouth County, New Jersey*. Research manuals focusing on genealogical study in Scotland, specific family histories, collected family works, and general histories round out the Scottish materials in the Library.

Scots-Irish (Ulster Scots) — Millions of Americans have ancestors from the Scottish settlement of northern Ireland and the major migrations to the colonies in the eighteenth century. Library holdings include many local, state and general studies on these immigrants. Most are historical accounts, but some contain genealogical information. One basic guide is Reintjes' *Scotch-Irish: Sources for Research* and many articles in genealogical periodicals offer additional advice.

Switzerland — Basic information sources on Swiss research and Swiss names are available.

Wales — Basic information sources for research in Wales are available.

West Indies — Important record abstracts from the seventeenth and eighteenth centuries offer researchers information on families which first settled in the Caribbean and later migrated to the mainland colonies. Abstracts of Barbados wills and vital records, the classic journal *Caribbeana* (v. 1, 2, 4-6), and other scattered sources provide useful coverage for this region. Grannum's *Tracing Your West Indian Ancestors: Sources in the Public Record Office* is an excellent source for British possessions in the area. Such current periodicals as *The Newsletter of the Saint-Domingue Special Interest Group* and *Caribbean Historical and Genealogical Journal* are very helpful.

13.12
GENEALOGICAL DIRECTORIES

Many directories are in print to help researchers locate various types of current information. They list family associations and their publications, genealogical researchers, genealogical and historical societies, research centers and libraries, and book publishers. Others provide addresses for county courts, federal courts, and cemeteries and funeral homes.

13.13
HERALDRY

The DAR Library has a small collection of basic books on heraldry and coats of arms including Siebmacher's *Wappenbuch*. During the 1920s and 1930s, *The DAR Magazine* ran a column "A Page in Heraldry," which offered coats of arms on specific surnames and commentary. This is not a subject in which the Library specializes. In Washington, the Library of Congress has a large number of books on heraldry and related topics.

An early view of Boston.

13.14
IMMIGRATION AND NATURALIZATION RESEARCH

Many sources to assist with immigration research are available in the Library. The DAR does not own, however, National Archives microfilm of passenger arrivals at U.S. ports.

The *Passenger and Immigration Lists Index*, edited by P. William Filby with Mary K. Meyer, is the standard source for gaining access to many **published** records of immigrants into the American colonies and the United States. The Library owns this multi-volume index along with the majority of sources therein referenced. Researchers should consult this set to determine if an ancestor appears in a **published** passenger list found in books and journals. As the editors locate new materials, they include these references in the next annual supplement to the set.

New publications of immigration records appear frequently. Some cover the colonial period and others the nineteenth and twentieth centuries. The DAR Library's holdings are not limited to any one period or to only a few national groups. While significant materials list immigrants from the British Isles, major indices also cover Czech, Dutch, German, Greek, Italian, Russian, and Swedish newcomers. Those sources for the British Isles concentrate on the colonial period movements of English, Scottish, Scots-Irish, and Irish to America, and on the Irish migrations relating to the Great Famine. Those for the rest of Europe concentrate on French Huguenot and German colonial migrations and nineteenth-century departures from across the continent. The series *Germans to America* (1850-1893) is one of the Library's most popular sets.

In 1910 the Connecticut DAR began a program to publish manuals to assist recent immigrants to the United States with their citizenship tests. These manuals were in the native language of several groups. By the early 1920s, the expense and popularity of the program made the Connecticut DAR enlist the involvement of the National Society. For the next three decades or so the DAR published many other manuals in numerous foreign languages of Europe, Asia and Latin America. Since the 1950s the manuals have been available only in English at the request of the Federal government.

Example above right:
– Russian (1947)

These materials can be found for the most part in the Library's General section under "Emigration." There are significant holdings, however, in many state sections, which contain studies and sources relating specifically to migrations into a specific state from Europe or other parts of North America. Examples include materials on German Palatine immigrants into New York, Germans into Pennsylvania, Dutch and Scandinavians into New Sweden and New Netherland, Spanish and French into Louisiana, Spanish into Florida, German Salzburgers into Georgia, and French Huguenots into Virginia and South Carolina. The variety of immigrants into this country over the centuries leads to the publication of new studies and lists on a regular basis. Particularly useful are volumes which examine the settlement and lives of immigrant groups in specific communities and counties. All shed light on the evolving American population.

One less obvious source for immigration information is DAR membership applications. Because many Revolutionary War soldiers and patriots were themselves the immigrant to North America, researchers will often discover a European place of origin for a family through the vital information these sources provide on the ancestor of a DAR member. Because documentation of colonial immigration is so difficult, this information could be crucial in developing a search strategy across the Atlantic.

Naturalization records are among the most difficult-to-locate, decentralized, and least frequently published of sources. Still, as these become available in print, the Library acquires them to provide clues for immigration research and the origins of families and individuals. Generally, abstracts of naturalization records will be located in the catalog under the name of the county or city in which the records were created.

13.15
JEWISH RESEARCH

A basic collection of materials for Jewish research is available at DAR. In the Library's General/Religion section are various sources such as collected family genealogies, research guides, histories of Judaism in the United States, and major genealogical and historical journals. For the latter, the Library owns a largely complete set from volumes 1 (1905) to 82 (1994) of the periodical *Publications of the American Jewish Historical Society/American Jewish Historical Quarterly/American Jewish History* (with indices), as well as an incomplete run of *American Jewish Archives* between volumes 6 (1954) and 47 (1995). In other sections of the Library, researchers will encounter studies of Jewish participation in the American Revolution and on Jewish communities around the United States, particularly those which date from the colonial period. Histories of Jewish settlements in specific states are also available. In the General/Names section are several recent and important volumes on the origins of Jewish family names.

In the Seimes Microfilm Center a collection of Jewish research sources is available on microfiche. These include "Jewish Applicants for Emergency Passports (1915-1924)," "Burials in the Old Section of the Washington Hebrew Congregation's Cemetery," "Jewish Genealogical Consolidated Surname Index," "Jewish Genealogical Societies Publications," "Gazetteers of Eastern Europe," and other sources relating to Holocaust Research.

13.16
LAND RECORDS

Land records are a fundamental source for genealogists. Abstracts, indices and guides concerning land abound throughout DAR collections. From original deeds in the Americana Collection to deed abstracts and CD-ROMs containing indices of federal land records, researchers will find much to investigate. Histories of land policies and ownership in the United States, guides to use and interpretation of land records, and studies on surveying offer background information for genealogists. *The American State Papers: Public Lands Series* [1789-1837] is a ten-volume set including the index *Grassroots of America* and offers much detail on the development of early federal land policies as well as the names of thousands of Americans involved with public land sales and purchases.

In the past several years the General Land Office of the Department of the Interior's Bureau of Land Management has published on CD-ROMs indices resulting from its "Automated Records Project." These provide access to pre-1908 homestead and cash entry patents from federal land offices in public land states in the eastern part of the country. At the present time CDs are available for Arkansas, Florida, Louisiana, Michigan, Minnesota, Ohio, and Wisconsin. The remaining states under the Eastern States Office of GLO are pending. With these indices researchers may determine whether an ancestor acquired land from the federal government and from there contact the GLO for additional information and copies of documents.

Throughout the state sections, researchers will find land materials specific to each state, especially records of colonial land patents. These include publications with a state-wide coverage or approach, studies interpreting the development of land ownership in some states, and important indices to land records. In many of the public land states, volumes examine and sometimes index the sales of public lands by the federal land offices in each state.

County deed abstracts from around the country fill the shelves in the Library. Most are from the seventeenth to the nineteenth centuries. Some counties have had extensive abstracting, while others only minimal. These volumes are among those which the Library collects as crucial sources. Microfilms of selected county deed books are in the Microfilm Center.

13.17
LAW SOURCES

General material to assist genealogists with interpretation of historical legal documents and sources are part of the Library collection. Legal dictionaries, citation guides, encyclopedia, and manuals are available along with historical analyses of such subjects as marriage, divorce, and common law. In the various state sections, researchers may also find legal materials specific to their state of interest such as legislative acts, codes or historical studies. *The U.S. Statutes at Large* 1789-1881 are available on microfiche. The massive quantity of law materials useful to genealogists and the unavailability of most historical legal publications precludes the DAR Library from collecting heavily in this area.

13.18
LINEAGE SOCIETY PUBLICATIONS

As a lineage society itself, the DAR has received many publications from other such organizations during the twentieth century. These are not always complete or current, but they may provide useful clues for further investigations. DAR does not have copies of application papers for these organizations with the exception of the General Society of the War of 1812 for which a partial collection is available on fifteen microfilm reels covering approximately 1914 to 1976.

Various lineage societies with similar membership requirements and objectives as the DAR are often confused with the latter organization. Several of these are listed below for general reference. Please note that although the DAR Library owns some of the publication of many of these societies, all are completely separate organizations from DAR. Each maintains its own files, application papers, and libraries. Additional information on these and other lineage societies may be found in the latest edition of *The Hereditary Register* and other similar directories found in genealogical collections nationwide.

National Society, Children of the American Revolution (C.A.R.)
C.A.R. was established in 1895 by the DAR and subsequently incorporated as a separate organization. Anyone under age 21 who can trace their direct ancestry to a person who "rendered aid to the cause of American Independence" may join on invitation from members of a local society. Although C.A.R.'s offices are located in DAR's Constitution Hall, it is completely separate and maintains its own application papers and files. All correspondence should be sent to N.S.C.A.R., 1776 D St., N.W., Washington, D.C. 20006-5392.

National Society, Sons of the American Revolution (SAR)

The SAR formed in 1889 and maintained its national headquarters in Washington, D.C. until 1979, when they moved to Louisville, Kentucky. Its membership is comprised of men over age 18 who are direct lineal descendants of "an ancestor who was at all times unfailingly loyal to, and rendered active service in, the cause of American Independence..." [NSSAR pamphlet, *General Information and Application Requirements*] The DAR does not own any SAR applications or files. SAR maintains an important genealogical library at its headquarters at 1000 South Fourth Street, Louisville, KY 40203. Telephone: 502-589-1776. The DAR Library has some SAR national and state publications.

National Society, Daughters of the Revolution of 1776 (DR)

This society formed in 1891 after a policy rift with the DAR. It disbanded several years ago. All papers of the DR were donated to the Suffolk County Historical Society, 300 W. Main Street, Riverhead, NY 11901; telephone, 516-727-2881. The Suffolk County Historical Society will check the records of the Daughters of the Revolution in reply to written inquiries. Researchers frequently confuse the DR with the DAR for obvious reasons, and the latter receives inquiries which may relate to DR members. The DAR Library has some older DR publications.

General Society, Sons of the Revolution (SR)

Founded in 1876, this society is headquartered at Fraunces Tavern, 54 Pearl Street, New York, NY 10004. It is composed of male lineal descendants over 21 of one who "assisted in the establishment of American Independence by services rendered during the War of the Revolution..." [Hereditary Register (1986), p. 50.] The DAR Library has some older SR publications.

Society of the Cincinnati

The Society is located at 2118 Massachusetts Avenue, N.W., Washington, D.C. 20008; telephone 202-785-2040. It maintains a library of 35,000 volumes. Contact the Society for additional information on research and membership. The DAR Library owns some Society of the Cincinnati publications.

The Library's collection of publications of other lineage societies includes some material for these major groups and a limited number of publications for other smaller groups. These publications may include lineage books, rosters, directories, yearbooks and histories. Check the catalog for listings. More recent information which updates listings in these publications may be available from each organization.

- National Society Daughters of Colonial Wars

- Colonial Daughters of the XVII Century

- Colonial Dames of America

- National Society U.S. Daughters of 1812

- General Society of the War of 1812

- National Society Daughters of the American Colonists

- National Society Daughters of Colonial Wars

- National Society Daughters of Founders and Patriots of America

- Order of Founders and Patriots of America

- The Society of Colonial Wars

- National Society of the Sons and Daughters of the Pilgrims

- United Daughters of the Confederacy

- Women Descendants of the Ancient and Honorable Artillery Company

13.19
MAPS, ATLASES AND GAZETTEERS

The Library has an eclectic map collection. Some are actual folded or rolled maps in the expected format. Others from are books and journals, removed by the staff years ago for reasons not entirely clear today. Retrospective cataloging of the maps is a slow, ongoing process.

Atlases represent an important source for genealogical study. The Library's collection ranges from modern state road and topographical atlases, to early property atlases and historical atlases. The recent, continuing series, *Atlas of Historic County Boundary Changes*, is a major addition to the literature and is published in state or regional volumes. Similar studies detailing the minute evolution of important jurisdictional lines, offer researchers crucial information for record location and ancestral residences.

Place names are essential clues in research and historical and contemporary gazetteers help locate forgotten, extinct, and current places. These guides may be found with many atlases in the "Geography" subsections within the state and regional sections as well as the General section of the Library.

Although, not part of DAR, researchers will be interested to know that the United States Geological Survey operates a map sales center in the Department of the Interior (E Street entrance). Here one will find a wide selection of USGS map publications, which are extremely useful tools for genealogical research. A photo ID or a DAR visitor's badge is required to enter the building just across 18th Street from DAR.

13.20
MILITARY RECORDS RESEARCH

Sources for research in the military records of the United States and the states are a significant part of DAR collections. Consequently any discussion of these sources must be within a broad historical context. Publications, microforms and manuscript materials for most of the nation's historical conflicts abound. Coverage for the American Revolution is naturally a major component of this material, but the War of 1812 and the Civil War also receive strong attention.

Each section on a specific war or on particular military records in this discussion highlights general and specific sources in DAR collections. References are also given as illustrations of the types of publications and records available.

The inclusion of a book or a source in this guide does not imply that it is an acceptable source for DAR Revolutionary War service. Consult *Is That Lineage Right?* for listings of what is acceptable.

13.20.1
EARLY COLONIAL WARS

The first English colonists to Virginia established Jamestown in the territory of the Powhatan Indians. Relations between the two cultures were tense at times, but relatively peaceful. Peace was shattered in 1622 and again in 1644 when Powhatans led by chief Opechancanough unsuccessfully attempted to annihilate the colonists. The story of the Anglo-Powhatan wars is included in general works on Virginia history. Some documents relating to Virginia's early Indian wars may be found in *The Records of the Virginia Company of London*.

After some thirty years of peace in Virginia, war erupted again in 1675, this time against the Susquehannocks, a tribe previously friendly to the colonists. When the Virginia government did not respond to the crisis, a Provincial Council member named Nathaniel Bacon led two expeditions against the Indians and later unsuccessfully attempted to seize control of the government. Documents relating to the upheaval can be found in *Bacon's Rebellion: Abstracts of Materials in the Colonial Records Project*.

New England colonists were no more successful in dealing with the Indians. A 1636 war between the Massachusetts Bay Colony and the Pequots and one from 1675-1676 against the Wampanoag and their chief King Philip resulted in English victories and near destruction of the tribes. General histories of the period with emphasis on the Pequot War and King Philip's War are available in the Library. An especially interesting source on the two wars is *The History of the Indian Wars in New England from the First Settlement to the Termination of the War with King Philip, in 1677* written by Rev. William Hubbard and originally published in 1677. Researchers interested in military records of the period should examine Bodge's *Soldiers in King Philip's War* which includes lists of Massachusetts soldiers involved, biographical sketches of the officers and documents related to the war. Additional official materials on the Pequot War and King Philip's War may be found in *Records of the Governor and Company of the Massachusetts Bay in New England, The Public Records of the Colony of Connecticut* and *Rhode Island Colonial Records*.

Heightened competition between England, France, Spain and the Netherlands led increasingly to armed conflict. The colonists found themselves pitted against an alliance of French and Indians in King William's War and Queen Anne's War, against the Spanish in the War of Jenkin's Ear and opposite both the Spanish and the French in King George's War. Between 1652 and 1674 the British fought three wars against the Netherlands. The Second Anglo-Dutch War (1664-1667) resulted in the British capture of New Amsterdam, now New York. Accounts of the surrender of New Amsterdam may be found in *Narratives of New Netherland 1609-1664* and *Documents Relating to the Colonial History of New York*.

Colonial participation in these wars varied. Rosters of the soldiers who served from the colonies are found in several sources including *Colonial Delaware Soldiers and Sailors, Virginia's Colonial Soldiers, The Military History of the State of New Hampshire 1623-1861* and *A List of Rhode Island Soldiers & Sailors in King George's War 1740-1748*. Massachusetts took a particularly active role in these conflicts. Rosters of Massachusetts men in the colonial wars include *Massachusetts Officers and Soldiers in the Seventeenth Century Conflicts, Massachusetts Officers and Soldiers 1702-1722, Massachusetts Officers and Soldiers 1723-1743* and *Massachusetts Soldiers in the French and Indian Wars 1744-1755*. Additional material on colonial involvement in these wars may be found in official records such as *Journals of the House of Representatives of Massachusetts*. Several general histories of these early colonial wars, as well as histories of specific tribes, are available in the Library.

13.20.2
THE FRENCH AND INDIAN WAR

In May 1754 a young Major George Washington of the Virginia militia, and a small group of soldiers under his command skirmished with French soldiers near what is now Uniontown, Pennsylvania. This engagement and Washington's subsequent surrender to the French after a month long siege in a hastily constructed fort was the beginning of the French and Indian War. Within a year, regular British troops were dispatched to North America under General Edward Braddock who found defeat and death at the hands of the French. The conflict expanded until it included most of the nations in Europe where it was known as the Seven Years War. Battles were fought around the globe. After initially suffering a number of defeats, the British army in North American successfully invaded Canada and captured Quebec. When the war was over, the British dominated North America and French influence was at an end.

The full story of the French and Indian War is recounted in a number of works including Schwartz's *The French and Indian War 1754-1763: The Imperial Struggle for North America*, Jennings' *Empire of Fortune*, Gipson's *The British Empire Before the American Revolution*, and Parkman's classic study *Montcalm and Wolfe*. Specific campaigns of the war are explored in Older's *The Braddock Expedition and Fox's Gap in Maryland*, Kopperman's *Braddock at the Monongahela*, Steele's *Betrayals: Fort William Henry and the "Massacre"* and Dunnigan's *Siege-1759: The*

Campaign Against Niagara. The experience of the French soldiers is portrayed in Gallup and Shaffer's *La Marine: The French Colonial Soldier in Canada 1745-1761* and in Bonin's *Memoir of a French and Indian War Soldier*. Hargreaves' *The Bloodybacks* depicts the life of the British enlisted man during this period and Ford's *British Officers Serving in America 1754-1774* lists individuals by name with rank, regiment and date of commission.

The French and Indian War saw the first extensive use of American troops to supplement British regulars. Some of these American units were highly specialized such as Rogers Rangers whose story is told in *Reminiscences of the French War with Robert Rogers' Journal and a Memoir of General Stark* and Loescher's *Genesis: Rogers Rangers, The First Green Berets*. Most Americans who served however, did so in "provincial" units of infantry like those examined in Anderson's *A People's Army: Massachusetts Soldiers and Society in the Seven Years' War*. A remarkable number of muster rolls have survived from this period. Examples of these rolls include Bockstruck's *Virginia's Colonial Soldiers*, De Lancey's *Muster Rolls of New York Provincial Troops 1755-1764*, Bradshaw's *Pennsylvania Soldiers in the Provincial Service 1746-1759, Massachusetts Officers and Soldiers in the French and Indian Wars 1755-1756* and *Massachusetts Officers in the French and Indian Wars 1748-1763*. Additional lists of provincial soldiers can be found in the *Pennsylvania Archives* and the *Delaware Archives, Military*. Each of these lists is useful for establishing military service during the war, but the rolls do not include information on the soldiers' spouses or descendants.

13.20.3
DUNMORE'S WAR AND THE BATTLE OF POINT PLEASANT

The frontier conflict in 1774 in the Ohio Valley known as Dunmore's War is viewed by some as the last colonial war and by others as the beginning of the American Revolution. The Library has materials on this conflict in general and on the Battle of Point Pleasant. The DAR accepts service in this battle in a limited way. Please contact the Genealogy Department for clarification. The best known source on this war is Thwaites' *Documentary History of Dunmore's War*.

13.20.4
Part 1
THE AMERICAN REVOLUTION

Some of the most enduring images of American popular culture comes from the Revolution. Paul Revere's ride, the "minute men" of Concord and Lexington, the defense of Bunker Hill, Washington crossing the Delaware, the winter at Valley Forge and Betsy Ross are the subjects of statutes, paintings and books. All of these images are based on the actions of real people although they are now legendary. Equally important are the contributions of the American officers and men who did not achieve fame, yet performed countless acts of heroism and sacrifice in the cause of the Revolution. Because of their celebrity, it is easy to find accounts on the service of George Washington, Paul Revere or Israel Putnam. Finding specific information on the common soldier is an altogether different prospect. This has always been a primary objective for the DAR.

A number of obstacles face any researcher interested in a Revolutionary soldier. The passage of time takes its toll on documents. Records are destroyed or deteriorate. Then too, the military establishments of the eighteenth century were not as well organized nor as exact in their record keeping as the modern army. As a result, the researcher should not expect to find the minutiae of a modern military personnel record for a Revolutionary War soldier. Finally, while the Continental Army was the national army during the Revolution, it was not the only organized body of American soldiers. Throughout the war, state and town militia units under the authority of the state governments supplemented and supported the Continental Army. Consequently, not one, but several different government bodies kept records on the American troops.

13.20.4.1
The Continental Line and the Militia

When they arrived in the New World, the English colonists brought with them the concept of militia, a military force for defense formed from the male population. In more densely populated New England one finds town militia, while in the South, militias included all the men in a county or an even wider area. Militiamen elected their own officers, practiced military drill and kept weapons in their homes. They served as a military unit only in times of crisis. By the time of the Revolution, the militia was an established feature of American colonial life. Militiamen stood on the green of Lexington and plagued the British retreat back to Boston the same day. Following the events in Lexington and Concord, the Massachusetts Provincial Congress called for the establishment of a New England army. Several colonies, including Massachusetts responded by forming regiments that were dispatched to Boston. In June 1775, the Continental Congress called for Pennsylvania, Maryland and Virginia to form companies of riflemen which, when added to the troops outside Boston, would form the nucleus of the Continental Army. Later Congress would expand the call for enlistments to include all of the colonies.

Continental Line Infantry, showing State Distinctions.
(From original drawing by Harry A. Ogden)

Large standing armies were not a feature of eighteenth century American life. In order to pursue the cause of independence it was necessary for the Congress to create the Continental Army from the only trained military force at its disposal: the existing state militia units. This was only a stop gap measure and a matter of some concern to the army's new commander, George Washington. The militiamen were nonprofessional soldiers and their enlistment was limited to a matter of months. It was not until late 1776 that Congress authorized enlistment periods in the Continental Army for a period of no less than three years or the duration of the war. At the same time, Congress asked that each state form a specific number of regiments for service in the Continental Army. The extended enlistment period gave Washington the opportunity to form the professional army he desired, but the army never grew to the point it could without the support offered by the militia. Throughout the war, whenever the Continental Army was on campaign it was joined by local militia who would assemble in time for the battle then leave once the shooting stopped.

A good one volume history of the army during the Revolution is Wright's *The Continental Army* published by the U.S. Army Center of Military History. Included in the book is a list of Continental Army units with an organizational history for each and a list of each regiment's engagements. Berg's *The Encyclopedia of Continental Army Units* has a brief history of every unit that served in the

Continental army and selected militia units with appendices on the organization of the Army, the size of the army and a list of the units at Valley Forge.

Individual histories of Revolutionary War regiments are relatively rare. Most state units are studied as a group in works such as *The North Carolina Continentals, The Pennsylvania Line: Regimental Organization and Operations, 1776-1783, The Virginia Continental Line.* E.M. Sanchez-Saavedra's *A Guide to Virginia Military Organizations in the American Revolution, 1774-1787* includes a description of every Virginia unit including the state navy, and identifies the officers in each unit. These books are available in the Library in the state sections.

For the most part these broader studies do not include the names of common soldiers. Exceptions to this rule are *The Commander-in-Chief's Guard, Revolutionary War* by Carlos E. Godfrey, *History of the First New Hampshire Regiment in the War of the Revolution* by Frederic Kidder and *The German Regiment of Maryland and Pennsylvania in the Continental Army* by Henry J. Retzer, which contain rosters. *Pierce's Register* preserves the names of officers and men of the Continental Army who received back pay from Paymaster General John Pierce in the form of certificates in 1783. A full listing of the officers in the Continental Army is available in Francis B. Heitman's *Historical Register of Officers of the Continental Army During the War of the Revolution.* Fortunately, records for the enlisted men of the Continental Army were preserved by the U.S. War Department, although not without some difficulty.

The Continental Line and the Continental Army are one and the same. The term "Line" is derived from the most common battlefield formation of the day. In battle infantry regiments advanced in long lines facing the enemy. The two opposing lines would then blaze away at each other until one side or the other retired from the field ending the battle. Any maneuvering on the battlefield was performed by Light Infantry or other auxiliary units whose efforts contributed little to the outcome of any engagement. Ultimately it was the Line regiments that determined the course of the battle. It was a matter of pride to be part of a "Line" regiment as it indicated the soldier was a professional.

13.20.4.2
Compiled Service Records

Accidental fires in 1800 and 1801 and a deliberate one set by the British in 1814 destroyed a number of federal records relating to Revolutionary War soldiers. No effort was made to replace these documents until the late nineteenth century, when the United States War Department acquired records from other federal departments or duplicated materials owned by the state governments. Using these sources, the War Department recreated service records for Revolutionary War soldiers. The compilations resulting from these efforts were later microfilmed by the National Archives and made available to the public under the title *Compiled Service Records of Soldiers Who Served in the American Army During the Revolutionary War*. The original documents are now permanently housed at the National Archives. All 1,096 rolls of this microfilm publication are available for use in the Seimes Microfilm Center. The service records are arranged first by state, then by regiment, and within the regiment alphabetically by the individual soldier's surname.

An index to the *Compiled Service Records* is also available on microfilm in the Microfilm Center. This index is the basis for a four volume publication by Virgil White entitled *Index to Revolutionary War Service Records*. Arranged after the style of its microfilm parent, White's work lists soldiers alphabetically and gives the regiment and rank for each soldier. In the *Compiled Service Records*, one finds the name and rank of the soldier, his known period of service, rate of pay, and notations of significant events during the service of the soldier.

Supplementing the *Compiled Service Records* is *Miscellaneous Numbered Records in the War Department Collection of Revolutionary War Records, 1775-1790's*. This microfilm series, also available in Seimes Microfilm Center, is a collection of documents primarily concerned with the administration of the Continental Army. As such, the materials include official correspondence, records of supplies, receipts, court martial proceedings, council minutes and payrolls. A *Special Index to the Numbered Records in the War Department Collection of Revolutionary Records* is also available on microfilm.

The *Compiled Service Records* and the *Miscellaneous Numbered Records* include the names of those soldiers who served in the Continental Army or in militia units that served with the Continental Army but were not incorporated into it. Militia units that did not participate in campaigns of the Continental Army are not listed in the *Compiled Service Records*.

13.20.4.3
Naval Records of the Revolution

The American Revolution was not restricted to land, yet the struggle at sea is one of the lesser known stories of the conflict. At the time of the Revolution, Great Britain had the most powerful fleet in the world. The Continental Navy never grew large enough to seriously contest the Royal Navy in large scale fleet actions. The single best known naval contest of the Revolution was the clash between the *Bonhomme Richard* commanded by John Paul Jones and the British *Serapis*. Yet there is more to the story of the war at sea than this single combat. Between them, the captains of the Continental Navy and American privateers amassed an impressive record. Several Continental Navy captains, most notably John Paul Jones, emerged victorious from engagements with British ships. Working in conjunction with the Navy, Continental Marines staged amphibious operations in the Bahamas and in Great Britain.

Commissioned by Congress specifically to seize British merchantmen in return for prize money, American privateers proved to be a constant annoyance to the Royal Navy and a menace to the merchant fleet. While none of these events proved to be decisive turning points in the Revolution, by the end of the war there was a well established American presence at sea. Two narrative histories, Miller's *Sea of Glory* and Allen's two volume *A Naval History of the American Revolution* tell the full story of American naval efforts during the Revolution.

The Continental Navy and Marines

The importance of the sea and the need for American ships was obvious from the first. Not long after he assumed command of the army, George Washington observed that the besieged British garrison in Boston was unlikely to suffer much hardship as long as supplies arrived by sea. Clearly, an American navy could hinder British shipping. Washington took matters into his own hands by creating a small "fleet" of eight vessels for the purpose of harassing British supply ships. *George Washington's Schooners: The First American Navy* contains a great deal of information on the officers and men of Washington's private navy. In October 1775, the Continental Congress established the Continental Navy partly in response to Washington's concerns and partly due to raids on Rhode Island by the Royal Navy. Congress established a Continental Marine Corps less than one month later on November 10, 1775.

Official papers dealing with Washington's navy and the establishment of the Continental Navy and Marines are found in *Naval Documents of the American Revolution*, a multivolume set that includes many contemporary materials dealing with naval operations. Because relatively few records of the Continental Navy still exist, *Naval Documents* draws from a wide range of sources including official correspondence from America, Great Britain and France, extracts from the journals of Parliament and the Continental Congress and reprints of contemporary newspaper articles. The full text of Congressional documents regarding the Continental Navy and American privateers is also found in *Journals of the Continental Congress*. Existing records of individual service for American mariners are available in the microfilm publication *Compiled Service Records of American Naval Personnel and Members of the Departments of the Quartermaster General and the Commissary General of Military Stores Who Served During the Revolutionary War*. These service records and a name index to the series are available in Seimes Microfilm Center.

Many of the commanders in the new Continental Navy had some experience in sea warfare, but were not professional military men. Of the captains, John Paul Jones is the best known, yet even he served only on merchantmen before the war. In spite of their varied backgrounds, all of these men would make a mark on the Continental Navy, beginning with Esek Hopkins who led a daring raid on the Bahamas in March 1776. *Naval Officers of the American Revolution: A Concise Biographical*

Dictionary has a brief biographical sketch of Hopkins and the other officers of the Continental Navy and Continental Marines while *Mariners of the American Revolution* includes the names of both officers and common seamen. A full biography of Hopkins and several biographies of John Paul Jones are available in the Library including Ellsbery's *Captain John Paul* and Morison's *John Paul Jones*.

No less important to the war at sea were the Continental Marines who served as the shock troops of the Navy. *Biographies of Continental Marine Officers* contains 130 biographical sketches with particular attention paid to service during the Revolution. In addition to the full story of Marine involvement, *Marines in the Revolution: A History of the Continental Marines in the American Revolution 1775-1783* has an appendix of Marine officer biographies and a ship-by-ship roster of Marines including officers, non-commissioned officers and privates.

Privateers

Much of the damage to British shipping came not from the Continental Navy, but from privateers. These were enterprising individuals who were commissioned by the Continental Congress, or its representatives to prey on British vessels. A list of the ships and their captains is found in *Naval Records of the American Revolution 1775-1788*. These ships and men were not amalgamated into the Continental Navy, the ownership of a privateering vessel remaining in private hands. Although armed, privateers rarely met the Royal Navy in open combat, preferring to seize merchant vessels. Maclay's *A History of American Privateers* gives a general overview of American privateers in the Revolution and the War of 1812 focusing on the more renowned ships and captains.

Typically privateers devoted all their energies to the capture of ships, but on occasion privateers were called on for other duties. While he was in France, Benjamin Franklin commissioned three privateers for the duty of rescuing American prisoners of war. An account of this episode is Clark's *Ben Franklin's Privateers* which identifies the captains of these vessels and names a number of seamen.

A more extensive study of the privateers is McManemin's *Captains of the Privateers During the Revolutionary War*. This study focuses on the careers of over sixty of the most successful privateering captains. Sanchez-Saavedra's *A Guide to Virginia Military Organizations in the American Revolution, 1774-1778* lists Virginia's privateering vessels with the names of the owners and captains. Additional information on privateers, both the ships and the men who sailed them, is found in Eatman's *Some Famous Privateers of New England* and Middlebrook's *Maritime Connecticut During the Revolution*.

State Navies

With so much of the population concentrated along the coastline it is no surprise that nearly every state was able to launch its own navy. Most of these navies were defensive in nature. Consequently, the duties of the state navies bound the ships to the coastline and the interior waterways. Some of the New England states however, particularly Massachusetts, ranged as far as the English Channel. It was not uncommon during these long voyages for the line between privateer and state navy to blur somewhat. Frequently, the defense of the coastline was an aggressive one. In the largest naval engagement of the war, excluding French operations, the Massachusetts Navy assaulted the British ships and garrison stationed at Penobscot. A history of this fiasco, which resulted in the near destruction of the Massachusetts Navy, is Cayford's *The Penobscot Expedition*.

The Library has several studies of these state navies including McManemin's *Revolution on the High Seas: A History of Maritime Massachusetts During the Revolutionary War,* Jackson's *The Pennsylvania Navy, 1775–1781*, Still's *North Carolina's Revolutionary War Navy* and Stewart's *Virginia's Navy of the Revolution*, which includes a roster of men who served in the Virginia Navy. Sanchez-Saavedra's *A Guide to Virginia Military Organizations in the American Revolution, 1774–1778* includes a list of Virginia State Navy vessels by type and by name and identifies the officers for each ship. As the name suggests, *Massachusetts Soldiers and Sailors of the Revolutionary War* identifies men of the Massachusetts Navy, and the *Pennsylvania Archives* names the mariners of the Pennsylvania Navy. In *Captains of the State Navies During the Revolutionary War*, McManemin details the lives and careers of 29 captains from various states. Also included is a brief description outlining the activities of each state navy.

13.20.4.4
State Records and Rosters

Many militia units never came within sight of the Continental Army but still performed valuable service during the Revolution both in battle and in more mundane tasks such as guard duty. Information on these militia men as well as muster rolls for state regiments that did serve with the Continental Army appear in a number of publications including many compiled and published by individual state governments.

State published rosters for the Revolution are as many and varied as the states themselves. Some of these publications such as *Georgia's Roster of the Revolution* are nothing more than lists of names. *Massachusetts Soldiers and Sailors of the Revolutionary War* arranges the names alphabetically and provides a brief description of service for each. Most of the entries in this seventeen volume set include the individual's place of residence at the time of the Revolution and some entries contain a physical description of the soldier or sailor. A supplement to this set that has names not included in the original seventeen volumes is available in the Seimes Microfilm Center. *Rolls of the Soldiers in the Revolutionary War 1775 to 1783* from the state of Vermont consists primarily of payrolls, showing rank, regiment and length of service. Roberts' *New York in the Revolution* lists officers and men of the Continental Line regiments from New York as well as county militia. Another source for New York soldiers is Fernow's *New York in the Revolution* which includes listings for every New York military unit during the war. Eckenrode's *Virginia Soldiers of the American Revolution* published by the Commonwealth of Virginia in 1912 is more of an index, with citations to other sources of information. *Official Register of the Officers and Men of New Jersey in the Revolutionary War* groups soldiers by rank and provides a brief description of military service for each. The *Delaware Archives, Military* devotes three volumes to the Revolution, lists soldiers by unit and includes rank, amount of pay, period of service and any significant events in the enlistment of the individual soldier. These lists and others are in the state sections of the Library.

Reverse of a Massachusetts Treasury Note

In some cases muster rolls are included as a part of a larger compilation of state records such as the *Pennsylvania Archives* and the *Maryland Archives*. The *Pennsylvania Archives* is a 128 volume compilation of early Pennsylvania documents. Revolutionary War records are scattered over four series in several volumes. These volumes include not only muster rolls, but can include official correspondence and even officers' journals. Like the *Pennsylvania Archives*, the *Archives of Maryland* is a large multivolume set that includes documents written before, during and after the Revolution. Maryland soldiers are identified in volume 18 of the *Archives of Maryland*, which carries the title *Muster Rolls and Other Records of Service of Maryland Troops in the American Revolution*.

Supplementing the official state publications are those rosters compiled by individual authors. Like the official ones, these rosters contain varying amounts of information depending on the intent of the compiler. John Gwathmey compiled a *Historical Register of Virginians in the Revolution* from a variety of sources to produce a list of names in alphabetical order with rank and unit of service for each individual and place of residence for most. Wright's *Maryland Revolutionary Records* uses pension applications and marriage records as sources for his list of soldiers. The Fishers' *Soldiers, Sailors and Patriots of the Revolutionary War–Vermont* and *Soldiers, Sailors, and Patriots of the Revolutionary War–Maine* lists individuals alphabetically by surname and include whatever genealogical information may be available such as marriages, children and place of burial. Bobby Gilmer Moss has compiled two works relating to the Revolution in South Carolina: *Roster of South Carolina Patriots in the American Revolution* and *The Patriots at Kings Mountain*. To compile the rosters in both books, Moss carefully consulted a variety of sources. As a result, while Moss' lists are as near to comprehensive as possible, the entries for each man do not have the same level of detail. Moss includes a description of service for every soldier, but for some entries he has information on post-Revolution activities and even some genealogical information such as birth and death dates, spouse and children. The emphasis is on genealogy in Burgess' *Virginia Soldiers of 1776*. Through the use of documents in the Virginia State Library, the Virginia State Archives, the Virginia Land Office and "other reliable sources" Burgess compiled not only service records for a number of Virginia veterans, but information on their families as well. Peden's *Revolutionary Patriots of Delaware 1775-1783* includes the names of both soldiers and women who contributed to the Revolution and genealogical information for some entries. In addition, information on individual soldiers and their families may be available in the Library's documentation files.

13.20.4.5
Patriotic and Civil Service

Not everyone who contributed to the Revolution served in the military. A number of individuals assisted the cause through patriotic and civil service. The *DAR Patriot Index* classifies civil service as "the holding of a Civil office such as: Constable; Jailor; Juror; Justice of Peace; Moderator; Ordinary; Selectman; Sheriff; Surveyor of Highways; Tax Collector; Town Clerk; Town Treasurer, etc." Patriotic service as defined by the DAR encompasses many occupations. According to the *DAR Patriot Index* patriotic service during the Revolution includes:

> An Associator; Collector of Provisions; Defender of Fort or Frontier; Delegate to a Continental Congress or to a Provincial Congress; Express Rider; Fence Viewer; Furnishing a substitute; Gunsmith who gave his services; Inspector of provisions; Legislator; Member of the Boston Tea Party, or the Cherokee Expedition, or the Galvez Expedition, or the Kaskaskia Campaign; Member of a Committee made necessary by the War; Minister who made patriotic sermons; Munitions maker; Nurse; Taking an Oath of Allegiance; Patroller; Prisoner of War or of the Indians; Ranger; Refugee; Rendering aid to the wounded; Rendering material aid; Signer of a petition or a non-importation agreement; Surgeon; Wheelwright.

Information is readily available on ranking politicians such as members of the Continental Congress in sources such as the *Papers of the Continental Congress*. Two sources for identifying local officials including selectmen, committeemen, grand-jurors, town clerks, fence viewers, surveyors and others are *Massachusetts Town Officials 1775-1783* and *Non-Military Service in the Revolutionary War from Extracts Connecticut Town Council Minutes 1774-1784*. A similar source for Maine is *Town Officers, Members of Wartime Committees, Preachers of Patriotic Sermons, Contributors of Material Aid 1774-1784*. All three works were compiled through the efforts of G.R.C. committees. Other sources for this type of service include state and county records for the period.

Another means of showing support to the Revolution was by taking an "Oath of Allegiance" to the Revolutionary governments in the individual states. Some of these oaths have been compiled and are available in a number of sources in the Library. Examples of these lists include *Delaware Signers of the Oath of Allegiance* and *New Jersey Oaths of Allegiance 1777-1778* both compiled by DAR chapters and such state records such as *The Pennsylvania Archives* and the *New Hampshire State Records* series.

Sources that are useful for identifying suppliers to the army and government are financial records or claims against the state. *Certificates and Receipts of Revolutionary New Jersey* is one such source that lists payments by the state to individuals for services rendered to the army or the government. Other examples of these records include the transcriptions of *Stub Entries to Indents Issued in Payment of Claims Against South Carolina Growing Out of the Revolution, Virginia Revolutionary Publick Claims*, which contains many but not all of the Virginia claims, and *North Carolina Revolutionary Army Public Accounts*. Each of these sources indicates the name of the claimant, the type of goods provided, and the amount of the claim. These sources are also available in Seimes Microfilm Center.

13.20.4
Part 3
GROUPS IN THE AMERICAN REVOLUTION

13.20.4.6
The Continental Congress

During the Revolution, the Continental Congress functioned as the national government. The documents of the Congress have been published in *Journals of the Continental Congress, Letters of Delegates to Congress, 1774–1789*, and Burnett's *Letters of Members of the Continental Congress. Index: Papers of the Continental Congress 1774–1789* provides subject and name access to the documents of the Congress except for the *Journals*, which has its own index. *The Papers of the Continental Congress*, a microfilm series from the National Archives is in the Seimes Microfilm Center.

The members of the Continental Congress are the subject of many books. Collected biographies of these men and general histories regarding the Congress and the signing of the Declaration of Independence are in the Library. A representative sample of more recent works on the Congressional delegates includes Ferris and Morris' *The Signers of the Declaration of Independence*, Wilson's *The Book of the Founding Fathers* and Thomson's *One Hundred Famous Founders*, which includes biographies of the signers of the Constitution as well.

Most of these books contain portraits of the Congressional Delegates and some brief information on their families. Heathcote's *The Signers of the Declaration of Independence* is unique in that it includes of photographs of the graves of the Signers. Fairhurst's *Homes of the Signers of the Declaration* presents photographs of the houses still standing that were owned by these men.

The Library owns several older works on the signers. These include Dwight's *Signers of the Declaration of Independence* published in 1895; the 1832, 1834 and 1844 editions of Goodrich's *Lives of the Signers to the Declaration of Independence;* and *Biography of the Signers to the Declaration of Independence* published in 1827. These volumes contain some information on the families of the Congressmen. Ancestral information on the delegates is available in *Lineage Lines of the Fifty-six Signers of the Declaration of Independence* from the New York G.R.C.

Some of the delegates to the Continental Congress went on to serve in the Constitutional Convention. The Library has a number of works dealing with the signers of the Constitution. These include the collected biographies found in Coleman's *The Constitution and Its Framers;* Charleton, Ferris and Ryan's *Framers of the Constitution;* Bradford's *Founding Fathers;* and Meister's *The Founding Fathers* which includes information on the families of the signers. General histories on the events surrounding the signing of the Constitution are available in the Library as well.

13.20.4.7
Prisoners of War

Neither side in the Revolution was prepared to deal with prisoners of war. In many cases, prisoners were housed in whatever facilities were available where overcrowding and poor sanitation became common problems. To alleviate these conditions in New York City, the British hit upon the expedient of housing American prisoners aboard prison ships where thousands died. Dandridge's *American Prisoners of the Revolution* includes the names of many American prisoners in the text and lists the names of eight thousand men known to have been held on the notorious prison ship "Jersey". This particular ship is the subject of two memoirs: Greene's *Recollections of the Jersey Prison-Ship* based on the manuscripts of Captain Thomas Dring and Andros' *The Old Jersey Captive.*

A listing of American prisoners held in Canada is found in McHenry's *Rebel Prisoners at Quebec 1778-1783.* Many captured American privateers and sailors were held in England. Their plight, and some prisoners' names are in Cohen's *Yankee Sailors in British Gaols.* A first person account of the experience is found in *The Prisoners of 1776; A Relic of the Revolution,* the journals of Charles Herbert, a Massachusetts sailor held in Old Mill Prison, Plymouth, England. Peterson's *Known Military Dead During the American Revolutionary War, 1775-1783* includes the names of some of the Americans who died in captivity. Rather than deal with the harsh conditions on prison ships, some of the Americans captured at Charleston enlisted in the British army. A transcript listing the names of these men is in *Continental Prisoners in His Majesty's Service, 1781.*

The largest single group of prisoners captured by the Americans were those British and German troops taken at Saratoga. Known as the "Convention Army" for the surrender convention between Gates and Bourgoyne, these men, and in some cases their dependents, were moved from one camp to another from Massachusetts to Virginia. Sampson's *Escape in America: The British Convention Prisoners 1777-1783* tells the story of these prisoners and includes the names of men who escaped or made the attempt. German troops who were prisoners are identified in Smith's *Muster Rolls and Prisoner-of-War Lists in American Archival Collections Pertaining to the German Mercenary Troops Who Served with the British Forces During the American Revolution.*

13.20.4.8
Women

Throughout the colonies women contributed to the Revolution in many ways. Their efforts have not gone unrecognized. The DAR pamphlet "Forgotten Patriots" addresses the role of women in an introductory way.

The Library maintains a file of articles and references to women in the Revolution and is compiling a bibliography of these studies for publication. DAR also published Somerville's *Women in the American Revolution* in 1974, and it is still available for purchase from the Corresponding Secretary General.

A number of women are listed in the *The DAR Patriot Index* as patriots and a few as soldiers. The third volume of the earlier edition of *The DAR Patriot Index* is an index to the spouses of soldiers and patriots. Naturally, this is overwhelmingly a list of the wives, and although there have been many corrections since this book was published in 1986, it remains a useful listing of thousands of American women alive during the Revolutionary period.

Many works on women in the Revolution are available in the Library. General overviews include Hoffman and Albert's *Women in the Age of the American Revolution* and Norton's *Liberty's Daughters*. Abstracts from diaries and journals of women from the Revolution are found in Evan's *Weathering the Storm*. Collected biographies of specific female patriots include Kelley and Feinstone's *Courage and Candlelight*, Laska's *"Remember the Ladies"*, Ellet's *The Women of the American Revolution*, Claghorn's *Women Patriots of the American Revolution: A Biographical Dictionary* and *Petticoat Patriots of the American Revolution*. Some of these accounts border on the legendary, others are more scholarly. Full length biographies of individual women include Freeman's *America's First Woman Warrior: the Courage of Deborah Sampson* and Seller's *Patience Wright: American Artist and Spy in George III's London*.

13.20.4.9
Minority Service

People from all walks of life and many ethnic groups served in the Revolution. African Americans in particular made significant contributions to the Revolution, from the death of Crispus Attucks in the Boston Massacre to victory at Yorktown. Several general works in the Library on the contributions of the African American to the Revolution including Quarles' *The Negro in the American Revolution*, Kaplan's *The Black Presence in the Era of the American Revolution* and Nash's *Race and Revolution*.

DAR promotes the Revolutionary War military service of African Americans and Native Americans in its series of works under the collective title of *Minority Military Service 1775–1783* by Elisabeth W. Schmidt and others. For each state, *Minority Military Service* lists the names of African Americans and Native Americans known to have served in the Revolution. Every name listed in each individual state booklet has referenced sources. In addition, a free six-page pamphlet, "The Forgotten Patriots," offers general information on minority participants in the Revolution. Robert Greene's *Black Courage 1775–1783*, also published by DAR, includes brief biographies of selected servicemen as well as a compiled list of African American pensioners. Nell's *The Colored Patriots of the American Revolution* written in 1855 and the Kaplans' *The Black Presence in the Era of the American Revolution* examine in depth the Revolutionary careers and lives of selected African Americans.

State-specific works on African Americans and Native Americans in the Revolution include Walling's *Men of Color at the Battle of Monmouth June 28, 1778* and White's *Connecticut's Black Soldiers, 1775-1783*. Both of these works include the names of African American soldiers and their regiments, but Walling's book includes the names of Native Americans as well. Other sources that identify African American and Native American troops include Moss' *Roster of South Carolina Patriots in the American Revolution*, Jackson's *Virginia Negro Soldiers and Seamen in the Revolutionary War*, *Massachusetts Soldiers and Sailors of the Revolutionary War*, Stryker's *Official Register of the Officers and Men of New Jersey in the Revolutionary War* and Newman's *List of Black Servicemen Compiled From the War Department Collection of Revolutionary War Records*.

13.20.4.10
George Rogers Clark

Through a series of daring campaigns in 1778 and 1779, Virginian George Rogers Clark and a small band of soldiers occupied what Virginia then considered its Illinois County and pushed out the British. The story of Clark's campaign is in several works including *George Rogers Clark Papers 1771-1781*, *The George Rogers Clark Adventure in the Illinois* and *George Rogers Clark and the Revolution in Illinois 1763-1787*. Muster rolls and payrolls for Clark's men are transcribed in Harding's *George Rogers Clark and His Men: Military Records, 1778-1784*. Also refer to section 13.20.4.17 for further information.

13.20.4.11
French Military Records

In spite of their traditional antagonism against Great Britain, the French did not immediately and openly ally themselves with the American patriots. Even more than Great Britain, France was left battered by the French and Indian War having lost not only her North American possessions, but a great deal of money in the process. Then too, the French government was not willing to commit to open war with Great Britain when the success of the Revolution was still very much in doubt. Thus, while individuals such as Lafayette did rally to the American cause, France was unwilling to support the Revolution until after the American victory at Saratoga. France recognized American independence in December 1777 and formally concluded an alliance one month later. A French fleet under Admiral d'Estaing was dispatched in the spring of 1778, but failed to achieve any success against the British. It was not until the arrival of a French army under Comte de Rochambeau in July 1780 that the French effectively contributed to the American cause. With Rochambeau's army and the addition of a French fleet under Comte de Grasse, Washington bottled up the army of Cornwallis at Yorktown and won a victory ensuring American independence.

The story of the negotiations that led to the French recognition of the American independence is told in *Yankees at the Court, French Policy and the American Alliance of 1778* and *New Materials for the History of the American Revolution*. General histories of French participation in the Revolution include *The French in American During the War of Independence of the United States, 1777-1783, France and North America: The Revolutionary Experience* and *The French Forces in America, 1780-1783. The French Army in the American War of Independence* has a brief history of the French military presence during the Revolution and includes full color illustration of French uniforms. In addition, the Library has an interesting memoir by Count William de Deux-Ponts, *My Campaigns in America* that covers French activities from 1780-1781.

The Library has two reference works that identify officers of the French army. Bodinier's *Les Officiers de L'Armeé Royale* includes a great deal of information of the organization of the French army and the opinions of the officers with regards to the Revolution and Americans in general. Also by Bodinier is *Dictionnaire des Officiers de L'Armée Royale qui ont Combattu aux Etats-Unis Pendant la Guerre d'Indépendance* which arranges the officers in alphabetical order by surname and includes a brief biography for each. Full length biographies of Rochambeau and de Grasse in English are also available. *Les Combattants Français de la Guerre Américaine* published by the French Ministere des Affaires Etrangeres in 1905 identifies soldiers and mariners of all ranks who served in America although some regiments list only the officers. The arrangement of the book is by regiment and then by rank within the regiment. An every name index aids the researcher in locating individual soldiers.

13.20.4.12
The Galvez Expeditions and Spanish Involvement

Like France, the Spanish government viewed the American Revolution as an opportunity to regain territories lost to Great Britain in previous wars, particularly Gibraltar and the Floridas. After Great Britain rebuffed Spanish attempts at negotiations, Spain formally allied herself with France in April 1779. A Spanish declaration of war against Great Britain followed two months later. At the time Bernardo de Galvez, a young professional soldier, was the governor of Spanish Louisiana. In the two years prior to Spain's declaration of war, Galvez used every means at his disposal to weaken British influence in the area, including financial assistance to Oliver Pollock, a patriot and a supplier for George Rogers Clark.

Although Spain declined to participate in the French North American campaigns, Galvez did not remain idle and launched his own offensive. With an army of professional Spanish soldiers and Louisiana militia Galvez captured Manchac, Baton Rouge and Natchez from the British in 1779. The following year Galvez seized Mobile and in 1781 captured Pensacola.

General histories of the Galvez campaigns are available in the Louisiana and Florida sections of the Library. Rosters of the officers and men who served with Galvez are available in *Spanish Records: List of Men Under General Don Bernardo de Galvez in his Campaigns Against the British, Officers Spanish and Natives of Louisiana Serving Under Gen. Don Bernardo de Galvez ...* and *General Archives of the Indies, Seville, Spain*. All three works are transcripts compiled from official documents by C. Robert Churchill. Other rosters include Schmidt's *Louisiana Patriots 1776-1783*, DeVille's *Louisiana Soldiers in the American Revolution* and Holmes' *Honor and Fidelity: The Louisiana Infantry Regiments and the Louisiana Militia Companies 1766-1821*. Official transcripts of original Spanish documents on the American Revolution are compiled in the multivolume set *Documentos Relativos a la Independencia de Norteamerica Existentes en Archivos Españoles*.

13.20.4.13
British Forces

**Uniforms of Officer and Private,
Seventeenth Foot (British)**
(Drawn by P. W. Reynolds, Chelsea, England)

At the time of the American Revolution, Great Britain possessed one of the best armies in the world. The Royal Navy was probably the strongest fleet on the face of the earth. Yet British leadership was ill equipped to win the war. Although they won victories, the generals consistently underestimated the resolve of the Americans, making victories such as Bunker Hill costly. Ultimately, the blunders of the British generals contributed to American independence.

A number of diaries, journals and memoirs by British soldiers have survived from the Revolution. Reprints of these personal accounts are available in the Library including *The Journal of Thomas Sullivan, A Soldier in the 49th Regiment of Foot in America* by Thomas Sullivan, an enlisted man and a participant in the Battle of Bunker Hill. Other sources include accounts by William Bamford, a captain in the 40th Foot, *The American Journals of Lt. John Enys*, *The Journal of Stephen Kemble, Lieutenant Colonel 60th Regiment of Foot* and *The Twilight of British Rule in Revolutionary America: The New York Letter Book of General James Robertson*. Additional sources on the British Army in the Library include general histories, studies on uniforms and organization and studies on how the army and the British public viewed the Revolution. A useful guide for researchers interested in the British Army is *In Search of the "Forlorn Hope": A Comprehensive Guide to Locating British Regiments and Their Records (1640–WWI)*. This guide includes a complete listing of British Army regiments, the battles in which they fought by year and the official number and nickname of the regiment.

Considering the power and reputation of the British fleet, the Royal Navy played a nearly negligible role in the Revolution. The Royal Navy suffered major defeats at Charleston, South Carolina in 1776 and at Yorktown in 1781. Although the Navy did capture a number of privateers and bested some American ships in combat, privateers continued to operate throughout the Revolution and single combat between ships had no great impact on the war. General histories of the Royal Navy during the Revolution are in the Library. A list of *The Commissioned Sea Officers of the Royal Navy 1660–1815* includes the names of officers who served in American waters during the war.

13.20.4.14
The Hessians

No group of Revolutionary War soldiers is more infamous than the Hessians. These German auxiliaries of the British army were hard professional soldiers accustomed to a harsh life of war and discipline. Their language and their manner was foreign. They had a reputation for cruelty. Initially feared and despised by the Americans, the Hessians' vulnerability became apparent when they surrendered to Americans at Trenton and Saratoga. That the Hessians were in the colonies at all was not a matter of their own choosing, but the result of an agreement between princes.

At the beginning of the Revolution Great Britain had a small professional army, not enough to combat the colonies in rebellion and protect British interests around the world. In order to press the war in America, the British were faced with the choice of enlarging their own army by recruiting from a largely unenthusiastic population or by hiring auxiliary troops from another source. Because the ancestors of George III were German, the Crown contracted with several German principalities for troops. Approximately 30,000 Germans served with the British army during the Revolution. The full story of the German involvement in the war is recounted in *The Hessians and the Other German Auxiliaries of Great Britain in the Revolutionary War* by Edward J. Lowell, *German Mercenaries in Canada* by J.P. Wilhelmy, and *The German Allied Troops in the North American War of Independence 1776–1783* by Max Von Eelking. A list of officers from ensign and above for each regiment that served in America is in the latter book.

**Uniform of a Hessian Grenadier
of Rall's Regiment**
(Drawn by Harry A. Ogden)

The best list of individual German soldiers, officers, non-commissioned officers and enlisted men, is a multivolume set originally published in Germany entitled *Hessiche Truppen im Amerikanischen Unabhängigheitskreig* or the "HETRINA" for short. The HETRINA includes the names of all soldiers who served from the regiments of the principalities of Hesse-Cassel and the Waldeck. The information for each soldier includes name, rank, regiment, date of birth, place of origin and remarks on the soldier's service. A brief history of the Hessian involvement in the war and an explanation of the list is included in both German and English. Another source on the Germans, derived in part from the HETRINA is Burgoyne's *Waldeck Soldiers of the American Revolutionary War*. This list is limited to the soldiers of the Third English-Waldeck Regiment and includes a timeline of significant events in the history of the regiment's American service and brief biographical sketches of the soldiers.

One of the most important sources of information on the Germans is *Hessian Documents of the American Revolution 1776–1783: Transcripts and Translations from the Lidgerwood Collection at Morristown National Historical Park, Morristown New Jersey*. This collection of 362 microfiche is in Seimes Microfilm Center. The Lidgerwood Collection of Hessian documents on microfiche consists of over 20,000 pages of original documents and 10,000 pages of translations detailing the service of Germans in America. Most of the information is taken from official journals, reports, order books and correspondence by the German officers involved. A guide to the collection is in the Library.

In addition to the observations recorded in the Lidgerwood Collection, the Library has a number of published journals and diaries by German troops. These include *A Hessian Officer's Diary of the*

American Revolution by Johann Ernst Prechtel, *A Hessian Diary of the American Revolution* by Johann Conrad Dohla, *The American Revolution, Garrison Life in French Canada and New York* translated by Helga Doblin and a collection of diaries and memoirs in *Hessian Journals: Unpublished Documents of the American Revolution.*

In spite of the method of their introduction to the American colonies many German soldiers elected to stay in America. Some deserted, others were prisoners of war who remained with their former captors and still others simply settled in the colonies at the expiration of their term of service. A list of Hessian prisoners is in *Muster Rolls and Prisoner of War Lists in American Archival Collections Pertaining to the German Mercenary Troops Who Served With the British Forces During the American Revolution* by Clifford Neal Smith. While imprisoned, many of these Germans were employed by the local population as laborers or in more skilled tasks. *Muster rolls and Prisoner of War Lists* shows if a prisoner was employed, the name of his employer and the soldier's trade before enlistment. Another source for tracing these soldiers is *Notes on Hessian Soldiers Who Remained in Canada and the United States After the American Revolution, 1775-1783* also by Smith. *Notes on Hessian Soldiers* is divided into three parts to provide the genealogists with different points of access: "Place of Origin", "Regiment and Company" and "Date of Defection".

A list of some German soldiers who remained in Canada after the war is *The Hessians of Nova Scotia* by Johannes Helmut Merz which includes some information of the descendants of these soldiers. Other works on the same topic by Merz include *He was a Hessian, Register of German Military Men,* and *Er War Ein Hesse! The Register of German Military Men* is a list of over 4000 soldiers known to have stayed in Canada after the Revolution. Each entry in the *Register* includes such information as the soldier's name, his regiment, last known place of residence in Canada and some brief notation regarding marriage or children. One of the sources used by Merz to compile the *Register* was *German Military Settlers in Canada After the American Revolution* by Virginia DeMarce. This work lists soldiers by surname and contains a great deal of genealogical information.

Some descendants of the Germans who remained after the war formed the Johannes Schwalm Historical Association in the late 1970s. Initially a society of descendants from Johannes Schwalm, a German soldier of the Revolution, the Association's interest expanded to include the study of all German auxiliaries and descendants. Their publication, *The Journal of the Johannes Schwalm Historical Association, Inc.* is an excellent source for genealogists and historians interested in the German auxiliaries.

The term "Hessian" is derived from the principalities of Hesse-Cassel and Hesse-Hanau. Although the Hessians constituted the largest group of German soldiers, other principalities supplied troops as well. These principalities were Brunswick, Waldeck, Ansbach-Bayreuth and Anhalt-Zerbst. Under the customs of the day, these Germans were considered "auxiliaries" rather than mercenaries, the distinction being that a mercenary hired himself to a foreign army while the auxiliaries were loaned out as a group. Their monarch received payment from the British crown while the soldiers remained on the payroll of their principalities.

13.20.4.15
Loyalists

In many respects, the Revolution was the first American civil war. A number of colonists were not eager for independence from the British crown. In fact, a number of American colonists actively opposed the Revolution and went so far as to form their own military units to resist the "rebel" armies in the field. These American opponents of the Revolution were termed "Tories" or "Loyalists". Some estimates put the total number of Loyalists as high as one-third of the population in the colonies.

The saga of the Loyalists is well represented in the DAR Library. One of the most comprehensive treatments is *The Loyalists of America and Their Times* (1880) by Egerton Ryerson which covers the development of revolutionary sentiment from 1620 forward and the experience of loyal Americans during the Revolution and the War of 1812. A more focused study is *Royal Raiders: The Tories of the American Revolution* by North Callahan, a narrative history of the Loyalist military and political experience during the Revolution. *The Loyalist Perception and Other Essays* concentrates on Loyalist opinions regarding the Revolution while *The Price of Loyalty* allows these people to speak for themselves through a collection of letters and other writings by loyal Americans. Loyalists lived in every colony during the Revolution, but two of the colonies with the highest Tory population were New York and Massachusetts. The story of Loyalists in these colonies is recounted in Potter's *The Liberty We Seek*. Loyalism in other colonies including East and West Florida receive attention through a series of essays in *Loyalists and Community in North America*. All of these works and others are in the DAR Library.

State Histories

Although strongest in New York, Massachusetts and the South, Loyalism was pervasive throughout the colonies. For nearly every one of the state sections that constitute the original thirteen colonies, the Library has a study or a list of Loyalists. While some of these books are not as comprehensive as others, each is useful in its own way. In the Virginia section one finds two concise studies on Loyalists with two different approaches. *Loyalism in Virginia* concentrates on the economic aspects of the conflict between the patriots and loyal Americans, while the emphasis of *Loyalism in Revolutionary Virginia* is on civil war among Virginians in the areas of Norfolk and the Eastern Shore. A broader approach is used by *A State Divided: Opposition in Pennsylvania to the American Revolution* by Anne Ousterhout and *The Loyalists of Revolutionary Delaware* by Harold B. Hancock, both of which examine Loyalism colony-wide during the Revolution. Neither book however, provides the user with a comprehensive list of Loyalists within those colonies. *Loyalists of New Jersey* on the other hand, lists Loyalists by name and gives a brief biographical entry for each. Loyalist biographical information is also found in *The Loyalists of Massachusetts* and *Divided Hearts: Massachusetts Loyalists 1765–1790 A Biographical Directory*.

Records of Confiscation

As supporters of the crown, the Loyalists were singled out for special treatment by the patriots. Throughout the colonies, Loyalists saw their homes looted and burned and their property confiscated. While much of the destruction was accomplished by marauding bands, most of the confiscated property was later sold by the states as official policy. Fortunately for genealogists, many states kept records of these seizures and the later disposal of the property. *Connecticut Loyalists* lists Loyalist landowners in Greenwich, Stamford and Norwalk, describes the confiscated property and names the purchaser. Similar lists are found in *The Loyalists in North Carolina During the Revolution; Sequestrations, Confiscations and Sale of Estates, State Papers of Vermont; Loyalism in New York During the Revolution* and *The Disposition of Loyalist Estates in the Southern District of the State of New York*.

A great deal of information on the land confiscations and the Loyalists themselves appear in state records. In the *Pennsylvania Archives*, 3rd series, v.10, one finds proclamations by the Supreme Executive Council of Pennsylvania to seize the property of loyal Americans. The names of these Loyalists are included in the proclamations. The disposition and sale of their former property is described in detail in the *Pennsylvania Archives*, 6th series, volumes 12 and 13. A similar list of names and sales of confiscated property is found in *The Revolutionary Records of the State of Georgia*, volume 1 and a list of disenfranchised Loyalists of New Hampshire is included in *State Papers. Documents and Records Relating to the State of New Hampshire*, volume 8.

Military Records

In response to the deprivations and assaults they suffered at the hands of the patriots, and in defense of the Crown, Loyalists armed themselves and organized into military units. Particularly in New York and in the South regular regiments of Loyalists fought in conjunction with the British or operated independently. Relatively few records exist for these Loyalist groups. The single best source in the Library for these soldiers is *Loyalists in the Southern Campaign of the Revolutionary War* by Murtie June Clark. This three volume set includes muster rolls for regiments formed in 1777 and after. Although all of the units listed served only in the Southern campaigns, the soldiers listed did not come exclusively from the South. The set does not have any biographical information on the soldiers, but it does include a complete roster of each regiment, the name and rank of the individuals in the regiment, and the period of service. One of the best known Loyalist formations was a brigade of three battalions formed in New York under the command of Brigadier General Oliver DeLancey. From its formation in 1776 until 1778 the DeLancey Brigade operated on Long Island and the area around New York City. After 1778 the First and Second Battalions were sent south. A reprint of the *Orderly Book of the DeLancey Brigade* for the period September 1776 to June 1778 is available in the Library. The DeLancey Brigade served the Loyalist cause until the end of the war and disbanded in Nova Scotia, Canada in 1783.

The Loyalists in Canada

In the wake of the British defeat at Yorktown and the subsequent Treaty of Paris, many Loyalists chose to leave the colonies and to start anew in the eastern provinces of Canada. These American exiles settled in New Brunswick, Nova Scotia and what became the province of Ontario. An overview of this exodus and the initial stages of settlement is found in the Mikas' *United Empire Loyalists: Pioneers of Upper Canada*. The thoughts and feelings of the Loyalists are found in *Eleven Exiles: Accounts of Loyalists of the American Revolution* and *Loyalist Narratives From Upper Canada* both of which focus on the lives and experiences of specific Loyal Americans.

With these Loyalists were over 3,000 Black Loyalists, some former slaves, who took refuge in New York during the War. Many of these African Americans settled in Nova Scotia although over 1,000 returned to Africa. A list of all the African Americans who departed from New York is found in The *Black Loyalist Directory* edited by Graham Russell Hodges. Included on the list are such details as age, sex, place of origin and name of former owner if previously a slave.

The sudden influx of American expatriates gave the British government the opportunity to move colonists into unsettled areas of Canada. As an added plus, many of the Loyalist settlers were veterans of the Loyalist regiments. Men with experience in warfare could only help to solidify British control of Canada. The land grants awarded to the Loyalists serve as the basis for several lists in the DAR Library. *Loyalist Lists* by E. Keith Fitzgerald records the arrival of three Loyalist regiments for settlement: Rogers' Rangers, Jessup's Rangers and the 1st Battalion of the King's Royal Regiment of New York. Also included is a list of nonmilitary exiles. Three of the four lists include not only the name of the head of the household and his original occupation, but also the number of women and children and the family's place of origin. The Jessup's Rangers list does not include any information on women and children. None of the lists indicate where these people settled. *Loyalists and Land Settlement in Nova Scotia* compiled by Marion Gilroy does indicate the acreage and general location of individual land grants, but includes only the land holder's name, former rank or place of origin.

The Claims Commission

In 1783, the British government established a American Claims Commission designed to financially compensate Loyalists for their losses. Initially, the Commission set a deadline of March 1784 to receive claims. Because this proved to be an unreasonable time frame for many claimants, the deadline was later extended to 1786. Hearings were held by the commissioners for each claim. A transcript of the testimony for many of these hearings is in Fraser's *Second Report of the Bureau of Archives for the Province of Ontario*. Transcripts missing from the earlier report are included in *Loyalist Settlements 1783–1789* published by the Archives of Ontario. The records of these hearings serve as the basis for several lists in the DAR Library.

One of the earliest lists of Loyalists is *Biographical Sketches of Loyalists of the American Revolution* (1864), a two volume set by Lorenzo Sabine. In these books, Sabine gives an overview of the Loyalist experience with emphasis on the political scene of the Revolution and after. This essay is followed by brief biographical entries on individual Loyalists. The content for these sketches varies considerably. Sabine includes such information as where the Tory lived before the Revolution, occupation and experience during and after the war. Although Sabine did not have access to the records of the commission, much of the information included in his sketches is based on papers used at the hearings and retained by the descendants of the original claimants.

Both *Biographical Sketches of Loyalists of the American Revolution* by Gregory Palmer and *American Loyalist Claims* by Peter Wilson Coldham base their sketches on the Audit Office records of the Loyalist Claims Commission. Palmer's book is essentially an updating of Sabine's work. Palmer does not have a historical essay on the plight of the Loyalists, but spends a good deal of time speculating on Sabine's sources in the earlier work. Using the records of the commission, Palmer is able to verify much of Sabine's information and add additional names to the list. In style, both Coldham and Palmer follow Sabine for the biographical sketches, but include a source for every entry. Because the only sources Palmer and Coldham use for their entries are the Audit Office records, each biographical sketch is only an abstract of the claim.

Perhaps the most complete list of loyal Americans is *The New Loyalist Index* by Paul J. Bunnell. To compile this list, Bunnell used a variety of sources including land grant records muster rolls and the Claims Commission records as abstracted by Coldham. Bunnell is also the author of *Research Guide to Loyalists* that lists the availability of primary and secondary source material in the United States and Canada.

United Empire Loyalists

On November 9, 1789 Lord Dorchester, then Governor General of Canada conferred the title of United Empire Loyalist on the American Loyalists who fought for the crown. This was a hereditary title to be passed down from generation to generation. Descendants of the original U.E. Loyalists perpetuate the memory of the early settlers in the United Empire Loyalists' Association. Among the publications of this society are the three volume *Loyalist Lineages of Canada*, a list of Loyal American settlers and their descendants and the periodical *The Loyalist Gazette*, a source of good general articles on Loyalists and the American Revolution.

13.20.4
Part 4
POST-REVOLUTION SOURCES

13.20.4.16
First Person Accounts

Filling in the details of an ancestor's life is an important part of genealogical research, and a fortunate few genealogists will benefit from diaries and journals kept by some individuals.

In the process of applying for pensions veterans supplied proof of their service either in testimony or with documentary evidence. This was a necessary part of the application process and is often the only written information on an individual's participation. Such manuscripts also mention many other persons with whom the author had contact, and consequently assume an importance to many researchers.

Most soldiers of the Revolution had neither the time nor the inclination to record their experiences or thoughts about the war. Nonetheless, several first person accounts by both officers and enlisted men have survived and some examples are owned by the Library. *March to Quebec* is a compilation of journals written by participants of Benedict Arnold's campaign in Canada. Personal accounts by officers include *The Revolutionary Journal of Col. Jeduthan Baldwin*, *The Journal and Order Book of Captain Robert Kirkwood of the Delaware Regiment of the Continental Line*, *The New-York Diary of Lieutenant Jabez Fitch* and the *Memoirs of Captain Lemuel Roberts*. The experiences of the enlisted soldier are recorded in *Diary of a Common Soldier in the American Revolution, 1775–1783* [by Jeremiah Greenman], *The 1777 Journal of Robert Treat of Orange, Connecticut*, and the *Memoirs of the Life of John Adlum in the Revolutionary War*. A number of journals and diaries of the period can also be found in the series *Eyewitness Accounts of the Revolution*. While none of these accounts contain a great deal of genealogical information, they are extremely useful in illustrating eighteenth century military life and the experience of the Revolutionary soldier.

It was a common practice before the Revolution for provincial governments to offer pensions for disability as a result of military service. On August 26, 1776 the Continental Congress passed a law allowing for half pay to disabled officers and men. The very early pensions awarded to invalid soldiers are found in *Abstract of Semi-Annual Payments to Invalid Pensioners of the Revolutionary War March 4, 1801 Through September 5, 1815* compiled by the Thomas Marshall Chapter, DAR. Congress continued to expand the pension program during the Revolution and after. Eventually the Federal government assumed responsibility for pensions issued by the state governments for Revolutionary service. The full text of the pension and land acts is contained in *Army and Navy Pension Laws and Bounty Land Laws of the United States* (1861).

Bounty Land Warrant of Thomas Denniston
Ohio Revolutionary War Bounty Land Warrants, #7030 Act of July 9, 1788.

In order to secure a pension, an applicant appeared in a court of record with proof of his military service. This proof could take the form of documents or witnesses. Widows who applied for pensions also needed documentary evidence to support their claims. The court certified the evidence then passed the documentation on to the Pension Office for final approval. Because the pension laws were restrictive, at least initially, the Pension Office rejected a number of applicants. A list of *Rejected and Suspended Applications for Revolutionary War Pensions* shows that lack of proof was the primary cause for rejection. Beyond name and place of residence, relatively little information on applicants is available from this list or from *Pensioners of Revolutionary War Struck Off the Roll* although the latter volume does indicate in many cases the regiment of the applicant. As time passed Congress modified the pension laws to include more individuals. The last pension law relating to the Revolution passed on March 9, 1878 and allowed widows to receive pensions if the veteran served at least two weeks.

In addition to pensions, the Continental Congress attempted to encourage enlistments by the offer of free land to veterans. Congress passed the first bounty land act on September 16, 1776. This act granted land to officers and soldiers who were engaged in military service and served to the end of the war and to representatives of veterans who were killed during the war. Enlisted men and non-commissioned officers were granted 100 acres by the act; an ensign up to 150 acres; a lieutenant was granted up to 200 acres; other officers up to colonel could receive 500 acres. Considering the first pension law offered half pay only if one was wounded or maimed in battle to the point of disability, the offer of free land was a much more attractive inducement for enlistment. Later acts expanded the eligibility requirements for bounty lands to include the widows and children of veterans.

Many men took full advantage of the bounty land offer. A number of lists in the DAR Library preserve the names of these individuals with varying degrees of additional information. *Kentucky Land Warrants, for the French, Indian, & Revolutionary Wars* gives the name of the Revolutionary War veteran, his rank, regiment of service, term of enlistment, date of land grant and amount of land. On the other hand *Ohio Military Land Warrants 1789-1801* lists only the names of recipients and the date of the grant. Patrick Wardell used land grants in part to produce his multivolume *Virginia/West Virginia Genealogical Data From Revolutionary War Pension and Bounty Land Warrant Records* and William Lindsay Hopkins was able to discover a great deal of military service information using rejected *Virginia Revolutionary War Land Grant Claims 1783-1850*.

State governments also made such awards of land to veterans. The names of state land grant recipients are found in *Revolutionary War Bounty Land Grants Awarded by State Governments* compiled by Lloyd DeWitt Bockstruck. *Georgia Revolutionary Bounty Land Records 1783-1785* lists the names of soldiers and refugees entitled to bounty lands in that state. Georgia veterans with three years of residence in the state were also entitled to land from a statewide lottery in 1827. *Authentic List of All Land Lottery Grants Made to Veterans of the Revolutionary War by the State of Georgia* preserves the names of these veterans. Microfilm copies of original land grants and warrants from North Carolina are available in the Seimes Microfilm center under the titles *Revolutionary Pay Vouchers, Land Grants, Wills, Tax Lists and Other Records from the North Carolina State Archives* and *North Carolina Warrants and Surveys, Western Territory, 1778-1791* [Tennessee].

Because proof was required for the approval of a pension or a bounty land warrant, the application files of Revolutionary veterans and their widows is an important source of information. A pension file contains not only proof of the veterans service, including testimony, affidavits, and documentary evidence, but frequently information on the veteran's family. All of the pension and bounty land files have been microfilmed and compiled by the National Archives under the title *Revolutionary War Pension and Bounty Land Warrant Application Files, 1800-1900*. These pension files are available in Seimes Microfilm Center. All of the files are arranged alphabetically by the surname of the veteran. The *Index of Revolutionary War Pension Applications in the National Archives* is available in the Library. All of the pension files have been abstracted by Virgil White in a four volume set entitled *Genealogical Abstracts of Revolutionary War Pension Files*. As the title suggests, the main emphasis in White's work is on genealogy, not military records, but he does include the branch of service, if not the regiment or rank, and the individual's pension application number. Entries are arranged alphabetically by the applicant's surname and include date of application, family names and some detail on the life of the veteran or his widow.

The DAR abstracted selected pension files in two series entitled *Pension Papers* (233 vols.) and *New Hampshire Pension Records* (101 vols.). More emphasis is placed on military service in these abstracts than in White's work however, with particular attention placed on testimonies of experiences during the war. Both sets are indexed by a Special Index in the Library. Grace M. Pierce compiled and abstracted *Rhode Island Pension Records* in six volumes and followed the format of the *Pension Papers*. These and other pension abstracts, including a five volume set of transcripts by Mabel Van Dyke Baer, are located in the DAR Library. Additional lists of pensioners compiled by the DAR or others are located in the state sections including *Pension Records of Soldiers of the Revolution Who Removed to Florida* by Jessie Fritot for the Jacksonville Chapter, DAR; Quisenberry's *Revolutionary Soldiers in Kentucky* and *Some Tennessee Heroes of the Revolution*.

During the course of their work DAR staff genealogists assembled a large collection of photocopies of federal pension applications either by extracting them from the documentation from DAR membership application or by ordering copies. Several years ago, after the Seimes Microfilm Center acquired the National Archives microfilm of these pensions, the Library received these paper copies. The Library staff placed these alphabetically arranged files in the manuscript collection. There are eighty-three boxes of these copies. Some have copies of the final pension payment papers attached. All are available to researchers.

On a periodic basis during the nineteenth century, the Federal government published lists of all living pensioners. These lists are not as informative as the pension application file but are useful in determining the pensioner's name, rank, or in the case of a widow her husband's rank, and place of residence. In *Revolutionary Pensioners: A Transcript of the Pension List of the United States for 1813* pensioners are listed in alphabetical order within their state of residence with their former rank and the amount of their pension. *The Pension List of 1820* adds place of residence during the Revolution to the information on the 1813 list. Copies of original pension payment records are available to the public on microfilm under the title *Ledgers of Payments to U.S. Pensioners Under Acts of 1818 Through 1858* in the Seimes Microfilm Center.

In 1840 a census was taken of surviving Revolutionary War pensioners. This census was published in 1841 under the title *A Census of Pensioners for Revolutionary or Military Services*. It includes the name, age, and place of residence for the pensioner along with the names of individuals with whom the pensioner resided in 1840. The source has been reprinted several times.

Most pensioners received their stipend through the application process, but it was not uncommon for individuals to petition Congress for a pension. These petitions were referred to the House Committee on Revolutionary Pensions. Some of these petitions are compiled in *Revolutionary Pensioners 1827-1831*, a bound copy of original house reports relating to pensions. Although these reports are confined to only a four year span, they contain a great deal of information relating to pensioners and to the petitioners in particular. Several petitions relate the military service of the veteran in great detail. *Revolutionary Pensioners 1827-1831* does not have an index, but the *CIS US Serial Set Index Part I, American State Papers and the 15th-34th Congress* provides limited access to these and other Congressional documents of the period.

13.20.4.18
The Draper Manuscript Collection

Fascinated by the George Rogers Clark story and the experience of the settlers across the Alleghany mountains, historian Lyman C. Draper spent much of the nineteenth century compiling a massive amount of material on the frontier during Revolutionary period. When Draper died in 1891, possession of his compiled manuscripts passed to the State Historical Society of Wisconsin. These manuscripts include diaries, journals, maps, muster rolls and other original documents concerning the early history of a number of states including Georgia, Illinois, Ohio, Kentucky and Tennessee and the western parts of Virginia and the Carolinas. In addition, Draper conducted interviews or corresponded with participants in the events of the frontier and their descendants.

The papers cover events from the 1740's until after the War of 1812 including incidents from the Revolution such as the battle of King's Mountain (the subject of Draper's only book *King's Mountain and its Heroes*), the George Rogers Clark expedition and Indian warfare on the frontier. The manuscripts include information on the famous, such as the "George Rogers Clark Papers," as well as the contributions of enlisted soldiers, women and minorities. This invaluable collection is available on microfilm in the Seimes Microfilm Center. Several subject guides to the manuscripts and an overall *Guide to the Draper Manuscripts* by Josephine Harper are in the Library.

13.20.4.19
Death and Burial Records

By modern standards the battle casualties of the Revolution seem relatively light, but at the time it was very shocking and left a major imprint on post-war society. It was not uncommon for the dead and wounded to number in the hundreds rather than in the thousands as was the case in the Civil War and later American wars. Before it was common for soldiers to wear identification, many of the fallen remained unknown. This was the case in the Revolution. After years of research, Clarence Stewart Peterson compiled a list of *Known Military Dead During the American Revolutionary War 1775-1783*. Stewart includes the names of those Americans killed in action or who died while in service. For those named in the book, Stewart includes rank, whether or not the soldier was killed or died of other unspecified causes and the date and place of death if known. His study is not, however, comprehensive.

Most of the men who served in the Revolution survived the war. Many followed the western movement of emigrants living to old age in a state far from their starting point. A special project of the DAR has been the marking of the graves of known Revolutionary War veterans and patriots. Many chapters have reported grave marking ceremonies in *The DAR Magazine* throughout the twentieth century. The Office of the Historian General maintains card files on reported located and marked graves. See Chapter 7 for further information.

One outgrowth of this activity is the large number of cemetery books and transcripts in the Library from DAR chapters around the country. In most cases several volumes have been issued for a state over a number of years such as *Graves of Revolutionary Soldiers in New Jersey* originally transcribed in 1926, *Revolutionary War Patriots Buried in New Jersey* and *Alphabetical Listing of Located Graves in New Jersey of Revolutionary War Patriots*. Most of these volumes are unique typescripts, but some such as *Roster of Soldiers and Patriots of the American Revolution Buried in Indiana* were commercially published and bound. The amount of information contained in each volume varies. *Graves of Revolutionary Soldiers, Located and Marked by the Peoria Chapter, NSDAR* contains photos of headstones, abstracts from pension applications and newspaper articles. *The Golden Book: Revolutionary Soldiers' Graves Pennsylvania* lists only the name, dates, location of cemetery and occasionally the veteran's regiment.

Researchers must be aware, however, that there are errors in these indices and publications. Use these sources for clues. Do not accept information in print without additional proof.

13.20.4.20
Lineage Societies

A number of lineage societies have been formed in the United States based on ancestral service in the Revolution. The DAR is the largest lineage society based on descent from a participant in the American Revolution. In addition to the *DAR Patriot Index*, the Library has a variety of state and national rosters for these societies. The rosters in the DAR Library include those of the National Society of the Sons of the American Revolution, the Society of the Cincinnati and the Sons of the Revolution. Information on Revolutionary War service may also be found in the *Order of Washington Lineage Book* and in the application papers of the Order of Lafayette (1917-1930) bound in book form. See section 13.18 for additional information on these groups.

13.20.4.21
DAR Rosters

Many state sections contain Revolutionary War rosters compiled by the DAR. Although a variety of information appears in these rosters, the changing nature of historical study and the number of individuals and styles involved in compiling these volumes, the researcher should not accept the evidence in total without first verifying the information from other sources. There are many unverified and erroneous listings in these books, and the staff genealogists do not accept them as proof of Revolutionary War service.

One of the largest such rosters is *Histories of Revolutionary Soldiers*, a set of over forty volumes compiled and transcribed by various chapters of the Georgia DAR from 1967 to 1987. The Georgia *Histories* lists the soldiers and patriots in alphabetical order within each volume, describes service, indicates where the individual is buried and lists family members. Every entry in the book includes a list of sources for the information. An index is available for the Georgia series. *Roster of Revolutionary Soldiers and Patriots in Alabama* compiled by Louise Milam Julich for the Alabama DAR follows an arrangement identical to that of the Georgia *Histories*.

The Rachel Caldwell Chapter of the DAR in Greensboro, North Carolina produced ten volumes of *Biographical Sketches of Soldiers and Patriots in the Battle of Guilford Courthouse, March 15, 1781* (1958-1971). Each entry includes service information and genealogical information if any was available. There is no comprehensive index for the set, but each volume is indexed separately and all the books are arranged alphabetically by the surname of the soldier or patriot. A state-wide *Roster of Soldiers from North Carolina in the American Revolution* was published by the North Carolina DAR in 1932. *The Official Roster of the Soldiers of the American Revolution Who Lived in the State of Ohio* published by the Ohio DAR uses a "*Who's Who*" style entry with a heavy use of abbreviations. The information in the three volumes of Ohio rosters is derived from a variety of sources; not all of these sources are verifiable. All of these DAR rosters and others are located in the state sections of the DAR Library.

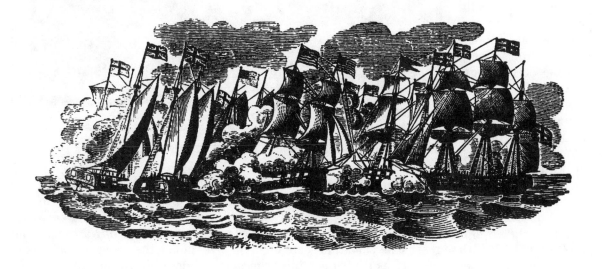

13.20.5
THE WAR OF 1812

Often called the "Second American Revolution" the War of 1812 was in reality simply an opportunity for Great Britain to give the Americans a sound thrashing. It was an ugly war for the United States. Ignoring heavy opposition to the war, particularly in the North East, President James Madison asked Congress for a declaration of war against Great Britain on June 1, 1812. Ostensibly fought to address American grievances against the British, including the concept of freedom of the seas, the war was caused at least in part by the desire of "western" politicians, such as Henry Clay, to expand the boundaries of the United States. To face British regulars, Indians and Canadian militia, the United States fielded a small professional army supplemented by state militia. In the process of the war, the United States invaded Canada, suffered stunning reversals on land, including the burning of Washington, D.C., enjoyed equally stunning success at sea, crushed Indian opposition in the Northwest and won a decisive victory against the British at New Orleans after the signing of a peace treaty.

For researchers interested in a general history of the war, the Library has a number of books available. These range from Lossing's classic *The Pictorial Field–Book of the War of 1812* (1868) to Cobbert's rare *The Late War Between Great Britain and the United States* (1815). More recent works on the war include Hickey's *The War of 1812: A Forgotten Conflict* and Stagg's *Mr. Madison's War*. Works on specific battles are found throughout the collection including Lord's *The Dawn's Early Light* on the 1814 Washington/Baltimore campaign and Whitehorne's *While Washington Burned: The Battle for Fort Erie*. Books on the Battle of New Orleans such as Albright's *New Orleans: The Battle of the Bayous* and Arthur's *The Story of the Battle of New Orleans* are found in the Louisiana section. Also in the state sections are works on the contributions of individual states during the war such as Quisenberry's *Kentucky in the War of 1812*.

When President Madison asked for a declaration of war, the United States had only a small standing army. As it did during the Revolution, the government turned to the state militias to supplement and support the national army. Despite early opposition to the war in some parts of the country, every state responded to the call. The names of these volunteers are pre-

British troops burning books in the Library of Congress

served in both official state publications and commercially published rosters. Muster rolls for the War of 1812 available in the Library include *Pennsylvania Archives; the Delaware Archives, Military; Roster of Soldiers in the War of 1812-14* [Vermont]; *Roster of Ohio Soldiers in the War of 1812;* and *Muster Rolls of the Soldiers of the War of 1812 Detached from the Militia of North Carolina in 1812 and 1814*. All of these state publications are useful in determining the regiment and rank of individual soldiers and some such as the Vermont roster include additional details on individual service, but these books do not include genealogical information.

The naval side to the War of 1812 is well represented by general works such as *War on the Great Lakes* and Shomette's *Flotilla: Battle for the Patuxent*. As was the case during the Revolution, licensed privateers preyed on British merchantmen or engaged British ships of war. Some of these privateers are identified in Cranwell and Crane's *Men of Marque: A History of Private Armed Vessels Out of Baltimore During the War of 1812*, Eastman's *Some Famous Privateers of New England* and Murphy's *Letters of Marque and British Aliens in the U.S. During the War of 1812 from official records*. Compiled naval correspondence, reports and other official documents can be found in *The Naval War of 1812: A Documentary History* which includes a name index for located individuals in the Navy. *Deep Water Sailors, Shallow Water Soldiers* identifies sailors, marines and soldiers who participated in the Lake Erie campaign. Brief biographical entries for soldiers and marines drawn primarily from pension records are included in an appendix. Dixon and Eberly's *Index to Seamen's Protection Certificate Applications: Port of Philadelphia 1796–1823* identifies mariners from the War of 1812 period. The information on each applicant includes name, age, ethnic group, and state or country of birth.

Like the soldiers and sailors of the Revolution, veterans of the War of 1812 were eligible for pensions and bounty land grants. Veterans' and widows application files are housed at the National Archives and available for research on microfilm. The names of both veterans and widows appear in the government publication *List of Pensioners on the Roll January 1, 1883* and White's *Index to Old Wars Pension Files 1815–1926*. Researchers are more likely to find widows in the *List of Pensioners* than veterans, because the list was published nearly seventy years after the end of the war. The *List of Pensioners* does not have an index and the arrangement is by state, then county, then by individuals listed in no particular order. White includes pensions from a much longer period of time and arranges the names in alphabetical order.

Abstracts for these pension applications appear in several different forms throughout the Library collection and contain much useful information for the genealogist. White's *Index to War of 1812 Pension Files* contains very brief entries which can include the name of the veteran, his regiment, place of residence and his wife's name. Longer abstracts appear in *Major Index to Pension List of the War of 1812* and Baer's *War of 1812 Bounty Lands and Pension Applications*. Entries in the latter work, a typed manuscript, run a page in length or more. State-specific works based on pension and bounty land lists in the collection include Gandrud's multivolume *Alabama Soldiers, Revolution, War of 1812, and Indian Wars*, Walker's *Illinois Pensioners List of the Revolution, 1812 & Indian Wars*, Wright's *Maryland Militia War of 1812* and Lontz's *Pennsylvania War of 1812 Pensioners*.

American battlefield casualties in this conflict were relatively light in comparison with later wars. Peterson's list of *Known Military Dead During the War of 1812* includes deaths in battle and by other causes. The names are arranged in alphabetical order and includes rank, regiment and date of death. Most of the soldiers survived the war and died of natural causes. The known burial sites of 1812 veterans can be found in several books throughout the collection including *An Index of Veterans of Connecticut During the Years 1812, 1813, 1814, 1815, 1816* and *Index to the Grave Records of Servicemen of the War of 1812 State of Ohio*, both compiled by the National Society of the United States Daughters of War of 1812.

The *1812 Ancestor Index* of the National Society of the United States Daughters of 1812 is available in two volumes in the Library. This index lists the names of the individuals recognized by the society as having served in some capacity during the War of 1812. Names are alphabetical and entries include rank and state, birth and death dates, and spouses and children. Additional lineage information on 1812 veterans can be found in volumes 13-39 of the applications of the General Society of the War of 1812. Microfilm copies of these applications are in the Seimes Microfilm Center. Indices to members and ancestors are found at the front of the reels.

13.20.6
THE MEXICAN WAR

Although it is now largely a forgotten conflict, the Mexican War had important consequences for the United States. In the Treaty of Guadalupe-Hidalgo that ended the war, Mexico ceded to the United States what became the states of New Mexico, Arizona, California, Nevada and Utah. It was the first foreign war of the United States to the extent that all of the battles were waged on Mexican soil. The DAR Library has several excellent histories of the Mexican War including Bauer's *The Mexican War 1846-1848*, Hamry's *The Story of the Mexican War*, Eisenhower's *So Far from God* and one of the first accounts of the war *A Complete History of the Mexican War 1846-1848* (1849) by Nathan Covington Brooks.

On the American side the Mexican War was fought by a combination of United States Army regulars and volunteer units from the states, particularly from the South. *North Carolina in the Mexican War 1846-1848* recounts that state's involvement in the war until the departure of North Carolina troops from Mexico in 1848. South Carolina sent the Palmetto Regiment to Mexico where it served with distinction from the landing at Vera Cruz to the assault on Mexico City. *South Carolina in the Mexican War* tells the story of the Palmetto Regiment and includes a roster and some photographs of its members. The *Military History of Mississippi 1803-1898* includes a section on the Mexican War with lists of casualties. In *Maryland and District of Columbia Volunteers in the Mexican War*, Charles J. Wells lists all of the soldiers in alphabetical order with rank, date of enlistment, age at time of enlistment and any remarks from the soldier's record. A separate section shows the muster rolls for the

Baltimore and District of Columbia Battalion and the Maryland and District of Columbia Regiment. *Official Roster of the Soldiers of the State of Ohio in the War With Mexico, 1846–1848* offers a brief history for each Ohio regiment in the war, with a company-by-company roster of each regiment. The rosters include the name of each soldier, his age, rank, period of enlistment and remarks on his service.

In order to pursue the war, the United States was forced to wage campaigns on three fronts: Mexico, California and New Mexico. These were alien landscapes to most of the American soldiers with a largely unfriendly climate. Supplies for the army were poor and disease a constant companion. *Army of Manifest Destiny* tells the story of this force and its hardships interspersing the narrative with first person accounts by the soldiers. The experiences of the army in California were recorded in letters by Napoleon Jackson Tecumseh Dana, a lieutenant with the U.S. Army. Dana's letters are compiled and transcribed in *Monterey Is Ours! The Mexican War Letters of Lt. Dana*. Graphically illustrating the American experience in the war is *Eyewitness to War: Prints and Daguerreotypes of the Mexican War, 1846–1848* which contains the first photographs of American soldiers on campaign and contemporary prints of the battles. The names of at least some of these soldiers are preserved in *Index to the Dispatches and to the Names of United States Soldiers Who Fought in the Final Battles of the Mexican War* compiled by Mary Emily Smith Witt. Through a careful reading of military correspondence, Witt produced a list of both enlisted men and officers who served during the assault on Mexico City. Abstracts of the dispatches are included as well.

The Battle of Monterey

When the shooting stopped, the ordeal was not over for many American troops. In California and New Mexico, especially around Santa Fe, a United States occupation force was necessary. The native Mexican citizens of these territories did not welcome the Americans. It was many years before tensions eased and the native New Mexicans and Californians accepted the American presence. The story of the first days of American occupation in New Mexico is told by *Seeds of Discord* and *Turmoil in New Mexico* and in California by *California Conquered* and *General M.G. Vallejo and the Advent of the Americans*.

Many of the soldiers who survived the war and the peace later received a pension from the federal government. From 1886 to 1926 the government accepted pension applications from Mexican War veterans and their widows. These applications are indexed by Wolfe's *Mexican War Pension Applications*, Troxel and Warner's multivolume set *Mexican War Index to Pension Files 1886–1926*, and White's *Index to Mexican War Pension Files*. Each of these works differs slightly from the others in terms of arrangement and information. White's compilation includes the soldier's name, pension number, date of application and regiment of service. Troxel and Warner include the same information as White, but add the soldier's date of death or dates during which the soldier or widow received a pension, if known. Wolfe's transcription does not include the rank or regiment of the soldier.

The memory of the soldiers is kept alive by the lineage society Descendants of Mexican War Veterans. A roster of members and their ancestors is located in the Library. The ancestor list is arranged alphabetically by surname, and includes the rank and regiment for each man.

13.20.7
THE CIVIL WAR

Most libraries have a number of books on the American Civil War consisting largely of biographies and battle histories. These books concentrate on the broad canvas of the war, and the dominating personalities who made policy and planned the strategy. In such studies, the common soldier, if mentioned by name at all, serves only to provide color to the narrative, to describe their feelings in battle, on campaign or in camp. For the genealogical researcher, such works provide the background, but not the detail of what the war did to a family. At the DAR Library the emphasis is on how the Civil War effected the community, the family and the individual.

Over three million men served in the armies of the Confederacy and the Union during the Civil War. Each one of these men left behind some record of service. The basic problem for the genealogist is pairing the name of an individual with a military unit. Until recently, this was something of a daunting task. While a researcher may know the state where an ancestor lived before the war, this information does not translate easily into proof of service during the war. For this proof one must turn to published regimental rosters.

Not long after the smoke cleared from the battlefields, the United States War Department produced the *Official Army Register of the Volunteer Force of the United States Army*. While useful, this set is not quite the genealogical bonanza suggested by the title, for the text lists only officers. Except for the U.S. Colored Infantry regiments and specialized units such as the U.S. Sharpshooters and the Veteran and Reserve units, regular U.S. Army officers are not included in the list. Arrangement in the books is by state, then by regimental number. Because the set has a name index, the researcher does not need to know a regimental number to find an individual soldier. Information on each man in the *Official Army Register* includes date of rank and whether or not the officer was promoted, discharged or killed in action. Naturally, the *Register* contains information only on Union officers. For similar information on Confederate soldiers, one must consult the state sections of the Library.

13.20.7.1
General History

One of the primary sources on the war is *War of the Rebellion: Official Records of the Union and Confederate Armies*. In the aftermath of the Civil War, the United States War Department collected and compiled the official papers of both the Union and the Confederacy. Wars generate records and the Civil War is no exception. The Civil War armies routinely used reams of paper to issue orders, send messages and describe troop movements. Commanders on every level wrote post-battle reports indicating the contributions of individuals and the accomplishments or failures of divisions, brigades and regiments. These records comprise the 128 volumes of the *Official Records*. The Library owns a copy of this set and the index.

For studies of the major battles of the Civil War turn to the state sections of the DAR Library. Several accounts of the Battle of Gettysburg are in the Pennsylvania section. Researchers interested in the Shiloh campaign or the battle for Chattanooga will find these studies in the Tennessee section. Similarly, overall accounts of how a state fared during the war are in the state sections such as William R. Trotter's three volume study *North Carolina in the Civil War*. Burton's *The Siege of Charleston 1861–1865*, Morris and Foutz's *Lynchburg in the Civil War* and similar works on specific cities or counties are located in the state sections with other books on the counties.

13.20.7.2
Research Guides

While researchers will find considerably more material available at the DAR Library than they might have expected, the collection is limited to published sources. There are several guides, however, to the larger repositories of Civil War records. The National Archives and Records Administration is custodian for the records of the Union and most of the national records for the Confederacy. Henry Putney Beers' *The Confederacy: A Guide to the Archives of the Government of the Confederate States of American* and a companion volume *The Union: A Guide to Federal Archives Relating to the Civil War* by Beers and Kenneth W. Munden describe the National Archives collection of Civil

War documents. The records of service for individual soldiers are available on microfilm at the National Archives. A description and index of these records is provided by *Military Service Records: A Select Catalog of National Archives Microfilm Publications*. The Library of Congress owns a number of Civil War papers and related material which are cataloged in *Civil War Manuscripts: A Guide to Collections in the Manuscript Division of the Library of Congress*. These and other guides are found in the Library.

It is one thing to know where a source is located, it is quite another to know how to use that source effectively. Neagles' *U.S. Military Records* describes what records are available to researchers at the federal and local level for American soldiers from 1776 to the present and how to access these records. Other works in the DAR Library concentrate solely on using Civil War materials from general overviews to narrower ones. Two basic guides, Schweitzer's *Civil War Genealogy* and Goene's *Tracing Your Civil War Ancestor* are available. In addition, one finds *Confederate Research Sources*, an earlier work by Neagles, and Secret's *Guide to Tracing Your African Ameripean* [sic.] *Civil War Ancestor*, both designed for specific research audiences. Those researchers interested in tracing a Civil War ancestor may also wish to consult the selected publications the Library has available from the United Daughters of the Confederacy.

Even for the DAR Library, the study of genealogy does not begin and end with the American Revolution. More books have been published on the American Civil War than on any other war in the nation's history. The official records left behind are more complete than any of the previous American wars. Because so many men saw duty, the Civil War a is boon to genealogists. The DAR Library's collection on the Civil War is designed to help the researcher find their ancestor among the three million men who served, and to offer some picture of what life was like for the common soldier.

13.20.7.3
State and National Rosters

To recognize the contributions of their citizens to the war, a number of state governments, North and South, published rosters of the veterans. Some of these books, such as *Roster and Record of Iowa Soldiers in the War of the Rebellion*, were printed within the lifetime of many veterans while others like *North Carolina Troops, 1861–1865, A Roster* were completed recently or are pending completion. The Library also owns many other rosters including those of Pennsylvania and Michigan. These lists are invaluable to the researcher, but the organization and content of the rosters vary considerably. The most common arrangement is by regiment, then by company and within the company alphabetically by surname as in *Rosters of the Confederate Soldiers of Georgia, 1861–1865*. Of the state rosters *Tennesseans in the Civil War* and *Records of Louisiana Confederate Soldiers and Commands*, use a purely alphabetical scheme listing all the soldiers by name followed by unit designation as does Hartzler's *Marylanders in the Confederacy*. Following the lead of the *Official Army Register*, *New York in the War of the Rebellion 1861–1865* and *The Official and Statistical Register of the State of Mississippi* include only the names of officers from the company level up. Many of the omissions and idiosyncrasies of the state rosters are corrected by *The Roster of Confederate Soldiers 1861–1865* and *The Roster of Union Soldiers 1861–1865*. These multivolume sets list in alphabetical order all of the soldiers for whom the National Archives has a service record. Both of these sets are located in the Library.

13.20.7.4
Regimental Histories

Because not all state histories include specific information on individuals, the researcher should turn to regimental histories for details from service records. Most recent regimental histories use these service records as a starting point. Unlike the state rosters, the regimental histories are more detailed, dedicating an entire book to the history of one regiment. One of the best examples of this genre is the *Virginia Regimental History Series*. Each of the eighty volumes in the series contains a complete roster of the regiment, abstracts of individual service records and a narrative of all the important actions of the regiment. The Library also owns individual regimental histories written by veterans such as Kirk's *History of the Fifteenth Pennsylvania Volunteer Cavalry* (1906) or more recent studies like Nikazy's *Forgotten Soldiers: History of the 4th Tennessee Volunteer Infantry Regiment (USA) 1863–1865* (1995). These and other regimental histories are in the state sections of the Library and *Ohio Civil War Regimental Histories and Reunions* is available in the Seimes Microfilm Center.

13.20.7.5
Veterans' Memoirs

Beyond the information found in secondary sources and that compiled by the federal and state governments, are the personal experiences of the soldiers themselves. Proud of their accomplishments, Union and Confederate veterans published their own accounts of the war. In the DAR Library, one finds a variety of memoirs spanning the spectrum of the Civil War experience. Some of these memoirs have been in print for over one hundred years, while others were published only recently. Reed's *Hardtack and Coffee* (1887) and *The Civil War Reminiscences of Major Silas T. Grisamore, C.S.A.*, originally printed from 1867 to 1871, were written and published during the lifetime of the authors. Private David Holt's *A Mississippi Rebel in the Army of Northern Virginia*, on the other hand, was edited and published long after Holt's death.

Confederate veterans in general were far from reluctant to reminisce and refight the war in print. Two series of the late nineteenth century provided retired Confederates with a forum to air their views: the *Confederate Veteran* and the *Southern Historical Society Papers*. Although obviously partisan, both series contain a number of interesting war accounts as well as reprints of official Confederate records.

13.20.7.6
Diaries and Letters

From general to private, Civil War literature is rich with diaries and letters. Both North and South sent a large number of literate men to the war, men who recorded their thoughts for their families and for the future. Quite a few diaries and letter collections have been published commercially, particularly in recent years. The library has a number of these including *All for the Union: The Civil War Diary and Letters of Elisha Hunt Rhodes* edited by Robert Hunt Rhodes and *The Diary of John*

K. Benefiel for the Year 1864: A Civil War Soldier, 46th Reg. Indiana Volunteers. In addition, under the auspices of the DAR's G.R.C. several members have compiled letters and diaries written by Civil War ancestors such as *Copy of a Diary Written Through the Civil War* by Capt. James Gibson copied by Mrs. Meta Russell for the Alamo Chapter, DAR; *The Civil War Journal of J.C. Wandling, Washington, N.J.* compiled by Alma Jackson Chambers and Esther W. Berner for the Jemima Cundict Chapter, DAR and *Civil War Diary of Peter F. Smith* compiled by Shirley Garmon for the General Robert Irwin Chapter, North Carolina DAR. These diaries and letters are located throughout the collection.

While it is unlikely the average researcher will come to the Library and find his or her ancestor's letters or diaries neatly compiled and waiting on the shelf, these thoughts recorded over a century ago are useful even if they are not penned by one's ancestor. Diaries and letters often mention the names of other individuals in the regiment. Moreover, these letters and journals chronicle the day-to-day existence of the soldier. Pieces of information take an ancestor from being a grim two dimensional figure staring from a faded photograph, to a living, breathing being.

13.20.7.7
Pension Lists and the 1890 Union Veterans' Census

On the instructions of the United States Senate, the Pension Bureau published a five volume list of all living pensioners in 1883. Although not identified as such, a large number of those listed were Union veterans; some were from earlier conflicts. The federal government, of course, did not pension Confederate veterans. The arrangement of the list is by state, county and town. Pensioners living abroad are included in volume 5 of the set. Names are not arranged in any particular fashion within the town and addenda of additional names are inserted at will. The lack of organization is due in large part to the Senate's insistence to have the list produced in less than one month. Despite its flaws, *The List of Pensioners on the Roll, January 1, 1883* contains a great deal of useful information. Each entry includes the pension number, the name of the pensioner, the reason for the pension, the amount of the pension, the date the pension was granted and where the pensioner was living at the time.

Less than seven years after the publication of the 1883 list, a special census enumerated Union veterans and widows of veterans. Had it remained intact, this census would have been an excellent resource for genealogists. Unfortunately, most of the schedules for Alabama through Kansas and the District of Columbia are missing. The Library has several volumes of these censuses including the *1890 Civil War Veterans Census: Tennessee* and *the Missouri 1890 Special Federal Census of Union Veterans and Widows of Veterans of the Civil War*.

The purpose of the 1890 veteran's census was to identify potential pensioners from the Union army. Consequently, the census takers excluded Confederate veterans, although the West Virginia schedules of this special census include former soldiers from both sides with the Confederate veterans crossed out.

The states of the former Confederacy offered pensions to their own aging veterans. The Library owns the indices to many of these state pension applications including *Tennessee Confederate Widows and Their Families, Mississippi Confederate Pension Applications* and *Register of Florida CSA Pension Applications*. Information contained in these indices varies from book to book, but all include the name of the pensioner, the regiment of service, the date of application and the home county of the applicant. Copies of a number of Virginia's printed pension lists for veterans and their widows in the early twentieth century are in the Library's collection.

13.20.7.8
Burial Records

After the war many veterans returned to the town of their birth to live out the rest of their days. Others moved in all directions of the compass, finding their final resting place hundreds of miles from where they were born. The DAR Library has a number of cemetery listings for Civil War veterans. For the most part, these listings are located in the county sections of the collection such as *839 Confederate Soldiers Buried in Clay, Cleborne and Randolph Counties, Ala.*, although the Florida section boasts a statewide directory of deceased veterans. Union war dead and place of interment are listed in *The Roll of Honor*, a publication of the United States Army Quartermaster Corps. *The Roll of Honor* has a name index. See also section 13.4.

13.20.7.9
County Histories

The period between the end of the Civil War and the turn of the century saw a boom in the publication of county histories, most of which are in the Library. Because nearly every county sent some men off to fight, the Civil War was an important part of these histories. When these men went as a regiment, the names of every man in the regiment were recorded in the county history. Individual entries often include a brief description of service and on occasion, some biographical information. *The History of Essex County, New Jersey*, (1884), examines the county's service during the war, describes the service of each regiment from the county and lists by name all ranks in the regiment. If the author of the history was a veteran however, considerably more information is available. Writing in 1913, Union veteran W. L. Curry devoted three-quarters of *History of Jerome Township, Union County, Ohio to the Civil War*, including photos of veterans, regimental rosters and histories and full individual service records. A number of more recent publications by local historians concentrate exclusively on the Civil War at the county level. *For Home and Honor* offers the service records of Madison County, Virginia veterans and describes how the county was effected by the war. As the title suggests, *Civil War Veterans of Athens County, Ohio: Biographical Sketches* includes biographical and genealogical information in addition to war experiences. These and similar histories are in the Library's state sections.

13.20.8
THE INDIAN WARS

From the formation of the Republic until 1890 the United States was almost constantly at war with one Native American tribe or another. A selection of studies on the individual wars and the tribes involved is available in the American Indian Collection. For more information on the soldiers involved, researchers should consult the abstracts of pension reports in the Library including *Index to Volunteer Soldiers 1784-1811, Index to Volunteer Soldiers in Indian Wars and Disturbances, 1815-1858, Index to Old Wars Pension Files 1815-1926* and *Index to Indian Wars Pension Files,*

1892-1926. State militia took an active role in the wars prior to 1861. Information on these soldiers is available in the state section in sources such as *Alabama Soldiers: Revolution, War of 1812, and Indian Wars; Abstracts of Pensions, Soldiers of the Revolution, 1812 & Indian Wars Who Settled on the Kentucky Side of the Ohio River;* and *The Battle of Tippecanoe.*

13.20.9
THE SPANISH AMERICAN WAR

America's "splendid little war" with Spain in 1898 was the first major conflict following the organization of the DAR in 1890. Naturally, the young, patriotic group supported the war effort against the aging Spanish Empire. The National Society's enthusiasm for the war is reflected in surviving publications from the period. One DAR activity, in particular, produced materials of potential genealogical value.

The DAR established a "Hospital Corps," and certified and sent out nearly 1,000 nurses for the United States Army. The DAR's first Librarian General and first Surgeon General, Dr. Anita Newcomb McGee, was very instrumental in this effort. For researchers with a Spanish American War nurse in their family "List of United States Army Nurses Appointed on Recommendation of the Daughters of the American Revolution Hospital Corps," *American Monthly Magazine* v. 15 (September 1899), 360-422, will be of interest. The Historian General's Office has some additional material on the DAR's participation in support of this war effort, including a rearranged list of the nurses in the above article sorted by state. Subsequent to the war many of the nurses were involved in the Spanish-American War Nurses Association.

Researchers at DAR will also find the occasional book listing the participants from a particular state in the Spanish American War. Examples of these include Riley's *Roster of the Soldiers and Sailors Who Served in Organizations from Maryland during the Spanish-American War* and *The Official Roster of Ohio Soldiers in the War with Spain 1898-1899.* Some county histories also contain rosters of local soldiers in this conflict.

13.20.10
WORLD WAR I

Genealogically, not much has been published on World War I. The DAR Library does not own a collection of general histories of this war. There are, however, a number of sources available at DAR of interest to those researching ancestors involved in "The Great War," some of which are unique.

Scattered throughout the Library collection, one will encounter various state or local rosters and histories describing the activities of that state or locality during the war. Some examples include Fraser's *Roster of Men and Women Who Served in the Army or Naval Service of the United States or Its Allies from the State of North Dakota*, Davis's *Virginians of Distinguished Service in the World War*, and *Indiana World War Records: Gold Star Honor Roll, 1914-1918.* These and others provide some coverage for the first major war of the twentieth century. Researchers will find rosters of local soldiers and sailors in some county histories. If the Library does not own such studies or listings for a particular state or locality, researchers will likely find works like those mentioned above in other libraries.

A recent set of books relating to World War I is *Deaths: American Expeditionary Force, 1917, 1918* compiled by Ashley K. Nuckols. Arranged by state, these volumes provide listings and some copies of photographs of those who died during the war. Each is indexed.

AU COMITE D. *[illegible]*
DES
"FATHERLESS·CHILDREN·OF·FRANCE·INC."
LA FRANCE RECONNAISSANTE

Certificate sent by the French Government, and signed by the President of France, to show
that country's gratitude to the National Society Daughters of the American Revolution,
for adopting over 5,000 French war orphans. The certificate was received by the
Treasurer General, NSDAR, through the Headquarters of the fatherless children of France.

The DAR's stated purpose to promote patriotic endeavor naturally resulted in involvement of DAR members in the country's war efforts. World War I was the second war in which the United States participated after the DAR's founding in 1890. Support for the war effort by DAR members took many forms, and one project in particular resulted in materials of genealogical significance.

Towards the end of the war and in the years immediately following it, the DAR urged its members to complete four-page, printed forms detailing the lives and service of men and women in their families who were in the military during the conflict. Some submissions are from DAR members, who were themselves involved. The result of this effort to preserve historical information and to honor war participants was a collection of 117 volumes of *War Service Records* for World War I. The set is divided into state volumes. Within each state's volumes, the forms are arranged in alphabetical order **by the submitting DAR chapters**. Then the forms themselves are in alphabetical order by the names of the subject of each brief report. Among the information requested (not all forms are filled in completely) are name, date of birth, place of birth, relationship of the submitter to the subject of the report, marriage, names of parents, names of children, education, fraternal orders, military service, and discharge information. Some of the submissions include excellent photographs of the subjects.

The *War Service Records* are in the custody of the Office of the Historian General. Depending on the condition of the paper and photographs, one may be able to obtain photocopies from these registers. Researchers interested in knowing of the availability of a volume for their state of interest and particulars relating to their use should contact the Archivist, Office of the Historian General **prior to making a visit**.

The collected questionnaires are not indexed, and they are by no means a complete listing of either all American participants in World War I or of all the relatives of DAR members who served. They do, however, illustrate the type of work the DAR has often performed. They are an interesting and unknown collection of information which DAR members gathered for posterity. Until a few years ago, the staff was unaware of their existance, until a locked storage cabinet needed relocation in the Library's storage area. The key emerged after some searching, and the contents revealed. The Library transferred the collection to the Historian General for preservation and safekeeping. A similar set of completed questionnaires for World War II already in the latter office's custody provided an excellent complement.

13.20.11
WORLD WAR II

The literature on World War II is enormous and is readily available in libraries nationwide. The DAR Library does not collect general studies on this war. There are various publications, however, similar to those for World War I mentioned previously, which detail the activities and military participants from states and localities during the conflict. Examples of these are Lutz's *Richmond in World War II*, Parlier's *Pursuits of War: The People of Charlottesville and Albemarle County, Virginia in the Second World War*, and Lindvahl's study for Effingham County, Illinois, *They Served With Honor*. Some recent county histories include sections on their military personnel who participated in World War II.

As it had during the First World War, the DAR developed a project asking members to complete printed forms detailing the basic biographical and service

> We wish we had the space to give you the detailed information from the reports of the state librarians. They show contributions from states of many thousands of books and magazines to U.S.O. centers, Army and Navy hospitals and military camps, as well as many books sent to our approved schools and to local libraries. All states have sent books to their adopted ships. Delaware sent a victrola to their adopted ship.
>
> Mabel J. Smith, Librarian General, in her April 1945 Board report in *National Historical Magazine*, June 1945, p. 407.

information of their relatives involved in the war effort. The result of this attempt to preserve historical information was a collection of ninety-four volumes of questionnaires, generally labeled *World War II Honor Roll* or *World War II War Service Records*. These are arranged by state, then by donating chapter, and then alphabetically by subject. Unlike their World War I predecessors, these questionnaires are one page long and contain much less information. Few photographs appear. The collection does not appear to be complete and several states are not represented. The Office of the Historian General maintains this set and the same conditions for use apply to it as with the World War I *War Service Records*. Similarly, not all members completed submissions for their relatives, and there is no index.

13.20.12
THE KOREAN WAR AND THE VIETNAM WAR

While histories of these conflicts are increasing in number, the DAR Library does not collect general military histories for them. The only significant source available at DAR is the *FamilySearch* CD ROM *Military Death Index*, which lists the names of those who died during these two wars. An occasional county history will include a roster of local participants, and some cemetery transcriptions list burials of Korean War and Vietnam War military personnel.

13.21
NAMES

Names are, of course, crucial to genealogical inquiry. The Library houses books useful to genealogists on given names, surname origins, nicknames, occupational names, naming patterns, and general studies of the subject. Many of these volumes examine names from specific national or ethnic groups.

13.22
NATIVE AMERICAN RESEARCH

The DAR has long had an interest in Native Americans, and its American Indians Committee, established in 1936 "provides financial assistance and educational aid to native American youth" through support of several schools and with a scholarship program. With this activity as background, the DAR Library established a special collection designed to assist with Native American research in 1987 using existing holdings and newly donated materials. It has continued to expand since its inception. Now numbering some 1,200 volumes, the American Indian Collection provides historical and genealogical information for first peoples across the United States.

While the focus of this collection is general history and culture, genealogical studies and guidebooks are becoming more numerous. Researchers will find histories of specific Native American nations, state studies, and materials on interactions with European settlers. There are five shelves concerning the Cherokee alone. In addition to the special collection itself, much information on Native Americans can be found throughout the collection under the states and their counties.

Many records maintained by the federal and state governments relating to Native Americans are now being published, republished, or indexed. The Library attempts to acquire these. Researchers in Washington will find much to consult on this subject at the National Archives, the Department of the Interior Library, and the Library of Congress. The DAR Library offers this general collection as a supplement to its outstanding materials on Americans of European descent.

Recent guides for Native American research include Byers' *Native American Genealogical Sourcebook*, Kavasch's *A Student's Guide to Native American Genealogy* and Gormley's *Cherokee Connections: An Introduction to Genealogical Sources Pertaining to Cherokee Ancestors*.

13.23
NEWSPAPERS

DAR does not maintain a newspaper collection per se. Certain genealogical compilations such as those containing query columns from *The Boston Transcript* (1924-1933 only) and *The Hartford Times* (1934-1964; also on microfiche) are available however. More commonly discovered in the stacks are compilations from local newspapers of vital and genealogically significant news. Obituary indices for newspapers as large as *The New York Times* and as small as *The Martinsburg Gazette* are among these publications. Announcements in religious newspapers which cover entire states or regions are the subjects of frequent new publications. Directories showing what newspapers were published in specific towns and cities are also available.

13.24
PERIODICALS

Numbering nearly 700 subscriptions, state and local genealogical and historical periodicals are a significant portion of the Library's holdings. Some of the longer runs of these publications have been relocated to conserve shelf space, but they are available to researchers. Coverage tends to be strongest for the eastern states. Family newsletters and journals, both historical and current, are also owned and are located in the Family section. Many of the Library's periodical holdings are not available elsewhere in the Washington area.

Many genealogists tend to overlook the important work historians have published in national, state and local historical journals. Conversely, historians often overlook the contents of genealogical publications. Both groups would benefit from the use of each other's materials. For genealogists, historical journals contain background on many events in the past which had a direct bearing on the lives of our ancestors. Frequently, a historical article will shed light on the interpretation of court records or a military engagement. Such studies may be the only place one will find such clarification. Proper historical context is crucial to correct application of the sources used in genealogical study.

Indices to periodicals include *The Periodical Source Index, the Genealogical Periodical Annual Index,* and *the Combined Retrospective Index to Journals in History 1838–1974.* In addition, many journals have their own cumulative indices.

13.25
PRESIDENTS AND THEIR FAMILIES

The Library has a focused collection of books on the Presidency, the Presidents, and the First Ladies. Sources on their families, ancestors, and descendants are included along with biographies and some collected papers of individual Presidents. Major books include Brogan and Mosley's *Burke's American Presidential Families*, Quinn-Musgrove and Kanter's *America's Royalty: All the Presidents' Children*, and Roberts' *Ancestors of American Presidents*. Studies on the ancestors or descendants of specific Presidents are also available, such as McLean's *The English Ancestry of Thomas Jefferson.* Considerable published material on George Washington is in the Library's biography collection and in the Historical Research Library of the Office of the Historian General.

13.26
RELIGIOUS/CHURCH RECORDS AND HISTORIES

The Library maintains basic histories and guides to the records for many Christian denominations and Jewish congregations in the United States. Histories of specific churches and abstracts of many historic church records populate the shelves in the state sections in large numbers, however. Burials in churchyards and associated cemeteries appear in the many cemetery transcriptions throughout the collection. Some church records are available in the Historian General's Americana Collection and in microform.

The CLERGYMAN

13.27
STATE AND REGIONAL RESEARCH

State records and histories offer sources and background not available in federal and local materials. The quantity of records for the fifty states is staggering and most are not published. The Library owns many state records which are in book form, and the Microfilm Center houses major microfilmed state government sources. The emphasis there is to offer materials not available in other research centers in the Washington area.

County, town, and community histories constitute a large portion of the Library's state sections. Not only are most late nineteenth and early twentieth century "mug books" and subscription histories for counties across the country available, but many more recent histories sparked by the Bicentennial, county and town anniversaries, and other historic events are as well. Recent county histories containing family sketches written by local residents are also plentiful. The published *DAR Library Catalog, Volumes Two and Three*, provides listings of the majority of these publications, but because many more have arrived since these catalogs were published, researchers will find numerous newer local histories throughout the collection.

The explosion in genealogical publishing in the past two decades centers in large part on record abstracts and transcriptions. These types of publications represent sources which the Library collects aggressively and nationwide. Marriages, deeds, wills, court minutes, tax lists, town minutes, militia lists, church records and cemetery transcriptions from Virginia to Oregon and Louisiana to Minnesota are collectively one of the Library's strengths. More arrive daily and are shelved shortly thereafter.

Copies of individual documents from these many sources are common types of documentation with DAR membership applications and are found in the Library's file collection. They will be portions of lineage proof and therefore in files under the names of Revolutionary War ancestors of DAR members.

When original deeds, wills, and similar items were found in these files, the staff photocopied them and placed the originals in the Americana Collection. This section within the Historian General's Office preserves many original pre–1860 documents mostly from donors and occasionally from transfers within the building. A card index to genealogical materials in the Americana Collection provides access to much of this information.

The following list highlights the major components of each state and regional section in the DAR Library and the Seimes Microfilm Center. These sections are not limited to the sources listed below, however. Selected State DAR bookplates also appear throughout this section.

Alabama
The Gandrud collection of county record abstracts provides the basis of Alabama materials, but many other abstracts are also available. Alabama has a 200 volume G.R.C. set. The *Internal Revenue Assessment Lists 1865–1866* are on microfilm.

Alaska

A very small amount of material on the 49th State includes some interesting genealogical sources. Some materials on Russian America are located in "The West" section.

Arizona

Basic historical and genealogical sources are available.

Arkansas

Many county record abstracts, a 200 volume G.R.C. set with guide, and Allen's series of *Arkansas Land Patents* provide good sources. Original land grants tract books are available on microfilm.

California

A large number of county histories and record abstracts, the 1852 state census in typescript and microform, and a 300 volume G.R.C. set which includes the subseries *Records of the Families of California Pioneers* highlight the California section. Nineteenth-century Los Angeles County marriages and birth, marriage and death abstracts from the *Sacramento Bee* (1857-1895) provide further coverage.

Colorado

County histories and record abstracts anchor the Colorado section, and a 70 volume G.R.C. set offers additional materials.

Connecticut

Many town histories and records compliment the Connecticut materials in microform. The latter include *The Charles R. Hale Collection of Cemetery Records, The Barbour Collection* (also in books as published), *The Hartford Times Genealogical Column Index*, and *Connecticut Revolutionary War Records from the Connecticut State Archives*. A 200 volume G.R.C. set includes much unique material.

Delaware

A good collection on a small state includes twelve G.R.C. volumes of Bible records.

District of Columbia

With a G.R.C. set of over 200 volumes, which includes many abstracts of church and vital records along with extensive surveys of cemeteries in the District, the D.C. section is essential for researchers working on families in the Potomac Valley. The excellent publications of the Historical Society of Washington, D.C., the Columbian Harmony Society covering D.C. cemetery and other vital records, and most twentieth century D.C. city directories add valuable coverage to the basic historical sources for the Nation's Capital.

Florida

A growing county records collection coupled with over 200 G.R.C. volumes provides good Florida coverage. The W.P.A.'s *Register of Deceased Veterans of Florida* and *Spanish Land Grants in Florida: Confirmed and Unconfirmed* offer good sources.

Georgia

A large collection of county histories and state and local record abstracts combined with an indexed, 500 volume G.R.C. set provide Georgia researchers with much material. Colonial and Revolutionary era records from the Georgia Archives in Atlanta are available on microfilm along with some county records.

Hawaii

Basic histories, some collected Hawaiian genealogies, and studies of early missionaries comprise the Hawaii section.

Idaho

A basic collection with some county record abstracts is available.

Illinois

A large set of county histories and record abstracts provides the basis for a good Illinois collection. Illinois has a 250 volume G.R.C. set as well. In microform researchers will find *The Illinois County History Index*, *The Illinois Name Index to Early Records*, *Illinois Public Domain Land Sales*, and *Illinois Marriage Record Index*.

Indiana

The Library has a very large Indiana collection, the result of an earlier exchange with the Allen County Public Library in Fort Wayne as well as existing holdings. W.P.A. indices to vital records of Indiana counties are a major resource. Indiana has an 87 volume G.R.C. set.

Iowa

A good set of county histories and record abstracts coupled with a 225 volume G.R.C. set, give substantial coverage for Iowa researchers.

Kansas

A basic collection of historical and genealogical materials and over 100 G.R.C. volumes is available.

Kentucky

An ever-expanding collection of country record abstracts results in an excellent Kentucky section. Over 400 G.R.C. volumes complement this material. County tax lists prior to 1850 are on microfilm.

Louisiana

A detailed set of parish histories and record abstracts serves as the basis for significant materials on Louisiana. Hebert's *South West Louisiana Vital Records* and *South Louisiana Vital Records* are major sources, along with *The Diocese of Baton Rouge Catholic Church Records* and *Archdiocese of New Orleans Sacramental Records* sets. Studies on the German coast, and a G.R.C. set of over 200 volumes add further depth.

Maine

Many town record abstracts, a statewide index to marriages (1892-1966) on CD ROM, and an indexed G.R.C. set of over 300 volumes await Maine researchers. Massachusetts land grants in Maine after the Revolution are on microfilm.

Maryland

The Library has an excellent Maryland collection with extensive published county record abstracts, obscure local publications, and a newly indexed (1996) G.R.C. set of 240 volumes. In microform, researchers will find *Unpublished Maryland Revolutionary Records* by Margaret R. Hodges; historic Catholic church records of the Diocese of Washington from the Georgetown University Archives; Anne Arundel County deeds, wills, and other sources; colonial county rent rolls; and Maryland Prerogative Court Wills 1635-1714, v. 1-13.

Massachusetts

One of the largest state collections at DAR, the Massachusetts section contains numerous town histories and record abstracts, some late nineteenth and early twentieth century town reports, published 1855 and 1865 state censuses for many towns, and a G.R.C. set of over 450 volumes. The standard Revolutionary War source is *Massachusetts Soldiers and Sailors of the Revolutionary War*, and there is also a microfilm supplement. The *Corbin Collection*, the *Rollin H. Cooke Collection* (printed index), and the *1798 U.S. Direct Tax for Maine and Massachusetts* are on microfilm. On microfiche, the Holbrook Research Institute's collection of statewide vital records indices 1841-1895 and of early town records for many localities is a major resource, along with a collection of Boston city directories from 1789-1869. A microfilm version of the card index to the *Massachusetts Archives* series at the Massachusetts State Archives is a recent addition.

Michigan

County histories and record abstracts, including 53 volumes of Wayne County land transfers form the basis of the Michigan section. A card index to the 40 volume set *Michigan Pioneer and Historical Collections* is a useful finding aid not only for Michigan and Midwest research, but for New York as well. Michigan has a G.R.C. set of over 200 volumes. The 1894 state census is available on microfilm for those counties with surviving schedules.

Midwest Region

General histories and periodicals provide background information on the Midwest as a region and on the Old Northwest Territory in particular.

Minnesota

A good, basic selection of county histories and record abstracts and a 50 volume G.R.C. set constitute the Minnesota section.

Mississippi

A good selection of county histories and record abstracts is available along with a G.R.C. set of 150 volumes. *Mississippi Marriages* prior to 1926 (white) are on microfilm.

Missouri

The Missouri collection is one of the better ones for a Midwestern state. In addition to the many county histories and record abstracts, researchers will find extensive printed abstracts from newspapers of Springfield and Greene County from the 1880s to the 1990s (120

volumes) and 600 G.R.C. volumes in the Library. On 400 microfilm rolls is a statewide set of the major index books of county records, including deeds, wills, and marriages in the nineteenth century.

Montana
Basic histories and county materials are available.

Nebraska
Basic histories and county materials are available.

Nevada
Basic histories and county materials are available.

New England Region
Collectively, as well as individually, the six New England states are well represented in DAR holdings. In the New England section of the Library, researchers will find much Mayflower material, collected family histories, *The New England Historic Genealogical Register* (also on CD ROM) with its indices, and other standard studies and compilations for history and families.

New Hampshire
Many town histories, published state records and a G.R.C. set of 127 volumes provide the basis for the New Hampshire collection, and the recent addition of the indices to births, marriages, divorces, and deaths to circa 1900 on microfilm provide good New Hampshire coverage.

New Jersey
A large collection of New Jersey materials is enhanced by over 500 volumes of G.R.C. books containing much local information. County tax ratables (1778-1882) and New Jersey Revolutionary War records, including service records and damage claims, from the New Jersey State Archives offer many sources for research.

New Mexico
Basic sources on this Southwestern state include several studies of early Spanish and Mexican families along with materials on later settlers.

New Netherland Region
A good, separate collection of materials relating to the former Dutch colony in America, along with sources in the New Jersey and New York sections provide researchers with considerable information.

New York
One of the Library's largest collections covers the Empire State. County abstracts, numerous church records, and a partially indexed G.R.C. set of nearly 1,000 volumes anchor the section. The liber-size *Index to the Public Records of the County of Albany* (37 volumes) provides information on settlers in major portions of northern and central New York when Albany County was much larger. The *Vosburgh Collection* of church records, *New York City Wills 1677-1879*, state Revolutionary War accounts and claims, and applications for state land grants 1665-1803 are available on microfilm.

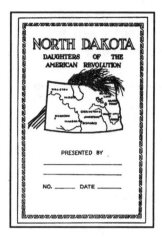

North Carolina

The Library has an excellent collection of North Carolina county histories and record abstracts along with many other useful sources. In microform are *North Carolina W.P.A Pre-1914 and Post-1914 Cemetery Card Indexes, North Carolina Revolutionary War Pay Vouchers, North Carolina Revolutionary War Army Accounts, North Carolina Treasurer's and Comptroller's Papers,* and various county court records. A microfiche *Marriage Bond Index of North Carolina 1741-1868* provides supplemental information to printed sources. A 200 volume G.R.C. set is also available.

North Dakota

A basic set of historical and genealogical materials, including the many county publications of the Red River Valley Genealogical Society represent North Dakota in the Library.

Ohio

A large collection of Ohio county histories and record abstracts is available and is supplemented by a G.R.C. set (with guide) of over 400 volumes. In microform are such sources as *Annals of Cleveland: Cleveland Newspaper Digest 1818-1876; Annals of Cleveland: Court Record Series 1837-1850; Hamilton County Deeds and Wills; Ohio Civil War Regimental Histories; Ohio Revolutionary War Bounty Land Warrants in the Virginia Military District,* and *The Ohio Surname Index to County Histories* from the Ohio Historical Society.

Oklahoma

A good, basic collection of local Oklahoma materials along with books in the American Indian Collection on tribes in Oklahoma and a 200 volume G.R.C. set are available.

Oregon

Basic county histories and record abstracts comprise the majority of the Oregon collection and various genealogical periodicals and a 50 volume G.R.C. set supplement them.

Pennsylvania

An excellent collection of county histories and records, church histories and records, and genealogical and historical periodicals is the core of the Pennsylvania section. The G.R.C. set contains over 200 volumes, and the published *Pennsylvania Archives* set is a popular source. Various county records are on microfilm along with *Abstracts Card File for Revolutionary War Active Duty Militia 1775-1783; Abstracts Card File of Revolutionary War Inactive Duty Militia; Military Abstract Cards, Philadelphia County, 1777-1783; Abstract Card File for Revolutionary War Continental Units 1775-1783; Pennsylvania Comptroller General Military Accounts, Militia 1775-1794;* and *Pennsylvania Comptroller General County Supply and Other Tax Lists.*

Rhode Island

An indexed, 90 volume G.R.C. set along with various county and town records is the basis for the Rhode Island section. On microfilm, the *Index to Military and Naval Records of Rhode Island 1774-1805* offers Revolutionary and post-Revolutionary military information.

The South Region

Many regional histories, periodicals, and record collections cover the states of the South as a region.

South Carolina

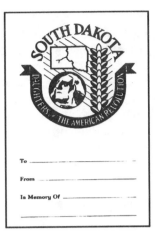

An excellent South Carolina collection is available to researchers. Beyond county histories and record abstracts, they will find a 200 volume G.R.C. set (with a microfiche index: *Name Index to Genealogical Records Collected by the South Carolina DAR*) and the following microform collections: *South Carolina Will Transcripts 1782-1868* (by county); *South Carolina Department of Archives and History Consolidated Index; South Carolina Auditor General's Records 1731-1775, Memorials COM Index; South Carolina Historical Magazine Index 1900-1983; Seventeenth and Eighteenth Century South Carolina Land Titles; South Carolina Department of Archives and History Individual and Combined Document Indexes to State Plats (Columbia and Charleston Series);* and *South Carolina State Plats, Charleston Series (1784-1860) and Columbia Series (1796-1868).*

South Dakota

A basic collection of sources and periodicals for South Dakota is supplemented on microfilm by a set of church vital and burial records and funeral home records numbering 160 reels from locations across the state.

Tennessee

Excellent county record abstracts and histories form the basis of the Tennessee section. A 200 volume G.R.C. set provides further sources. Two important microfilm collections are *North Carolina Secretary of State Land Grants in Tennessee and Tennessee Index to Land Grants 1775-1905.*

Texas

A large, but by no means comprehensive, county collection comprises the majority of the Texas section. The Texas DAR's G.R.C. has produced a set of 500 volumes. Many genealogical periodicals and early military record abstracts provide further depth of coverage.

Utah

A basic historical and genealogical collection of Utah materials is available.

Vermont

Many town histories and records, published state records, and an indexed G.R.C. set of 56 volumes give good Vermont information. The G.R.C. set contains many very complete cemetery listings from around the state. *The General Index to Vermont Vital Records to 1870* is available on microfilm.

Virginia

One of the Library's best state collections is that for the Old Dominion. County histories and many record abstracts, join with an

---

indexed G.R.C. set of 300 volumes and all Virginia genealogical periodicals for detailed coverage. *The Virginia Civil War Regimental Histories* series expands the information available on that period. *Virginia Land Office Patents and Grants, 1623–1784, Virginia Revolutionary War manuscript volumes "War 0–62,"* and *Virginia Revolutionary War Bounty Warrants* and index are available on microfilm along with various county and church records. Many traditional and newer published indices to Virginia materials offer access to family information.

Washington

A basic collection of historical and genealogical books forms the basis of the Washington section. The G.R.C. set of 65 volumes includes the subseries *Family Records of Washington Pioneers.*

The West Region

Overview histories and other studies provide background information on the Western states, on Russian America, and on the Spanish and Mexican periods in the history of the Southwest.

West Virginia

A good, growing collection of county histories, record abstracts, and genealogical periodicals forms the West Virginia section. The *Smith–Riffe Collection* of West Virginia and southwest Virginia families and a 184 roll set of microfilm reproducing abstracts of country records are available.

Wisconsin

Many county histories with recent indices and basic historical studies constitute this section.

Wyoming

Basic histories and some genealogical material are available for Wyoming.

13.28
VITAL RECORDS

These essential sources are found throughout DAR collections and in many forms. Researchers will find marriage registers, birth and death registers, New England town vital records, church records, cemetery surveys and transcriptions, and other similar sources. In the catalog, check the name of the locality with the subheadings "Vital records," "Birth records," "Death records," etc.

New England vital records are the best in the country and are represented in large numbers at DAR. Besides published volumes of many of these sources, the following are available on microfilm:

- Index to Vermont vital records to 1870

- Indices to New Hampshire vital records to 1900

- The Massachusetts Town Records series on microfiche from Holbrook Research, Inc.

- The Barbour Collection and Index of Connecticut vital records

Other state-wide indices include:

- Mississippi marriages prior to 1926 (white)

- North Carolina marriage bond index 1741–1868; separate bride and groom indices

- Illinois Marriage record index

Many individual vital records have accompanied DAR membership applications as proof of lineage. These have included birth, marriage, and death certificates or register entries. Bible records abound as well. The DAR Library maintains the files of this material, **but does not make available for research or provide copies of post–1910 records obtained from state health and vital records departments** for privacy reasons. There are no exceptions to this policy.

13.29
WOMEN'S HISTORY

Records relating to women in American history are found throughout DAR collections. The Library maintains a growing Women's History Collection, which focuses on the role and experience of women. A natural focus of this and other materials is women during the period of the American Revolution, but coverage is much wider. Also see sections 13.1 and 13.20.4.6.

The state sections include a subdivision "Women," which includes studies on women's experiences in the life and development of each state. Some books examine legal, cultural, and family ties in broad social contexts.

As a women's organization itself, the DAR owns much material on its own activities since 1890. The Office of the Historian General maintains the archival collections, which may require special permission to use, and the Historical Research Library, which includes various studies on American women's history. Catalogs and checklists from various exhibits on women's history and related topics in the DAR Museum are discussed in Chapter 10.

Chapter 14

CITING, QUOTING AND REPRODUCING DAR SOURCES

*D*AR staff often see vague references in books or in letters to materials which are supposedly found in DAR collections. Such phrases as "in the DAR Library" or "in the DAR files" are all too frequent. They provide no useful information to help other researchers or the staff locate the material again. Proper citation or reference to documents and their locations is essential when noting a source from all libraries and archives. The examples of bibliographic records given in this chapter are for the most frequently used DAR sources and provide guidelines for proper citation.

Although many DAR publications and compilations were never registered for copyright, reseachers should give proper credit for any reference in any publication or source they quote in their writing and note-taking. A proper credit line or footnote is important. This will avoid problems and misunderstandings in the future.

To reproduce or to quote extensively from any DAR publication, one must obtain permission from the appropriate part of DAR. Permission may or may not be granted, depending on the circumstances and purpose. For general DAR publications, write to the Corresponding Secretary General. For the *DAR Magazine*, contact the Magazine Office. For publications from state organizations including *Genealogical Records Committee Reports*, write to the appropriate state regent. DAR appreciates a copy of any work including significant portions of DAR-produced material.

CITATION FOR DAR MEMBERSHIP APPLICATION
[See Section 6.6.1 for a discussion of membership applications.]

"Membership application of [member's name](National Number) on [ancestor's name (dates, state)]," National Society Daughters of the American Revolution, Office of the Registrar General, Washington, D.C., [date application was approved].

Fictious example:
"Membership application of Elizabeth Jones Smith (1,111,111) on Josiah Walden (1750-1806, Vermont)," National Society Daughters of the American Revolution, Office of the Registrar General, Washington, D.C., April 19, 2003.

CITATION FOR DAR SUPPLEMENTAL APPLICATION PAPER
[See Section 6.6.3 for a discussion of supplemental applications.]

"Supplemental application paper of [member's name] (National Number, Add volume number) on [ancestor's name (dates, state)]," National Society Daughters of the American Revolution, Office of the Registrar General, Washington, D.C., [date supplemental application was approved].

"Supplemental application paper of Evelyn Green Brown (1,000,001, Add volume 1,236) on Stephen Butler (1743-1810, Virginia)," National Society Daughters of the American Revolution, Office of the Registrar General, Washington, D.C., October 11, 2001.

CITATION FOR DOCUMENTATION FILE SUPPORTING A MEMBERSHIP OR SUPPLEMENTAL APPLICATION

[See Section 6.9 for a discussion of documentation files.]

"[type of record] in Documentation file supporting the Membership Application [or Supplemental Application Paper] of [name of member], approved [date application was approved], (National Number) on [name of ancestor, dates, state]," National Society Daughters of the American Revolution, DAR Library, Washington, D.C.

Fictious example:

"Marriage record of Josiah Walden and Hannah Jones, 20 July 1772, Putney, Vermont, in Documentation file supporting the Membership Application of Elizabeth Jones Smith, approved April 19, 2003, (1,111,111) on Josiah Walden (1750-1806, Vermont)," National Society Daughters of the American Revolution, DAR Library, Washington, D.C.

CITATION FOR A GENEALOGICAL RECORDS COMMITTEE REPORT

The Genealogical Records Committee [G.R.C] *Reports* contain many genealogical materials which DAR members have collected since the late 1910s. There are now approximately 14,000 volumes of varying length, format and content.

These typescripts have arrived at DAR with numerous titles and much creativity in arrangement. Until 1988 there was little standardization and most state sets did not have proper volume numbering. In that year the Library imposed such a system on all new *G.R.C. Reports* for those state sets without one. Everything prior to 1988 automatically became "Series 1," and everything from 1988 to the present is in "Series 2."

To achieve uniformity, the Library's catalogers have assigned volume numbers for all books in Series 1 based on their compilation dates. Slowly order has arisen. The Library considers its national set of *G.R.C. Reports* as the master set. The volume numbering for Series 1 only applies to this set and not to any copies maintained by the states. This is primarily because there are no exact records showing where the state sets are located. A few states such as New York and Vermont, used a proper numbering system before 1988, and those systems remain in place from the very first book.

In addition to the volume numbering, the Library set the title for all of these volumes in both series as [a state's name + DAR] *Genealogical Records Committee Report*. The new titles are followed by a descriptive subtitle, which would have been formerly the title.

The following fictious models for a proper citation are given. For more detailed information, please contact the DAR Library, Cataloging Section.

For pre-1988 reports:

Wisconsin DAR, Genealogical Records Committee Report: Miscellaneous Records, Series 1, Volume 64 (1951), DAR Library, Washington, D.C. [Formerly referred to as *Wisconsin DAR, Miscellaneous Records*, 1951, with no other identifying information.]

For reports 1988 to the present:

Wisconsin DAR, Genealogical Records Committee Report: Cemetery Records of Dane and Wood Counties, Series 2, Volume 139 (2006), DAR Library, Washington, D.C.

CITATION FOR DAUGHTERS OF THE AMERICAN REVOLUTION MAGAZINE

The DAR Magazine has had several title changes during its existence which affect bibliographic citations. [Note: Until v. 51 (July-December 1917) a volume comprised half a year or six issues.] See Chapter 9 for a discussion of *The DAR Magazine*.

- *American Monthly Magazine*, v.1 (July 1892)–v.42 (June 1913)

- *Daughters of the American Revolution Magazine*, v.43 (July 1913)–v.72 (December 1938)

- *The National Historical Magazine*, v.73 (1939)–v.79 (1945)

- *Daughters of the American Revolution Magazine*, v.80 (1946) to the present

CITATION FOR NSDAR REPORT TO THE SMITHSONIAN

Annually, until 1974, the DAR was required to submit its annual report to the Secretary of the Smithsonian Institution. These then became United States Senate Documents and parts of the U.S. Government's *Serial Set*. Included within these reports over the years are various lists and compilations of Revolutionary War soldiers, cemetery records, and other genealogically important material. These volumes should be cited as is this last such report:

Seventy-seventh Report of the National Society of the Daughters of the American Revolution, March 1, 1973 to March 1, 1974. 94th Congress, 1st Session, Senate Document No. 94-117. Washington, D.C.: U.S. Government Printing Office, 1975.

References to any subsection of these reports should be treated as an article in a journal with the inclusive page numbers shown.

"The Ancient Burying Ground of Hartford: Names on the gravestones standing in 1835," Appendix C, *Third Report of the National Society of the Daughters of the American Revolution, October 11, 1898–October 11, 1900.* 56th Congress, 2d Session, Senate Document No. 219 (Washington, D.C.: Government Printing Office, 1901), 306-315.

★ ★ ★ ★ ★ ★ ★ ★ ★ ★ ★ ★ ★ ★ ABOUT THE AUTHORS

Eric G. Grundset has been Library Director for the DAR Library since May 1983. He holds a B.A. in history from James Madison University, undertook graduate study in Russian history at the University of Wisconsin, Madison, and holds a Masters Degree in Library Science from The Catholic University of America. A native Virginian of Norwegian and colonial Virginian descent, he is active in historical and genealogical organizations in the Old Dominion. Mr. Grundset is a former employee of the Virginia Room, Fairfax County Public Library System, a former president of the Virginia Genealogical Society, and a current member of that society's Board of Governors. Presently the First Vice President of the National Genealogical Society, he has served previously as an N.G.S. councilor and national conference chairman and program chairman. A genealogist, historian, lecturer and writer, Mr. Grundset resides in Fairfax, Virginia with his wife, also a public librarian, and their two daughters.

Steven B. Rhodes has been the Assistant Director of the DAR Library since March 1995. He holds a B.A. in History from Virginia Commonwealth University, a History of M.A. from Virginia Tech and an M.L.S. from the University of Maryland. In the past he has held positions at university, government and law libraries. A native Virginian, he currently resides in Maryland with his wife, a professional medical librarian, and their two sons.

Librarian General, Office of the – see DAR Library
Library of Congress 14, 21, 24, 112
Lineage Research National Committee 45, 80
Lineage societies 30, 73, 103, 115, 116, 146
Louisiana 39, 83, 88, 100, 111, 113, 114, 134, 148, 153, 165
Loyalists 138-141

M

Maine 39, 83, 88, 94, 128, 129, 165
Manuscript collections 23, 31, 32, 66, 67, 100, 145
Maps 117
Marriage records 72
Maryland 23, 27, 37, 39, 42, 79, 83, 88, 94, 99, 110, 123, 128, 148-150, 153, 157, 166
Massachusetts 39, 42, 69, 83, 88, 94, 101, 102, 103, 118, 119, 120, 122, 127, 129, 131, 133, 138, 161, 166, 171
McGee, Anita Newcomb 35, 157
Metrorail 13
Metrobus 13
Mexican War 149-151
Mexico 9, 92, 149-151
Michigan 39, 83, 88, 101, 108, 114, 153, 166
Michigan Pioneer and Historical Collections, Index to 23
Midwest 166
Military records 118-160
Minority Military Service, 1775-1783 63, 80, 94, 132, 133
Minnesota 39, 83, 88, 114, 166
Mississippi 83, 88, 101, 149, 153, 154, 166, 171
Missouri 42, 83, 88, 101, 166, 167
Montana 39, 83, 89, 100, 167
Mortality schedules (federal census) 100, 101

N

Names 160
National Archives 10, 11, 14, 24, 107, 108, 112, 124, 143, 144, 153, 161
National Historical Magazine 75
Native American Research 11, 29, 63, 118, 119, 132, 133, 160, 161

Naturalization records 114
Nebraska 39, 83, 89, 101, 167
Needlework, genealogical 78, 79
Netherlands 11, 113, 118, 119
Nevada 83, 89, 99, 100, 149, 167
New England 27, 110, 118, 119, 122, 126, 127, 148, 167, 170
New Hampshire 23, 39, 42, 83, 88, 94, 101, 119, 123, 129, 139, 144, 167, 171
New Jersey 39, 42, 69, 84, 89, 111, 128, 129, 130, 133, 136, 138, 146, 156, 167
New Mexico 84, 89, 101, 149, 150, 151, 167
New Netherland 27, 111, 113, 167
New York 23, 36, 39, 69, 84, 89, 101, 111, 113, 119, 120, 128, 135, 139, 153, 161, 167
Newspapers 161
North Carolina 39, 42, 84, 89, 93, 95, 101, 123, 127, 130, 139, 143, 146, 147, 148, 149, 151, 153, 168, 171
North Dakota 39, 84, 90, 99, 157, 168

O

Ohio 39, 84, 90, 94, 114, 142, 143, 145, 147, 148, 149, 150, 154, 156, 157, 168
Oklahoma 39, 84, 90, 168
Organizing Secretary General, Office of the 52, 65, 68, 72-74, 92, 104, 106
Oregon 37, 38, 84, 90, 168

P

Passenger lists 103
Pennsylvania 39, 69, 84, 90, 110, 113, 119, 120, 123, 127, 128, 129, 138, 139, 146, 148, 149, 153, 154, 168
Periodicals 161, 162
Philippines 92
Pierce's Register 70, 123
Poland and Poles 111
Presidents and First Families 71, 162

Q

Quilts 78, 79

R

"Real Daughters" 51, 70, 104
"Real Granddaughters" 51, 104
Reddy, Ann Waller 22, 31
Registrar General, Office of the 41, 44-65, 104
Religious records 162
Rhode Island 23, 39, 84, 90, 94, 101, 118, 119, 144, 168
Roots 93
Russia and Russians 111, 113
Russian America 111, 164, 170

S

Santo Domingo 112
Scandinavia 111
Scotland 111, 113
Scots Irish 10, 31, 111, 113
Seimes Microfilm Center 11, 21, 41-43, 46, 52, 53, 54, 98, 99, 102, 104, 124-171 (passim)
Sierra Leone 108
Smithsonian Institution, DAR Reports to the Secretary of the 68-70, 174
Society of the Cincinnati 115, 146
Sons of the American Revolution, National Society (SAR) 18, 115, 146
Sons of the Revolution 18, 115, 146
The South 23, 27, 38, 139, 169
South Carolina 39, 42, 69, 84, 90, 94, 110, 113, 128, 130, 133, 135, 149, 169
South Dakota 84, 90, 169
Spain 111, 118, 134, 164
Spanish American War 68, 157
State research sources 22, 23, 27, 28, 30, 36-39, 42, 68, 69, 70, 81-91, 97, 100-103, 114, 115, 163-170
Sweden 111, 113
Switzerland 111

T

Tennessee 39, 42, 84, 91, 100, 108, 143, 144, 145, 154, 169

Texas 39, 84, 91, 169
Tories — see Loyalists

U

United Empire Loyalists — see Loyalists
United Kingdom 9, 92
United States Daughters of the War of 1812, 149
Utah 85, 91, 101, 149, 169

V

Vermont 39, 42, 69, 85, 91, 94, 101, 128, 139, 148, 169, 171
Vietnam War 160
Virginia 22, 27, 31, 37, 39, 78, 85, 91, 94, 95, 100, 101, 103, 110, 113, 118, 119, 120, 123, 126, 127, 128, 129, 130, 131, 133, 138, 143, 154, 156, 157, 169, 170
Vital records 23, 38, 72, 145, 146, 156, 170, 171
The Vital Record Compendium 23, 38

W

Wales 112
War of 1812, 118, 147-149
Washington (state) 85, 91, 170
Washington, George 71, 79, 119, 120, 122, 125, 162
The West 27, 79, 85, 164, 170
West Indies 112
West Virginia 37, 39, 85, 91, 101, 108, 143, 170
Wisconsin 85, 91, 114, 145, 170
Women's history and records 22, 29, 70, 77, 78, 79, 132, 171
Works Progress Administration/Work Projects Administration (W.P.A.) 10, 29, 71, 108
World War I 157-159
World War II 11, 159, 160
Wyoming 85, 91, 100, 170

NOTES

NOTES